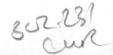

Praise for this book

'A deliciously fact-driven corrective to Internet hype of all kinds. Highly recommended.'

Fred Turner, *Stanford University, USA*

'This is a very important book; scholarly, informative and full of useful references, it offers a piercing critique of old mythologies about new media. It is essential reading for students and teachers of mass communications and all those who wish to understand the real impact of new media on our society.'

Professor Greg Philo, *Director of the Glasgow University Media Group*

'*Misunderstanding the Internet* is the book I have been waiting for since the late 1990s. It is a superb examination of the internet, how we got to this point and what our options are going forward. James Curran, Natalie Fenton and Des Freedman have combined to produce a signature work in the political economy of communication. They have combined hard research with piercing insight and a general command of the pertinent literature. This is a book I will be using in my classes for years to come.'

Robert W. McChesney, *University of Illinois at Urbana-Champaign, USA*

'This clear-sighted book provides a sometimes provocative yet solidly grounded guide through the competing claims and hyperbole that surround the internet's place in society. Deeply sceptical about the transformative potential of the internet, the authors combine an incisive history of the recent past with a call to action to embed public values in the internet of the future.'

Sonia Livingstone, *LSE, UK*

Misunderstanding the Internet

James Curran, Natalie Fenton and
Des Freedman

Routledge
Taylor & Francis Group

LONDON AND NEW YORK

First published 2012
by Routledge
2 Park Square, Milton Park, Abingdon, Oxon OX14 4RN

Simultaneously published in the USA and Canada
by Routledge
711 Third Avenue, New York, NY 10017

Routledge is an imprint of the Taylor & Francis Group, an informa business

© 2012 James Curran, Natalie Fenton and Des Freedman

British Library Cataloguing in Publication Data
A catalogue record for this book is available from the British Library

Library of Congress Cataloging in Publication Data
Curran, James.
Misunderstanding the Internet / James Curran, Natalie Fenton,
and Des Freedman.
p. cm. -- (Communication and society)
1. Internet--Social aspects. 2. Internet--Economic aspects. 3. Internet--Political
aspects. 4. Social networking. I. Fenton, Natalie. II. Friedman, Des,
1962- III. Title.
HM851.C87 2012
302.231--dc23
2011037305

ISBN: 978-0-415-57956-8 (hbk)
ISBN: 978-0-415-57958-2 (pbk)
ISBN: 978-0-203-14648-4 (ebk)

Typeset in Baskerville
by Taylor & Francis Books

MIX
Paper from
responsible sources
FSC® C004839
www.fsc.org

Printed and bound in Great Britain by
CPI Antony Rowe, Chippenham, Wiltshire

Contents

Part 1

Overview

Chapter 1

Reinterpreting the internet

James Curran

In the 1990s, leading experts, politicians, public officials, business leaders and journalists predicted that the internet would transform the world.[1] The internet would revolutionise, we were told, the organisation of business, and lead to a surge of prosperity (Gates 1995).[2] It would inaugurate a new era of cultural democracy in which sovereign users – later dubbed 'prosumers' – would call the shots, and old media leviathans would decay and die (Negroponte 1996). It would rejuvenate democracy – in some versions by enabling direct e-government through popular referenda (Grossman 1995). All over the world, the weak and marginal would be empowered, leading to the fall of autocrats and the reordering of power relations (Gilder 1994). More generally, the global medium of the internet would shrink the universe, promote dialogue between nations and foster global understanding (Jipguep 1995; Bulashova and Cole 1995). In brief, the internet would be an unstoppable force: like the invention of print and gunpowder, it would change society permanently and irrevocably.

These arguments were mostly inferences derived from the internet's technology. It was assumed that the distinctive technological attributes of the internet – its interactivity, global reach, cheapness, speed, networking facility, storage capacity, and alleged uncontrollability – would change the world beyond all recognition. Underlying these predictions was the assumption that the internet's technology would reconfigure all environments. Internet-centrism, a belief that the internet is the alpha and omega of technologies, an agency that overrides all obstacles, lies at the heart of most of these prophecies.

These predictions gained ever greater authority when, seemingly, they were fulfilled. From popular uprisings in the Middle East to the new ways we shop and interact, society is said to be changing in response to new communications technology. Only technophobes, stuck in a time warp of the past, remain blind to what is apparent to everyone else: namely that the world is being remade by the internet.

But as pronouncements about the internet's impact became ever more assured, and shifted from the future to the present tense, a backlash developed. A straw in the wind was the apostasy of MIT guru Sherry Turkle. In 1995, she had celebrated anonymous online encounters between people on the grounds that they could extend imaginative insight into the 'other', and forge more emancipated sensibilities (Turkle 1995).[3] Sixteen years later, she changed tack. Online communication, she lamented, could be shallow and addictive, and get in the way of developing richer, more fulfilling interpersonal relationships (Turkle 2011).[4] Another apostate was the Belarus activist Evgeny Morozov. His former belief that the internet would undermine dictators was, he declared, a 'delusion' (Morozov 2011). There were also others whose initial, more guarded hope in the emancipatory power of the internet turned into outright scepticism. Typical of this latter group are John Foster and Robert McChesney (2011: 17), who write that 'the enormous potential of the Internet ... has vaporized in a couple of decades'.

We are thus faced with a baffling contradiction of testimony. Most informed commentators view the internet as a transforming technology. Their predictions are now seemingly being confirmed by events. However, there is an unsettling minority who confidently decry the majority view as perverse. Who – and what – is right?

We will attempt to sketch an answer in this introductory chapter by identifying four key sets of predictions about the impact of the internet, and then check to see whether these have come true or not.[5] We will conclude by reflecting upon the nature of the conditions that result in the internet having a larger or smaller effect.

Economic transformation

In the 1990s, it was widely claimed that the internet would generate wealth and prosperity for all. Typifying this prediction was a long article in *Wired*, the bible of the American internet community, written by the magazine's editor, Kevin Kelly (1999). Its title and standfirst set the article's tone: 'The Roaring Zeros: The good news is, you'll be a millionaire soon. The bad news is, so will everybody else'.

Speculative fever had infected mainstream media as early as 1995. 'The Internet gold rush is under way', declared the *Seattle Post-Intelligencer* (6 December 1995). 'Thousands of people and companies are staking claims. Without a doubt there is lots of gold because the Internet is the beginning of something immensely important.' Across the Atlantic Ocean, the same message was being proclaimed with undisguised relish. The 'fortunes' of 'Web whiz-kids', according to the *Independent on Sunday* (25 July 1999), 'reduce National Lottery jackpots to peanuts and make City bonuses seem like restaurant tips ... '. Punters could become rich too, it was promised, if they invested in whiz-kids' IPOs (initial public offerings). This invitation to personal enrichment was backed up by authoritative reports in the business press that the internet was a geyser of prosperity. 'We have entered the Age of the Internet', declaimed *BusinessWeek* (October 1999). 'The result: an *explosion* of economic and productivity growth first in the U.S., with the rest of the world soon to follow' (emphasis added).

This forecast was reprised in the 2000s, accompanied by an explanation of why it had been wrong before but would soon be fulfilled. The 1990s represented the internet's pioneer phase, we are informed, when egregious mistakes were made. But the internet has now entered the full deployment phase, and is coming into its own as a transformative economic force (Atkinson et al. 2010).

Central to this resilient prophetic tradition is the idea that the internet and digital communication are giving rise to the 'New Economy'. While this concept is amorphous and mutable, it usually invokes certain themes. The internet provides, we are told, a new, more efficient means of connecting suppliers, producers and consumers that is increasing productivity and growth. The internet is a disruptive technology that is generating a Schumpeterian wave of innovation. And it is contributing to the growth of a new information economy that will replace heavy industry as the main source of wealth in de-industrialising, Western societies.

At the heart of this theorising is a mystical core. This proclaims that the internet is changing the terms of competition by establishing *a level playing field* between corporate giants and new start-ups. The internet is consequently renewing the dynamism of the market, and unleashing a whirlwind force of business creativity. By bypassing established retail intermediaries, the internet is carving out new market opportunities. It is lowering costs, and enabling low-volume producers to satisfy neglected niche demand in a global market. The internet also favours, we are informed, horizontal, flexible network enterprise, able to respond rapidly to changes in market demand, unlike heavy-footed, top-down, Fordist, giant corporations. 'Small' is not only nimble but empowered in the internet-based New Economy. As Steve Jobs asserted in 1996, the internet is an 'incredible democratiser', since 'a small company can look as large as a big company and be accessible … ' (cited Ryan 2010: 179).

The concept of the New Economy is often cloaked in specialist language. To understand its insights, it is seemingly neccessary to learn a new vocabulary: to distinguish between portal and vortal, to differentiate between internet, intranet and extranet, to assimilate buzz concepts like 'click-and-mortar' and 'data-warehousing', and to be familiar with endless acronyms like CRM (customer relationship management), VAN (value-added network), ERP (enterprise resource planning), OLTP (online transaction processing) and ETL (extract, transform and load). To be part of the novitiate who understands the future, it is first necessary to master a new catechism.

Since the economic impact of the internet is cumulative and incomplete, it is difficult at this stage to make an assured assessment. But sufficient evidence has accumulated to enable formulation of certain cautious conclusions. The first is that the internet has modified the nerve system of the economy, affecting the collection of data, the interactions between suppliers, producers and consumers, the configuration of markets, the volume and velocity of global financial transactions, and the nature of communication within business organisations, as well as giving rise to major corporations such as Google and Amazon, and the launch of new products and services. However, the internet does not represent a complete rupture with the past, since it was preceded by the widespread corporate use of computers, and by earlier electronic data interchange systems (like the telex and fax) (Bar and Simard 2002).

The second conclusion is that the internet has not proved to be a geyser of wealth cascading down on investors and the general public. There was an enormous increase in the stock market value of internet companies between 1995 and 2000. But this was partly a bubble, like the subsequent US housing bubble, fuelled by the credit boom produced by financial de-regulation in the mid-1990s (Blodget 2008; Cassidy 2002). The bubble was exacerbated by financial incentives that encouraged investment analysts to recommend unsound investment in the internet sector (Wheale and Amin 2003). This was reinforced by group-think that encouraged a belief that conventional investment criteria did not apply to the New Economy, leading to speculative bets on the future profitability of dotcom ventures, many of which had ill-considered, unrealistic business plans (Valliere and Peterson 2004). In the event, the internet gold mine proved to be made of fool's gold. Most dotcom start-ups that attracted heavy investment folded without ever making a profit, in some cases after burning through large quantities of money in less than two years (Cellan-Jones 2001). These losses were so severe that it tipped the US economy into recession in 2001.

There were clear signs that there was about to be another boom in internet stock in the mid-2000s. But this was overtaken by the credit crunch of 2007 and the financial crash of 2008. In the extended aftermath (still continuing over three years later), share prices fell; incomes in the West flat-lined or fell in real terms; and Western economic growth declined sharply. The internet was manifestly not the fount of a new era of prosperity.

The third conclusion is that the value of the 'internet economy' was probably oversold. Thus, a Harvard Business School study, using an employment income approach, concluded that the advertising-supported internet in America contributed approximately 2 per cent to GDP, or perhaps 3 per cent if the internet's indirect contribution to domestic economic activity is taken into account (Deighton and Quelch 2009). An alternative calculation estimated that business-to-consumer e-commerce in Europe accounted for 1.35 per cent of GDP (Eskelsen et al. 2009), while a booster consultant report, commissioned by Google, claimed that the internet contributed 7 per cent of the UK's GDP in 2009 (Kalapese et al. 2010). Even this last questionable estimate is modest by comparison with what was forecast in the late 1990s.

The fourth conclusion is that the internet has not revolutionised shopping. While over 40 per cent of Japanese, Norwegians, Koreans, Britons, Danes and Germans bought something online in 2007, fewer than 10 per cent did so in Hungary, Italy, Portugal, Greece, Mexico and Turkey (OECD cited in Atkinson et al. 2010: 22). Even in countries where online shopping is widespread, it tends to be concentrated on a limited range of products and services. In 2007, online sales accounted for 7 per cent of total sales turnover in the UK, and 4 per cent in Europe (European Commission 2009). However, the comparable figure for the UK in 2010 was 16 per cent, registering a big increase that was only partly the product of different methodology (Atkinson et al. 2010).

Online shopping will become more extensive in the future because internet access will increase, and security concerns will probably decline. But consumer resistance also derives partly from the pleasure that some people take in shopping in the real world, and their desire for immediate purchase, which are likely to persist. There is also a more fundamental obstacle: e-retail confers a large economic advantage only in sectors where warehousing and distribution costs are low. This is one reason why, so far, online selling has taken off in some sectors, like travel and insurance, but not in others, like automobiles and food.

The fifth, and much the most important, conclusion is that the internet has not created a level playing field between small and large enterprise. The belief that it would was the principal evangelical component of the 'New Economy' thesis, and lay at the heart of its conviction that the internet would generate a surge of innovation and growth.[6] This article of faith did not anticipate the difficulty that small and medium firms would continue to have in penetrating foreign markets. As it turned out, the usefulness of the internet as a tool for securing foreign market access was constrained by language, cultural knowledge, the quality of telecommunications infrastructures and computer access (Chrysostome and Rosson 2004). More importantly, the New Economy thesis failed to take adequate account of the continuing economic advantage of corporate size.[7] Large corporations have bigger budgets, and greater access to capital, than small companies. Big corporations also have greater economies of scale, enabling lower unit costs of production; generally greater economies of scope, based on the sharing of services and cross-promotion; and concentrations of expertise and resources that assist the launch of new products and services. They can seek to undermine under-resourced competition by temporarily lowering prices and by exploiting their marketing and promotional advantage. In addition, they can try to 'buy success' by acquiring promising young companies – the standard strategy of conglomerates.

This is why, in the internet age, large corporations continue to dominate leading market sectors, from car manufacture to grocery supermarkets. Indeed, in the leading economy (US), the number of *manufacturing* industries, in which the largest four companies accounted for at least 50 per cent of shipment value, steadily increased between 1997 and 2007 (Foster et al. 2011: chart 1). There was also a truly remarkable increase between 1997 and 2007 in the market share of the four largest firms in leading sectors of the US *retail* industry (Foster et al. 2011: table 1). To take just two examples, the big four computer and software stores' share soared from 35 per cent to 73 per cent, while the share of the big four merchandising stores rose from 56 per cent to 73 per cent, during this period. More generally, the gross profits of the top 200 US corporations as a percentage of total gross profits in the US economy very sharply increased between 1995 and 2008 (Foster et al. 2011: chart 3).

In brief, the triumph of the small business in the internet era never happened because competition remained unequal. Corporate Goliaths continued to squash commercial Davids armed only with a virtual sling and pebble.

Global understanding

During the 1990s, there was a broad consensus that the internet would promote greater global understanding. 'The internet', declared the Republican politician Vern Ehlers (1995), 'will create a community of informed, interacting, and tolerant world citizens'. The internet, concurred Bulashova and Cole (1995), offers 'a tremendous "peace dividend" resulting from improved communications with and improved knowledge of other people, countries and cultures'. One key reason for this, argues the writer Harley Hahn (1993), is not just that the internet is a global medium but also that it offers greater opportunity for ordinary people to communicate with each other than do traditional media. 'I see the Net', he concludes, 'as being our best hope ... for the world finally starting to become a global community and everybody just getting along with everyone else'. Another reason for optimism, advanced by numerous commentators, is that the internet is less subject to state censorship than traditional media, and is thus better able to host a free, unconstrained global discourse between citizens. It is partly because 'people will communicate more freely and learn more about the aspirations of human beings in other parts of the globe', according to Frances Cairncross (1997: xvi), that 'the effect will be to increase understanding, foster tolerance, and ultimately promote worldwide peace'. These themes – the internet's international reach, user participation, and freedom – continued to be invoked in the 2000s as grounds for thinking that the internet would bond the world in growing amity.

These arguments have been given a distinctive academic imprint by critical cultural theorists. Jon Stratton (1997: 257) argues that internet encourages the 'globalization of culture', and 'hyper-deterritorialization' – by which he means the loosening of ties to nation and place. This argument is part of a well-established cultural studies tradition which sees media globalisation as fostering cosmopolitanism and an opening up to other people and places (e.g. Tomlinson 1999).

Critical political theorists advance a parallel argument (Fraser 2007; Bohman 2004; Ugarteche 2007, among others). Their contention is that what Nancy Fraser (2007: 18–19) calls the 'denationalization of communication infrastructure' and the rise of 'decentered internet networks' are creating webs of communication that interconnect with one another to create an international public sphere of dialogue and debate. From this is beginning to emerge allegedly a 'transnational ethic', 'global public norms' and 'international public opinion'. This offers, it is suggested, a new basis of popular power capable of holding to account transnational, economic and political power. While these theorists vary in terms of how far they push this argument (Fraser 2007, for example, is notably circumspect), they are advancing a thesis that goes beyond the standard humanist understanding of the internet as the midwife of global understanding. The internet is presented as a stepping-stone in the building of a new, progressive social order.

The central weakness of this theorising is that it assesses the impact of the internet not on the basis of evidence but on the basis of inference from internet technology. Yet, readily available information tells a different story: the impact of the internet does not follow a single direction dictated by its technology. Instead the influence of the internet is filtered through the structures and processes of society. This constrains in at least seven different ways the role of the internet in promoting global understanding.

First, the world is very unequal, and this limits participation in an internet-mediated global dialogue. Not only are there enormous disparities of wealth and resources but these seem to be increasing (Woolcock 2008: 184; Torres 2008). The richest 2 per cent of adults in the world own more than half of global household wealth, with the richest 1 per cent of adults alone possessing 40 per cent of global assets in 2000 (Davies et al. 2006). Adults making up the bottom half of the world population own barely 1 per cent of global wealth. Davies et al. note that wealth is concentrated in North America, Europe and high-income Asia-Pacific countries; people in these countries hold almost 90 per cent of total world wealth.

These rich regions of the world have much higher internet access than poor regions. Thus, 77 per cent of North Americans have internet access, 61 per cent in Oceania/Australia and 58 per cent of Europeans (Internet World Stats 2010a). Yet, there are many developing countries with internet penetration rates that are less than 1/100th of those in wealthy countries (Wunnava and Leiter 2009: 413). The influence of per capita income on national internet penetration is corroborated by Beilock and Dimitrova (2003), who found that it is the most important determinant, followed by infrastructure and the degree of openness in a society.[8] Economic disparity thus skews the composition of the internet community. As Wunnava and Leiter (2009: 414) conclude: 'to date, Europe and North America, which represent a mere 17.5 percent of the total world population, house close to 50 percent of worldwide internet users'.

This will be modified over time, as poorer countries become more affluent. But because the world is so unequal, it will be a very long time before poor countries even approach current levels of net penetration in affluent countries. Meanwhile, the internet is not bringing the world together: it is bringing primarily the affluent into communion with each other. The total proportion of population in 2011 who are internet users is 30 per cent (Internet World Stats 2011a). Most of the world's poor are not part of this magic circle of 'mutual understanding'.

Second, the world is divided by language. Most people can speak only one language, and so cannot understand foreigners when they communicate online. The nearest thing to a shared online language is English, which, according to the International Telecommunications Union (2010), only 15 per cent of the world's population understands. The role of the internet in bringing people together is thus necessarily hampered by mutual incomprehension.

Third, language is a medium of power. Those writing or speaking in English can reach, in relative terms, a large global public. By contrast, those conversing in Arabic are able to communicate, potentially, to only 3 per cent of internet users (Internet World Stats 2010b); and those communicating in Marathi potentially reach a proportion of internet users so small as to be measurable only in decimal points. Who gets to be heard in the 'medium of global understanding' often depends on what language they speak.

Fourth, the world is divided by bitter conflicts of value, belief and interest. These can find expression in websites that foment – rather than assuage – animosity. Thus, race hate groups were internet pioneers, with former Klansman Tom Metzger, then leader of White Aryan Resistance, setting up a community bulletin board in 1985 (Gerstenfeld et al. 2003). From these cyber-frontier origins, racist websites have proliferated. The Raymond Franklin list of hate sites runs to over 170 pages (Perry and Olsson 2009), while the Simon Wiesenthal Centre (2011) documents 14,000 social network websites, forums, blogs, Twitter sites and other online sources in its *Digital Terror and Hate* report. Some of these websites have a large base: Stormfront, one of the earliest white-only websites, had 52,566 active users in 2005 (Daniels 2008: 134).

Detailed studies of hate sites conclude that they maintain and extend racial hatred in a variety of ways (Back 2001; Perry and Olsson 2009; Gerstenfeld et al. 2003). Race hate sites can foster a sense of collective identity, reassuring militant racists that they are not alone. Some foster a sense of community not only through features like an 'Aryan Dating Page' but also through more conventional content such as forums discussing health, fitness and home making. The more sophisticated are adept at targeting children and young people by offering, for example, online games and practical help. Race hate groups increasingly use the internet to develop international networks of support in which ideas and information are shared. And of course their staple content is designed to promote fear and hatred, typified by warnings of the 'demographic time bomb' of alien procreation in their midst. These 'white fortresses' of cyberspace promote not just disharmony. There is a relationship between racist discourse and racist violence (Akdeniz 2009).

This illustrates one central point: the internet can spew out hatred, foster misunderstanding, and perpetuate animosity. Because the internet is both international and interactive, it does not mean necessarily that it encourages only 'sweetness and light'. Indeed, there is evidence that active terror groups have used the internet to win converts and extend international links, in addition to transferring and laundering money (Conway 2006; Hunt 2011: Freiburger and Crane 2008).

Fifth, nationalist cultures are strongly embedded in most societies, and this constrains the internationalism of the web. Nation-centred cultures have been built up over centuries, and are strongly supported by traditional media. Thus, in 2007 American network TV news devoted only 20 per cent of its time to foreign news, while even its counterparts in two internationalist Nordic countries allocated just 30 per cent (Curran et al. 2009). Insular news values also shape the content of the press in these and other countries (Aalberg and Curran 2012).

This cultural inheritance shapes the content of the web. Thus, a study of the leading news websites in nine nations, spread over four continents, found that these report mainly national news. In fact, these premier news websites are, in general, only slightly less nation-centred than leading TV news programmes.[9]

National cultures can also influence user participation on the net. Thus, China is a strongly nationalistic society. This is a consequence of national humiliations visited upon it by Western and Eastern imperial powers in the past; pride in the country's remarkable economic success; and the product of the Communist regime's deliberate cultivation of nationalism as a way of maintaining public support and social cohesion. Intense nationalism finds expression in Chinese websites and in online chat rooms. This can spill over into visceral hostility towards the Japanese in which not much understanding is displayed (Morozov 2011).[10]

Sixth, authoritarian governments have developed ways of managing the net and of intimidating would-be critics. These will be discussed more fully later.[11] It is sufficient to note here that in many parts of the world people cannot, without fear, interact and say what they want online. Global internet discourse is distorted by state intimidation and censorship.

Seventh, inequalities within countries – not just between them – can distort online dialogue. This is not simply because a higher proportion of those on high incomes have home internet access than of those on low incomes (Van Dijk 2005; Jansen 2010). Those with cultural capital have a head start. Thus 81 per cent of writers of articles in the leading international e-zine, *openDemocracy*, in 2008 had elite occupations. They were also unrepresentative in other ways: 71 per cent lived in the Europe/Americas and 72 per cent were men. The context of the real world in which elites have greater time, knowledge and written fluency, in which men are better represented than women in politics, and in which knowledge of English tends to be geographically concentrated all shaped in this instance who got to hold forth (Curran and Witschge 2010). More generally, leading bloggers often come from elite backgrounds in Britain, America and elsewhere (Cammaerts 2008).

In short, the idea that cyberspace is a free, open space where people from different backgrounds and nations can commune with each other and build a more deliberative, tolerant world overlooks a number of things. The world is unequal and mutually uncomprehending (in a literal sense); it is torn asunder by conflicting values and interests; it is subdivided by deeply embedded national and local cultures (and other nodes of identity such as religion and ethnicity); and some countries are ruled by authoritarian regimes. These different aspects of the real world penetrate cyberspace, producing a ruined tower of Babel with multiple languages, hate websites, nationalist discourses, censored speech and over-representation of the advantaged.

Yet there are forces of a different kind influencing the development of society. Increasing migration, cheap travel, mass tourism, global market integration and the globalisation of entertainment have encouraged an increased sense of transnational connection. Some of these developments find support in the internet. YouTube showcases shared experience, taste, music and humour from around the world that promotes a 'we-feeling' (revealing, for example, that stand-up comedy in Chinese can be enormously funny, overriding the deadening effect of subtitles).[12] The internet also facilitates the rapid global distribution of arresting images that strengthen a sense of solidarity with beleaguered groups, whether these are earthquake victims or protesters facing repression in distant lands. The internet has the potential to assist the building of a more cohesive, understanding and fairer world. But the mainspring of change will come from society, not the microchip.

One key way of effecting change is democracy. Is the prediction that the internet would spread and rejuvenate democracy borne out by what has happened?

Internet and democracy

It was regularly proclaimed that the internet would undermine dictators by ending their monopoly of information (e.g. Fukuyama 2002). What this forecast failed to anticipate was that the internet could be controlled. Take, for example, Saudi Arabia, where an internet connection was first established in 1994. Public access to the internet was deferred until 1999, to give the government time to perfect its censorship arrangements. This included funnelling of all international connections through the state-controlled Internet Services Unit, the pre-set blocking of proscribed websites, and the creation of a volunteer vigilante force to recommend further proscriptions (Boas 2006). During a similar period, a more sophisticated apparatus was established in China to cope with a much larger volume of internet traffic. This included blocking websites through the state-controlled International Connection Bureau and state-licensed internet service providers, the limitation of bulletin board discussions to government-approved topics, concerted pressure on intermediaries to regulate internet cafes, and software monitoring of web content (Boas 2006).

In normal conditions, state internet censorship in authoritarian countries was not comprehensive, but effective enough. Indeed, a comparative study of eight nations concluded that 'many authoritarian regimes are proactively promoting the development of an Internet that serves state-defined interests rather than challenging them' (Kalathil and Boas 2003: 3). As we shall see in the next chapter, censorship could be undermined when authoritarian regimes faced organised resistance. But, even in these circumstances, the internet did not 'cause' resistance but merely strengthened it.

Another prediction, especially fashionable in the mid-1990s, was that the internet would install a new form of democracy. 'It will not be long', Lawrence Grossman wrote in 1995, 'before many Americans sitting at home or at work will be able to use telecomputer terminals, microprocessors, and computer-driven keypads to push the buttons that will tell their government what should be done about any important matter of state' (Grossman 1995). This did not happen, which is just as well, since online direct democracy would have disenfranchised those without ready internet access, made up disproportionately of the poor and elderly in Western countries. The 'e-government' that emerged usually took the form of inviting the public to comment, petition or otherwise respond online to an official website. This could be useful: for example, in Britain, 30 per cent of online responses to a proposed new law in 1997 came from private individuals – a much higher proportion than in the era before online consultation (Coleman 1999). However, the cumulative evidence suggests that online dialogue with government has, in general, three limitations. Citizens' inputs are often disconnected from real structures of decision making; citizens tend not to take part in these consultations partly for this reason; and sometimes 'e-democracy' means no more than one-sided communication in which the government provides information about services and promotes their use (Slevin 2000; Chadwick 2006; Livingstone 2010). In short, online consultation has added something to the functioning of democracy without making a great deal of difference.[13]

However, it has long been proclaimed that the internet will revitalise liberal democracy in other ways. The public will be better able to control government through its unparalleled access to information (Toffler and Toffler 1995). The internet will also undermine elite control of politics because, according to Mark Poster (2001: 175), the internet is 'empowering previously excluded groups'. Indeed, the internet will extend horizontal channels of communication between social groups while undermining top-down communication between elites and the general public. In this brave new world, it is hoped, the grassroots will reclaim power and inaugurate a 'renaissance of democracy' (Agre 1994).[14]

In America, some argued that the internet would dispense with the need for expensive television advertising and corporate funding, and create the conditions for a grassroots-driven politics that would take America in a new direction. For some, in 2008, Barack Obama embodied this dream. In fact, the internet did help Obama to raise substantial financial contributions from ordinary citizens and to win votes in the primaries and subsequent 2008 presidential election. Even so, the deepening economic crisis was probably the principal reason why Obama won the presidency.[15] More significantly for our purposes, Barack Obama combined old and new methods of electioneering. His team spent $235.9 million on television political advertising and his campaign (winning the Marketer of the Year award) was guided by costly professionals. To bankroll this, Barack Obama had to secure large corporate donations in addition to citizen funding (Curran 2011). In the event, Obama's administration employed numerous political and financial sector insiders and followed a liberal rather than radical agenda. The internet did not give birth, as it had been hoped, to a new kind of politics.

Nor does the internet seem to have 'empowered' low-income households (as distinct from high-income ones) in Western countries. Smith et al. (2009) discovered that, in the US, the advantaged tend to be the most active in politics, and this imbalance is reproduced in online activism. Similarly, Di Genarro and Dutton (2006) found that in Britain the politically active tend to be drawn from the higher socio-economic groups, the more highly educated and older people.

Those engaged in political online participation were even more skewed towards the affluent and highly educated, though they were more often younger. Di Genarro and Dutton's conclusion was that the internet seems to be promoting political exclusion rather than inclusion.

One reason why low-income groups are less politically active online is because an internet service costs money. However, a further reason has to do with political disaffection. In a comparative study of 22 countries, Frederick Solt (2008) found that economic inequality depresses political interest, political discussion and voting, save among the affluent. In very unequal societies (like the US), the privileged have a powerful incentive to participate in politics because they tend to do well out of it. By contrast, the disadvantaged have much less reason to engage in politics because they tend to obtain less advantage from participation. Low participation is thus presented by Solt as being, in a sense, a rational response to lack of influence. He is able to point out that extensive research does in fact corroborate that wealthy and powerful groups in the US, and elsewhere, have a disproportionate influence on public policy.

Poverty can marginalise and de-motivate in other ways. The UK Commission on Poverty, Participation and Power (2000: 4) highlights the way in which the repeated, bruising experience of being poor and not being treated with respect encourages a sense of powerlessness, while 'long-term poverty can make people feel that it is impossible to change things'. Ruth Lister (2004) also points out that some on low incomes embrace individual deficiency explanations of poverty, making them oriented towards individual rather than collective, political solutions. Studies also show repeatedly that children of poor families in Britain can acquire low expectations and a diminished sense of confidence and entitlement through early socialisation (Hirsch 2007; Sutton et al. 2007; Horgan 2007). Emollient generalisations about the 'empowering' technology of the internet often fail to take into account the powerful influences in the real world that can keep people disempowered.

Of course, the internet places a cheap tool of communication in the hands of citizens. But an enhanced ability to communicate at low cost should not be equated with being heard.[16] Activist groups have found it difficult to get the attention of mainstream media (Fenton 2010b). What they say can also be lost on the web. This is partly because their statements tend to get a low search engine listing. As Hindman (2009: 14) succinctly puts it, the internet is not 'eliminating exclusivity in political life: instead, it is shifting the bar of exclusivity from the production to the filtering of political information'. Activist groups also face the additional problem that public interest in politics can be limited. Thus, a recent survey of American internet users found that on a typical day 38 per cent go online 'just for fun' or 'to pass the time', compared with 25 per cent who say that they go online for news or information about politics (Pew 2009a).

However, the internet is a very effective mode of communication *between* activists. It can link them together, facilitate interaction between them and mobilise them to assemble in one place at short notice. This can result in activity that wins both media and public attention.

For example, a group of around ten activists met in a north London pub in October 2010 and decided to set up a blog called UK Uncut. In a remarkably short space of time, they put corporate tax avoidance on the public agenda. They began by organising a public protest against Vodafone, a company that had negotiated an advantageous back-tax settlement and had been the subject of a recent exposé in the satirical magazine *Private Eye*. This was followed by protests against other named large corporations which, at the time of public spending cuts, were avoiding tax. In early 2001, the campaign group organised 'teach-ins' in publicly bailed-out banks to coincide with the announcement of large bank executive bonuses, under the slogan 'bail-in' to cuts. Within six months, UK Uncut had been reported in numerous TV and radio reports and had featured in 40 articles in leading newspapers.[17] Without the internet, this pub group could not have made the impact that it did.

UK Uncut was helped by the fact that it connected to an undercurrent of public indignation. However, the next example illustrates the way in which the internet can help activists to huddle together when they are out of step with the national mood. MoveOn was set up in America in the wake of the 9/11 terrorist incidents to oppose militarism. Interviews and observations suggested that its online activity provided an anonymous safe haven for dissent at a time of intimidating patriotism. The online campaign also helped to put sympathisers in touch with other like-minded people in their district, and spurred some armchair dissenters into becoming politically active. In a rapid expansion facilitated by the internet, MoveOn grew from 500,000 US members in 2001 to 3 million by December 2005 (Rohlinger and Brown 2008). A relative failure in terms of its campaign objectives, MoveOn nevertheless rallied and sustained dissent.

If one democratic use of the internet is to connect activists, another is to make a 'blind' appeal to consumer power. Thus, an internet-aided campaign was initiated against Nike in the 1990s on the grounds that its expensive trainers were being made by workers who were employed for long hours in unsafe conditions and earned subsistence wages. In response, the company argued that it was not responsible for conditions in factories that it did not own. Under public pressure, Nike shifted its position in 2001 and gave a public undertaking that it would exert 'leverage' on contractors if they were bad employers. The campaign then focused on publicly assessing Nike's claims to greater corporate responsibility (Bennett 2003).

Similarly, a part-time British DJ, Jon Morter, and his friends decided to launch a protest against the commercial manipulation of pop music. They chose as their target the way in which the media's saturation coverage of the television talent contest *X Factor* in the UK regularly propels the show's winner to head the Christmas music chart. Through Facebook and Twitter, they launched a counter-campaign for Rage against the Machine, selecting the track 'Fuck you I won't do what you tell me' as their Christmas choice. The campaign took off, securing celebrity endorsements and extensive media publicity. The protest track secured the No. 1 Christmas spot in 2009, in a collective expression of resentment against commercial control.

The internet can also enable citizens to hold the media to account. Thus, in the much-cited Trent Lott saga, an indignant blogosphere objected in 2002 to the failure of mainstream media to report prominently, and condemn, a speech by a leading Republican politician, Senator Trent Lott, who referred nostalgically to the race-segregation politics of the past. Bloggers' protests were endorsed by a *New York Times* columnist, Paul Krugman, and were then investigated by the TV networks, which discovered that Senator Lott had made similar remarks in the past. In the ensuing political row, Trent Lott was forced to stand down as Senate majority leader. Through the internet, individuals – both Republicans and Democrats – successfully challenged conventional news values and a tacit understanding of the boundaries of the politically acceptable (Scott 2004).

Above all, the international reach of the internet makes it an effective agency for coordinating NGOs in different countries. An early example of this is the launch of the International Campaign to Ban Land Mines in 1992. Its founder, Jody Williams, had been alerted to the terrible injuries that left-behind landmines could inflict when she visited Nicaragua. She started an educational campaign in the United States, but made little progress. Realising that there were numerous anti-landmine organisations around the world, she concluded that the way forward was to link them together. Armed with the internet, phone and fax, Jody Williams and her colleagues brought together more than seven hundred groups in a concerted campaign for an international treaty. Their efforts were rewarded with the signing of the 1997 [anti-personnel] Mine Ban Treaty by 120 states, leading to the award of a Nobel Peace prize (Klotz 2004; Price 1998). However, both the United States and China refused to sign.

Similarly, an internet campaign was launched in 1997 against the Multilateral Agreement on Investments (MAI) prepared for ratification by OECD countries. Progressive activists around the world received e-mails warning that MAI would lead to an international race to the bottom in terms of labour, human rights, environmental and consumer regulation. The ensuing NGO agitation found a champion in the French socialist government, which successfully opposed MAI's adoption (and also publicly saluted the internet campaign) (Smith and Smythe 2004). This was followed by mass protests organised at the World Trade Organisation meeting in Seattle (1999) and at the G8 summit at Genoa (2001), greatly assisted by the internet (Juris 2005). Both these occasions were marked by violence, in contrast to the peaceful protests at the G8 meeting at Gleneagles (2005), when debt relief measures for poorer countries were publicly announced. However, some of these debt relief commitments were not, in fact, honoured.

These case studies leave little doubt that the internet has increased the effectiveness of political activists. Yet, despite the very selective case-study agenda of internet researchers, there is nothing particularly left-wing about the internet. Indeed, American conservatives became better organised, earlier, on the net than liberals (Hill and Hughes 1998), while the internet seems to have played a significant role in the more recent rise of the right-wing Tea Party Movement (Thompson 2010).

The utilisation of the internet by people of different persuasions has strengthened the infrastructure of democracy. But this positive input has been offset by negative trends in the wider political environment. Since the 1980s, there has been an enormous increase of investment in corporate and state public relations (Davis 2002; Dinan and Miller 2007). This was accompanied by a drift towards populist politics, supported by focus groups, private polling and political consultants (Crouch 2004; Marquand 2008; Davis 2010, among others). Meanwhile political parties became in many countries increasingly hollowed-out organisations with shrinking memberships – a trend almost caricatured by Berlusconi's very successful launch of Forza Italia, a 'plastic party' with few members (Ginsborg 2004; Lane 2004). All these developments contributed to a growing centralisation of political power.

The role of the internet in coordinating international political protest also needs to be put into perspective. The development of a global system of governance became closely aligned to the ascendant neoliberal order (Sklair 2002). Major institutions like the World Trade Organisation and International Monetary Fund are relatively unaccountable (Stiglitz 2002). As Peter Dahlgren (2005) notes, 'there are simply few established mechanisms for democratically based and binding transnational decision making'. The international forces galvanised by the net are still relatively weak, with little purchase for influencing global policy.

The major public institution most accessible to democratic influence, at least by comparison with intermediate and global structures of governance, is the nation-state. Yet, the nation-state has been rendered less effective by the rise of deregulated global financial markets and mobile transnational corporations. This has weakened the democratic power of national electorates (Curran 2002).

In short, the internet has energised activism. But in the context of political disaffection, increasing political manipulation at the centre, an unaccountable global order and the weakening of electoral power, the internet has not revitalised democracy[18].

Renaissance of journalism

The internet, according to Rupert Murdoch, is democratising journalism. 'Power is moving away', he declares, 'from the old elite in our industry – the editors, the chief executives and, let's face it, the proprietors', and is being transferred to bloggers, social networks and consumers downloading from the web (Murdoch 2006). This view is echoed by the leading British conservative blogger Guido Fawkes, who proclaimed that 'the days of media conglomerates determining the news in a top-down Fordist fashion are over ... Big media are going to be disintermediated because the technology has drastically reduced the cost of dissemination' (Fawkes cited Beckett 2008: 108). The radical academic lawyer Yochai Benkler (2006) concurs, arguing that a monopolistic industrial model of journalism is giving way to a pluralistic networked model based on profit and non-profit, individual and organised journalistic practices. The radical press historian John Nerone goes further, pronouncing the *ancien régime* to be a thing of the past. 'The biggest thing to lament about the death of the old order [of journalism]', he chortles, 'is that it is not there for us to piss on any more' (Nerone 2009: 355). Numerous commentators, drawn from the left as well as the right, and including news industry leaders, citizen journalists and academic experts, have reached the same conclusion: the internet is bringing to an end the era of media moguls and conglomerate control of journalism.

The second related theme of this euphoric commentary is that the internet will lead to the reinvention of journalism in a better form. The internet will be 'journalism's ultimate liberation', according to Philip Elmer-Dewitt (1994), because 'anyone with a computer and a modem can be his own reporter, editor and publisher – spreading news and views to millions of readers around the world'. One version of this vision sees traditional media being largely displaced by citizen journalists who will generate 'a back-to-basics, Jeffersonian conversation among the citizenry' (Mallery cited Schwartz 1994). An alternative version sees professional journalists working in tandem with enthusiastic volunteers to produce a reinvigorated form of journalism (e.g. Beckett 2008; Deuze 2009). This is a view now coming out of the heart of the news industry. 'Journalism will thrive', proclaims Chris Ahearn, Media President at Thomson Reuter, 'as creators and publishers embrace the collaborative power of new technologies, retool production and distribution strategies and we stop trying to do everything ourselves' (Ahearn 2009).

The dethroning of traditional news controllers and the renewal of journalism are thus the two central themes of this forecast. Superficially at least, it looks as if some elements of this forecast are coming true. In certain circumstances, citizen journalists have made an impact. Thus, the bystanders who, in 2009, caught on camera the killing of Nada Soltan in a Tehran demonstration and the manslaughter of Ian Tomlinson in a London demonstration recorded news stories that went around the world. Similarly, participants' footage of the uprisings in the Middle East, and of repressive attempts to contain them, was widely used by news organisations in 2011.

There has also been an outpouring of self-communication, with an estimated 14 per cent of adults in the US in 2010 writing a blog (Zickuhr 2010). This has been accompanied by a spectacular increase in social media traffic (Nielsen 2011), though most social media content has little to do with journalism. In addition, new independent online publications, such as *Huffington Post*,[19] *Politico* and *openDemocracy*, have made their mark.

But the millenarian prophecy of death and renewal is wishful thinking. One reason for thinking that the old order persists is that television is still the most important source of news in most countries. Thus, in all six countries surveyed – Britain, France, Germany, Italy, United States and Japan – more respondents said that they relied on television than the internet as the main source of news about their country (Ofcom 2010b).

More importantly, leading news organisations colonised the news segment of cyberspace. To pre-empt competition, they set up satellite news websites. These quickly became dominant because they were heavily cross-subsidised; and exploited the news-gathering resources and established reputations of their powerful parent companies. Thus, Pew (2011) found that in 2010, 80 per cent of the internet traffic to news and information sites was concentrated on the top 7 per cent of sites. The majority of these sites (67 per cent) were controlled by 'legacy' news organisations from the pre-internet era. Another 13 per cent were accounted for by content aggregators. Only 14 per cent of these top sites were online-only operations that produced mostly original reportorial content.

In other words, the rise of the internet has not undermined leading news organisations. On the contrary, it has enabled them to extend their hegemony across technologies. In concrete terms, this means that the ten most-visited *news* websites in the world in 2010/11 included only one online independent (*Huffington Post*); the remaining nine were leading news organisations, like the *New York Times* and Xinhua News Agency, from the pre-internet era (Guardian 2011). The top ten news websites in the US in March 2011 included only one online independent (again the *Huffington Post*); the remainder were four leading TV organisations, three leading newspapers and two content aggregators (Moos 2011). In Britain, there was no online independent among the top ten news sites in 2011: all the top spots were filled by leading 'legacy' television and newspaper organisations and content aggregators (Nielsen 2011).

Content aggregators do not usually give prominence to alternative news sources. Thus Joanna Redden and Tamara Witschge (2010) examined Google's and Yahoo!'s listing of content, over time, in relation to five major public affairs issues, only to find that 'no alternative news sites were returned in the first page of search results'. This prioritisation matters, they point out, because research shows that the first page is much more likely to be sampled than subsequent pages. Redden and Witschge also found that Google and Yahoo! tended to privilege leading news providers, reproducing their ascendancy.

The leading news brands' successful defence of their oligopoly has been helped by the weakness of their challengers. Independent online news ventures have failed to develop a business model that works. Most have found it difficult to build a subscription base because the public has become accustomed to having free web content. And because these online independents have generally attracted small audiences, they have low advertising returns. A Pew Research Center study (2009b) in the US concluded that 'despite enthusiasm and good work, few if any of these are profitable or even self-financing'. Similarly, a 2009 *Columbia Journalism Review* study concluded that 'it is unlikely that any but the smallest of these [web-based] news organisations can be supported primarily by existing online revenue' (Downie and Schudson 2010). Often with skeletal resources, their most pressing priority has usually been to stay alive.

Nor has the internet connected the legion of bloggers to a mass audience. In Britain, for instance, 79 per cent of *internet users* in 2008 had not read a single blog during the previous three months (ONS 2008). Most bloggers lack the time to investigate stories. They are amateurs, who need their regular day job to pay their way (Couldry 2010). This reduces their ability to build a large audience.

What about the claim that the quality of journalism is being improved by the internet? This seems eminently persuasive, at first sight. After all, as a consequence of the internet, journalists have faster access to more information and to a wider range of news sources. This should make it easier to verify stories and to give expression to different viewpoints. Journalists can also draw more easily upon feedback and input from their audiences.

However, what this optimistic expectation leaves out of account is the devastating consequences of lost advertising. In economically advanced countries, the internet now reaches a large audience; it is cheap, and good at targeting specific consumers (which is why 'search' is the internet's biggest category of advertising). After a slow start, these strengths generated a meteoric increase of internet advertising at the expense of television and the press. In the US, advertising on the internet overtook that in newspapers in 2010 (having earlier overtaken cable TV) (Gobry 2011). In Britain, internet advertising already took a larger share (25 per cent) of advertising expenditure in 2010 than the newspaper press (18 per cent) (Nielsen 2011). The scale of redistribution that was involved is perhaps most dramatically illustrated in relation to classified advertising. In the UK, the internet's share of classified expenditure soared from 2 per cent to 45 per cent between 2000 and 2008, while that of the local and regional press plummeted from 47 per cent to 26 per cent. The classified advertising share of national papers fell from 14 per cent to 6 per cent during the same period (Office of Fair Trading 2009).

This loss of advertising has led to closure and contraction. In Britain, 101 British local newspapers folded between January 2008 and September 2009[20], while in the US some major newspapers like the *Christian Science Monitor* ceased print publication. Numerous local TV channels in the US now no longer originate local news, while the main commercial TV channel (ITV) in the UK wants to discontinue local news coverage. The number of journalists employed in the US declined by 26 per cent between 2000 and 2009 (Pew 2011), while those employed in the UK's 'mainstream journalism corps' shrank by between 27 per cent and 33 per cent between 2001 and 2010 (Nel 2010). News budgets were cut, with the result that even the large metropolitan dailies and television network news in the US have been forced to economise on high-cost investigative and foreign journalism.

A major study of British journalism also concludes that a more profound and pervasive process of deterioration is taking place, in marked contrast to hyped predictions of regeneration (Fenton 2010a; Lee-Wright et al. 2011). It found that fewer journalists are being expected to produce more content, as a consequence of newsroom redundancies, the integration of online and offline news production, and the need to update stories in a 24-hour news cycle. This is encouraging journalists to rely more on tried-and-tested, mainstream news sources as a way of boosting output. It is also fostering the lifting of stories from rivals' websites as a way of increasing productivity, even to the extent of using the same news frames, quotes and pictures. Depleted resources are contributing in general to increased reliance on scissors-and-paste, deskbound journalism. To judge from an Argentinian study, a very similar trend towards imitative, office-centred journalism is also taking place elsewhere (Boczkowski 2009).

In brief, the dominant news organisations have entrenched their ascendancy because they have gained a commanding position in both the offline and online production and consumption of news. In addition, the rise of the internet as an advertising medium has led to budget cuts, increased time pressure on journalists and, sometimes, declining quality in mainstream journalism. This has not been offset by new independent news start-ups because these have been mostly too small and with too little firepower to ride to the rescue.

That said, there are significant variations between countries. For example, internet-based citizen journalism has been a relative flop in Britain, whereas it has been a great success in South Korea. We need to take a closer look at this not least because it illustrates the way in which the external context affects the internet's impact.

Different contexts/different outcomes

At the turn of the century there was little demand for radical political and cultural change in Britain. The 2002 general election witnessed the lowest turnout ever, registering public disaffection with politics (Couldry et al. 2007). The left was disoriented by the neoliberal trajectory of the Labour government and its decision to join the US-led invasion of Iraq in 2003. A youth-based cultural revolt lay in the past, having taken place more than a quarter of a century earlier. So when the website *openDemocracy* (*OD*) started in 2001, it was in a relatively becalmed period in which the winds of change had died down in Britain. It was also an international project, only partly connected to a British base. With substantial foundation support, an able team at the centre, and drawing upon a talented network of contributors, the website became the leading British venture of its kind. But its total, gross number of visitors per month peaked at 441,000 in 2005 before falling rapidly thereafter. Indeed, the venture went into financial crisis in 2007 from which it has never fully recovered (Curran and Witschge 2010).

In sharp contrast, there was a pressure-cooker build-up in favour of political and cultural change in South Korea. The short-lived attempt to create a parliamentary democracy in 1960 had been overtaken by a military coup. However, the democracy movement gained increased momentum in the subsequent period, securing major constitutional reforms in 1987. A civilian president was elected in 1992, and this opened the way to further liberalisation. The number of civil society organisations doubled in the 1990s, having doubled in the previous decade (Kim and Hamilton 2006: 553, table 5). There was a long-running campaign for greater media independence from government that gained support from increasingly disaffected journalists (Park et al. 2000). Public attacks were also made on collusion between big business and government, the neoliberal policies pursued in the wake of the Asian 1997–98 economic crisis, and the continued presence of a large, unaccountable American army in the country. The politician Moo-hyun Roh came to represent this gathering tide of opposition, and was elected President in 2002. This upsurge of political radicalism was accompanied by a cultural revolt against authoritarian conformity.

OhmyNews (OMN), launched in 2000, became the focal point of this political and generational protest.[21] It was different from the three dominant national dailies, all of which were closely identified with the establishment and became associated with the political mobilisation that led to the election of President Roh. It also became a vehicle of cultural dissent, giving space to views that did not conform to the precepts of Confucian civility and obedience.

In these very special circumstances, OMN took off like a balloon. Established by a young, radical journalist, Yeon Ho Oh, in 2000 with a modest launch fund of $85,000, OMN had initially a skeletal staff of four, supported by 727 volunteer 'citizen journalists' (Kim and Hamilton 2006). The website's registered citizen journalists grew to 14,000 in 2001, 20,000 in 2002, 30,000 in 2003 and 34,000 in 2004, while its core staff increased to 60 people by 2004 (of whom 35 were full-time journalists). This expansion in the number of volunteers was accompanied by a meteoric growth in readership. A survey undertaken for an independent investor company estimated that OMN had, in 2004, 2.2 million visitors a month. Winning this volume of young, mostly affluent users solved the perennial problem of independent web publishing – lack of income. OMN became profitable by 2003 because it attracted substantial online advertising. By contrast, the donations and voluntary subscriptions from users remained low, very much less than the modest proceeds of its print edition (Kim and Hamilton 2006: 548, table 1).

OMN 'reinvented' journalism by skilfully harnessing professional and amateur inputs. By the mid-2000s, its core group of professional journalists wrote only about 20 per cent of website content. However, they selected and edited the articles sent in by 'citizen journalists' that were published in the main sections of the website. Space was created beside articles for readers' responses, and the website hosted chat rooms on different topics. Citizen journalists received a token payment if their articles were accepted in the main section. Articles, unpaid and unedited, were also published in the 'kindling' sections of the website. The whole operation was overseen by a committee made up of both professionals and representatives of citizen journalists. By 2004, OMN published between 150 and 200 articles each day, becoming in effect a website 'daily'.

This remarkable achievement – attracting volunteers, building a mass audience, achieving solvency and influencing public life – was only possible because there was a ground-swell of progressive support behind the website. However, this ground-swell declined because there was growing disappointment with President Roh's government. Anticipated reforms were not enacted, or were discontinued in the face of determined political and business opposition. The Korean economy also underperformed on Roh's watch. In the next presidential election (2007), the conservative (GNP) candidate won in a very low poll. In 2009, former President Roh – facing the prospect of criminal charges for bribery and corruption – committed suicide.

OMN suffered as a consequence of its close association with a 'failed' President, and from the decline of the left. The proliferation of new websites meant also that OMN ceased to be the natural home of cultural dissent. It also became apparent that its volunteer base was relatively narrow: in 2005, registered volunteers were heavily concentrated in greater Seoul, almost entirely under the age of 40, and 77 per cent were male (Joyce 2007: 'exhibit' 2). The website ceased to be profitable in 2006, and ran into increasing financial difficulty. The glory days of OMN now seem to be over.

In hindsight, it is clear that new technology was crucial to OMN's success because it lowered costs, facilitated contributions from volunteers and enabled lively interactions on its website. But without a strongly prevailing wind, OMN would never have lifted off in the way that it did. And when that wind subsided, OMN lost momentum.

The importance of the external context in enabling or disabling the realisation of the technological potential of the internet can be illustrated in another way. When OMN was launched in Japan in 2006, it had substantial resources because it went into partnership with a telecommunications corporation. But Japan, a deeply consensual corporatist society, did not provide fertile soil for the new venture. OMN Japan found it difficult to recruit good disaffected journalists; its more professionally oriented staff had running conflicts with voluntary contributors (who objected to heavy editing). Web traffic stayed low, and voluntary contributors to OMN Japan remained fewer than a tenth of their counterparts in Korea (Joyce 2007). An attempt was made to save the website by giving it a softer, lifestyle focus, but to no avail. The venture closed in 2008, a failure from the very outset, in contrast to its sister paper.

OMN also set up in 2004 an English-language, international website. Again there was not the same political momentum behind it as there was for the domestic website. OMN International attracted a relatively small number of contributors and users. This detracted from its quality (reflected in its very erratic and uneven coverage of news and issues around the world), and saddled it with financial problems that seem unlikely to be resolved (Dencik 2011).

Empowerment/disempowerment

The importance of context can also be illustrated in another way by comparing two countries. Both Malaysia and Singapore seem at first glance rather similar.

They are authoritarian democracies, whose ruling parties have been in power ever since national independence. Both countries have illiberal laws, including the licensing of traditional media outlets and the annual licensing of civil society organisations. Yet, they both have adopted a liberal policy towards the internet in order to further their economic modernisation programmes. While Singapore's internet policy is notionally more restrictive, since it entails formal website licensing, in actual practice it is little different from that in Malaysia.

Internet penetration is higher in Singapore than in Malaysia. In 2011, 77 per cent of the Singapore population were internet users, compared with 59 per cent in Malaysia (Internet World Stats 2011b). This might lead us to expect that the rise of a relatively free internet would be more empowering in Singapore than Malaysia. In fact, the reverse is the case, due to crucial differences in the political environment of the two countries.

The ruling elite are less cohesive in Malaysia than in Singapore. Malaysia is run by a coalition of parties within which there have been perennial tensions. These became dysfunctional when the Prime Minister, Dr Mohamad Mahathir, turned on his deputy, Ibrahim Anwar, following extensive disagreements over economic policy. Anwar was sacked, beaten up by the police, and jailed on what were widely suspected to be trumped up charges of corruption and sodomy. This led to the creation of the opposition *reformasi* movement in 1998, which won support both from within and outside the political establishment (Sani 2009).

Malaysia has a more developed civil society than Singapore (George 2007). Malaysia's civil society includes active civil rights, constitutional reform and important Islamic groups. Its political opposition also became increasingly outspoken in the 1990s, partly because Malaysia was worse hit than Singapore by the 1997–98 Asian economic crisis, and took longer to recover. The tiger of Islamic fundamentalism in Malaysia – for which there is no equivalent in Singapore – also showed signs of slipping its government leash.

Against this background, the internet developed as an increasingly important space of dissent and criticism in Malaysia. Civil society groups set up independent websites. A dissenting minority press that had survived in Malaysia also developed an online presence. By the mid-2000s, internet activists became organised, and developed strong links with each other, in a way that did not happen in Singapore. Cherian George (2005) found that Malaysian websites more frequently updated their content, were better resourced, more critical and reached a very much larger audience than their counterparts in Singapore.

Malaysian political websites gained an increasing audience partly because mainstream media came to be distrusted. As opposition to the government grew (though in a discontinuous way), independent websites became a focal point of public criticism. This contributed in turn to the cumulative erosion of support for the governing bloc (Kenyon 2010). In 2008, the newly formed opposition coalition made substantial gains, winning nearly 37 per cent of federal lower house seats. For the first time since independence in 1957, the governing coalition ceased to have a two-thirds majority.

By contrast, Singapore is ruled not by a coalition but by a single, united party (PAP). The opposition is so little supported that it regularly secures the election of only a handful of MPs. Underpinning the ruling party's dominion are not only coercive laws but also a hegemonic national ideology that stresses Asian values, public morality and social harmony (Worthington 2003; Rodan 2004; George 2007). This hegemony is also underwritten by the city-state's economic success that encourages pragmatic acceptance of the regime. So great has been the ruling elite's domination of Singaporean society that the internet was largely neutralised as a space of dissent (Ibrahim 2006). Indeed, when Andrew Kenyon (2010) undertook a comparative analysis of critical reporting in three countries – Australia, Malaysia and Singapore – he had to omit Singaporean online content because there were too few critical articles to constitute an adequate sample.[22]

In brief, the wider political context encouraged the development of the internet as an agency of dissent in Malaysia, but of co-option and control in Singapore. This illustrates our concluding point: different contexts produce different outcomes, something that is repeatedly obscured by overarching theories of the internet centred on its technology.

Notes

1 My thanks for the exceptional research assistance of Joanna Redden on Chapters 1 and 2. My thanks go also to Nick Couldry for his insightful comments on a draft version of Chapters 1 and 2.

2 The Harvard reference system turns multiple citations into rebarbative obstructions between sentences. In this opening paragraph, only one publication per theme has been cited, usually for the sake of accessibility. Numerous other examples of these arguments will be encountered later in this chapter.

3 A central theme of this book was anticipated in a satirical 1993 *New Yorker* cartoon featuring a dog sitting in front of a computer, with the caption: 'On the Internet, nobody knows that you're a dog' (reproduced in Anderson 2005: 227).

4 Sherry Turkle did not change tack by 180 degrees, since what she wrote in both her optimistic and pessimistic phases was hedged with qualifications.

5 This approach differs from that of Vincent Mosco (2005), who examines internet prophecies as a discourse that illuminates the assumptions and contexts that produced them. This leads him to describe these prophecies as 'myths' without empirically investigating whether they became true or false. Our approach differs also from that of Anderson (2005), who looks at internet predictions in a more historically descriptive way.

6 In passing, it should be noted that a subsidiary theme of this thesis is that companies whose structure and functioning exploited to the full the interactivity of the internet would flourish in the New Economy. Thus, Castells (2001: 68) presents Cisco Systems as 'the pioneer of the [network] business model characterizing the Internet economy' that exemplified its dynamism. Yet, in 2000–01, Cisco's shares declined by 78 per cent, and the company laid off 8,500 workers. In 2011, Cisco announced further mass lay-offs, and its CEO, John Chambers, wrote: 'we are disappointed for our investors, our employees are confused. Basically, we lost some of … [our]success based on credibility, we must win back reputation' (Solaria Sun 2011). The company's rollercoaster history underlines the simple point that skilled structural utilisation of new communications technology is only one ingredient, among many, of economic success.

7 The literature on this is vast. For useful introductions, see Porter (2008a and b); Dranove and Schaefer (2010); and Ghoshal (1992).
8 Fuchs (2009) offers a similar but slightly different analysis that stresses internal inequality within nations, level of democracy and degree of urbanisation as variables influencing the level of national internet take-up.
9 The results of this ESRC co-funded comparative study will be published in 2012.
10 The way nationalist cultures can shape the web and internet use is discussed further in the next chapter, page 57.
11 See page 5, and pages 49–51 and 53 in Chapter 2.
12 See http://www.youtube.com/watch?v=iailMSUVenA (accessed 15 August 2011).
13 Coleman and Blumler (2008: 169 ff) argue eloquently that online consultation could make more of a difference if a *publicly supported* 'civic commons in cyberspace' is created that is linked to political decision making.
14 For more predictions in this vein, see Anderson (2005).
15 For more on the limits of internet influence in the 2008 US election, see Chapter 5.
16 For more on this, see Chapter 5.
17 See http://www.ukuncut.org.uk/press/coverage?articles_page=5 (accessed 4 April 2011).
18 For discussion of the role of the internet in 'spreading democracy', see the next chapter.
19 In 2011 *Huffington Post* ceased to be independent, and was acquired by AOL.
20 Information supplied by the Newspaper Society, UK, in e-mail correspondence, 19 February 2010.
21 My thanks to Elisabeth Baumann-Meurer for researching the historical context of OhmyNews.
22 In the 2011 general election, PAP sustained a small loss, perhaps influenced by increased online criticism. But PAP still won all but six seats.

References

Aalberg, T. and Curran, J. (2012) (eds) *How Media Inform Democracy*, New York: Routledge.
Agre, P. (1994) 'Networking and Democracy', *The Network Observer*, 1 (4). Online. Available HTTP: <http://polaris.gseis.ucla.edu/pagre/tno/april-1994.html> (accessed 4 May 2011).
Ahearn, C. (2009) 'How Will Journalism Survive the Internet Age?', *Reuters*, 11 December. Online. Available HTTP: <http://blogs.reuters.com/from-reuterscom/2009/12/11/how-will-journalism-survive-the-internet-age/> (accessed 10 June 2011).
Akdeniz, Y. (2009) *Racism on the Internet*, Strasbourg: Council of Europe Publishing.
Anderson, J. (2005) *Imagining the Internet*, Lanham, MD: Rowman and Littlefield.
Atkinson, R., Ezell, S. J., Andes, S. M., Castro, D. D. and Bennett, R. (2010) 'The Internet Economy 25 Years After .Com: Transforming Commerce and Life', The Information Technology & Innovation Foundation. Online. Available HTTP: <http://www.itif.org/files/2010-25-years.pdf> (accessed 2 February 2011).
Back, L. (2001) 'White Fortresses in Cyberspace', UNESCO Points of View. Online. Available HTTP: <http://www.unesco.org/webworld/points_of_views/back.shtml> (accessed 4 June 2011).
Bar, F. with Simard, C. (2002) 'New Media implementation and Industrial Organization', in L. Lievrouw and S. Livingstone (eds) *The Handbook of New Media*, London: Sage.
Bartels, L. M. (2008) *Unequal Democracy: The Political Economy of the New Gilded Age*, Princeton: Princeton University Press.
Beckett, C. (2008) *Supermedia*, Oxford: Blackwell.

Beilock, R. and Dimitrova, D. V. (2003) 'An Exploratory Model of Inter-country Internet Diffusion', *Telecommunications Policy*, 27: 237–52.

Benkler, Y. (2006) *The Wealth of Networks*, New Haven: Yale University Press.

Bennett, L. W. (2003) 'Communicating Global Activism', *Information, Communication & Society*, 6 (2): 143–68.

Blodget, H. (2008) 'Why Wall Street Always Blows It … ', *The Atlantic Online*. Online. Available HTTP: <http://www.theatlantic.com/magazine/archive/2008/12/why-wall-street-always-blows-it/7147/> (accessed 12 February 2011).

Boas, T. C. (2006) 'Weaving the Authoritarian Web: The Control of Internet Use in Nondemocratic Regimes', in J. Zysman and A. Newman (eds) *How Revolutionary Was the Digital Revolution? National Responses, Market Transitions, and Global Technology*, Stanford, CA: Stanford Business Books.

Boczkowski, P. (2009) 'Technology, Monitoring and Imitation in Contemporary News Work', *Communication, Culture and Critique*, 2: 39–59.

Bohman, J. (2004) 'Expanding Dialogue: The Internet, the Public Sphere and Prospects for Transnational Democracy', *Sociological Review*, 131–55.

Bulashova, N. and Cole, G. (1995) 'Friends and Partners: Building Global Community on the Internet', paper presented at the Internet Society International Networking Conference, Honolulu, Hawaii, June.

Cairncross, F. (1997) *The Death of Distance*, Boston: Harvard Business School Press.

Cammaerts, B. (2008) 'Critiques on the Participatory Potentials of Web 2.0', *Communication, Culture and Critique*, 1 (4): 358–77.

Cassidy, J. (2002) *Dot.con: How America Lost its Mind and Money in the Internet Era*, New York: Harper Collins.

Castells, M. (2001) *The Internet Galaxy*, Oxford: Oxford University Press.

Cellan-Jones, R. (2001) *Dot.bomb: The Rise and Fall of Dot.com Britain*, London: Aurum.

Chadwick, A. (2006) *Internet Politics: States, Citizens and New Communication Technologies*, Oxford: Oxford University Press.

Chrysostome, E. and Rosson, P. (2004) 'The Internet and SMES Internationalization: Promises and Illusions', paper delivered at Conference of ASAC, Quebec, Canada, 5 June. Online. Available HTTP: <http://libra.acadiau.ca/library/ASAC/ v25/articles/ Chrysostome-Rosson.pdf> (accessed 23 October 2011).

Coleman, S. (1999) 'New Media and Democratic Politics', *New Media and Society*, 1 (1): 62–74.

Coleman, S. and Blumler, J. (2008) *The Internet and Democratic Citizenship*, Cambridge: Cambridge University Press.

Commission on Poverty, Participation and Power (2000) 'Listen Hear: The Right to be Heard', Report of the Commission on Poverty, Participation and Power, Bristol: Policy Press. Online. Available HTTP: <http://www.jrf.org.uk/publications/listen-hear-right-be-heard> (accessed 10 January 2011).

Conway, M. (2006) 'Terrorism and the Internet: New Media – New Threat?', *Parliamentary Affairs*, 59 (2): 283–98.

Cook, E. (1999) 'Web Whiz-kids Count Their Cool Millions', *Independent*, 25 July, p. 10.

Couldry, N. (2010) 'New Online Sources and Writer-Gatherers', in N. Fenton (ed.) *New Media, Old News*, London: Sage.

Couldry, N., Livingstone, S. and Markham, T. (2007) *Media Consumption and Public Engagement*, Basingstoke: Palgrave Macmillan.

Crouch, C. (2004) *Post-Democracy*, Cambridge: Polity.

Curran, J. (2002) *Media and Power*, London: Routledge.

——(2011) *Media and Democracy*, London: Routledge.

Curran, J. and Witschge, T. (2010) 'Liberal Dreams and the Internet' in N. Fenton (ed.) *New Media, Old News: Journalism and Democracy in the Digital Age*, London: Sage.

Curran, J., Lund, A., Iyengar, S. and Salovaara-Moring, I. (2009) 'Media System, Public Knowledge and Democracy: A Comparative Study', *European Journal of Communication*, 24 (1): 5–26.

Dahlgren, P. (2005) 'The Internet, Public Spheres, and Political Communication: Dispersion and Deliberation', *Political Communication*, 22: 147–62.

Daniels, J. (2008) 'Race, Civil Rights, and Hate Speech in the Digital Era', in A. Everett (ed.) *Learning Race and Ethnicity: Youth and Digital Media*, The John D. and Catherine T. MacArthur Foundation Series on Digital Media and Learning, Cambridge, MA: MIT Press, 129–54.

Davies, J., Sandström, S., Shorrocks, A. and Wolff, E. (2006) 'The World Distribution of Household Wealth', United Nations University, World Institute for Development Economics Research. Online. Available HTTP: <http://www.wider.unu.edu/events/past-events/2006-events/en_GB/05-12-2006/> (accessed 10 January 2011).

Davis, A. (2002) *Public Relations Democracy*, Manchester: Manchester University Press.

——(2010) *Political Communication and Social Theory*, London: Routledge.

Deighton, J. and Quelch, J. (2009) *Economic Value of the Advertising-Supported Internet Ecosystem*, Cambridge, MA: Hamilton Consultants Inc.

Dencik, L. (2011) *Media and Global Civil Society*, Basingstoke: Palgrave Macmillan.

Deuze, M. (2009) 'The People Formerly Known as the Employers', *Journalism*, 10 (3): 315–18.

Di Genarro, C. and Dutton, W. (2006) 'The Internet and the Public: Online and Offline Political Participation in the United Kingdom', *Parliamentary Affairs*, 59 (2): 299–313.

Dinan, W. and Miller, D. (2007) *Thinker, Faker, Spinner, Spy*, London: Pluto.

Downie, L. and Schudson, M. (2010) 'The Reconstruction of American Journalism', *Columbia Journalism Review*. Online. Available HTTP: <http://www.cjr.org/reconstruction/the_reconstruction_of_american.php> (accessed 10 January 2010).

Dranove, B. and Schaefer, S. (2010) *Economics of Strategy*, 5th edn, Hoboken, NJ: John Wiley.

Edmunds, R., Guskin, E. and Rosenstiel, T. (2011) 'Newspapers: Missed the 2010 Media Rally', *The State of the News Media 2011*, Pew Research Center's Project for Excellence in Journalism. Online. Available HTTP: <http://stateofthemedia.org/2011/newspapers-essay/> (accessed 20 August 2011).

Ehlers, V. (1995) 'Beyond the Cyberhype: What the Internet Means to the Congressman of the Future', *Roll Call*, 1 October.

Elmer-Dewitt, P. (1994) 'Battle for the Soul of the Internet', *Time*, 144 (4): 50–57.

Eskelsen, G., Marcus, A., and Ferree, W. K. (2009) *The Digital Economy Fact Book*, 10th edn, The Progress and Freedom Foundation. Online. Available HTTP: <http://www.pff.org/issues-pubs/books/factbook_10th_Ed.pdf> (accessed 2 April 2011).

European Commission (2009) *Eurostat*. Online. Available HTTP: <http://epp.eurostat.ec.europa.eu/portal/page/portal/eurostat/home/> (accessed 14 August 2011).

Fenton, N. (2008) 'Mediating Hope: New Media, Politics and Resistance', *International Journal of Cultural Studies*, 11: 230–48.

——(ed.) (2010a) *New Media, Old News: Journalism and Democracy in the Digital Age*, London: Sage.

——(2010b) 'NGOs, New Media and the Mainstream News: News from Everywhere' in N. Fenton (ed.) *New Media, Old News*, London: Sage.

Foster, J. and McChesney, R. (2011) 'The Internet's Unholy Marriage to Capitalism', *Monthly Review* (March). Online. Available HTTP: <http://monthlyreview.org/110301foster-mchesney.php> (accessed 4 June 2011).

Foster, J., McChesney, R. and Jonna, R. (2011) 'Monopoly and Competition in Twenty-First Century Capitalism', *Monthly Review*, 62: 11.

Fraser, N. (2007) 'Transnationalizing the Public Sphere: On the Legitimacy and Efficacy of Public Opinion in a Post-Westphalian World', *Theory, Culture and Society*, 24 (4): 7–30.

Freiburger, T. and Crane, J. S. (2008) 'A Systematic Examination of Terrorist Use of the Internet', *International Journal of Cyber Criminology*, 2 (1): 309–19.

Fuchs, C. (2009) 'The Role of Income Inequality in a Multivariate Cross-National Analysis of the Digital Divide', *Social Science Computer Review*, 27 (1): 41–58.

Fukuyama, F. (2002) *Our Posthuman Future*, New York: Farrar, Straus and Giroux.

Gates, B. (1995) 'To Make a Fortune on the Internet, Find a Niche and Fill it', *Seattle Post-Intelligencer*, 6 December, p. B4.

George, C. (2005) 'The Internet's Political Impact and the Penetration/Particpation Paradox in Malaysia and Singapore', *Media, Culture and Society*, 27 (6): 903–20.

——(2007) *Contentious Journalism and the Internet*, Seattle: University of Washington Press.

Gerstenfeld, P. B., Grant, D. R. and Chiang, C. (2003) 'Hate Online: A Content Analysis of Extremist Internet Sites', *Analyses of Social Issues and Public Policy*, 3 (1): 29–44.

Ghoshal, S. (1992) 'Global Strategy: An Organizing Framework', in F. Root and K. Visudtibhan (eds) *International Strategic Management: Challenges and Opportunities*, New York: Taylor and Francis.

Gilder, G. (1994) *Life After Television*, New York: Norton.

Ginsborg, P. (2004) *Silvio Berlusconi: Television, Power and Patrimony*, London: Verso.

Gobry, P.-E. (2011) 'It's Official: Internet Advertising is Bigger than Newspaper Advertising', *Business Insider*, 14 April. Online. Available HTTP: <http://www.businessinsider.com/internet-advertising-bigger-than-newspaper-advertising-2011-4> (accessed 15 August 2011).

Grossman, L. K. (1995) *The Electronic Republic: Reshaping Democracy in the Information Age*, New York: Viking.

Guardian (2011) 'The World's Top 10 Newspaper Websites', 19 April. Online. Available HTTP: <http://www.guardian.co.uk/media/table/2011/apr/19/worlds-top-10-newspaper-websites?intcmp=239> (accessed 20 August 2011).

Hahn, H. (1993) *Voices from the Net*, 1.3, 27 October. Online. Available HTTP: <http://www.spunk.org/library/comms/sp000317.txt> (accessed 7 November 2010).

Hill, K. and Hughes, J. (1998) *Cyberpolitics*, Lanham, MD: Rowman and Littlefield.

Hindman, M. (2009) *The Myth of Digital Democracy*, Princeton: Princeton University Press.

Hirsch, D. (2007) 'Experiences of Poverty and Educational Disadvantage', Joseph Rowntree Foundation. Online. Available HTTP: <http://www.jrf.org.uk/publications/experiences-poverty-and-educational-disadvantage> (accessed 5 January 2011).

Horgan, G. (2007) 'The Impact of Poverty on Young Children's Experience of School', Joseph Rowntree Foundation. Online. Available HTTP: <http://www.jrf.org.uk/publications/impact-poverty-young-childrens-experience-school> (accessed 20 January 2011).

Hunt, J. (2011) 'The New Frontier of Money Laundering: How Terrorist Organizations use Cyberlaundering to Fund Their Activities, and How Governments are Trying to Stop Them', *Information & Communications Technology Law*, 20 (2): 133–52.

Ibrahim, Y. (2006) 'The Role of Regulations and Social Norms in Mediating Online Political Discourse', PhD dissertation, LSE, University of London.

International Telecommunications Union (2010) 'ITU Calls for Broadband Internet Access for Half of the World's Population by 2015', *ITU News*, 5 June. Online. Available HTTP: <http://www.itu.int/net/itunews/issues/2010/05/pdf/201005_12.pdf> (accessed 10 January 2011).

Internet World Stats (2010a) 'Internet Usage Statistics, the Internet Big Picture', Miniwatts Marketing Group. Online. Available HTTP: <http:www.internetworldstats.com/stats.htm> (accessed 10 January 2011).

——(2010b) 'Internet World Users by Language: Top 10 Languages', Miniwatts Marketing Group. Online. Available HTTP: <http://www.Internetworldstats.com/stats7.htm> (accessed 10 January 2011).

——(2011a) 'Internet World Stats: Usage and Population Statistics'. Online. Available HTTP: <http://www.internetworldstats.com/stats.htm> (accessed 14 August 2011).

——(2011b) 'Asia Internet Usage'. Online. Available HTTP: <http://www.internet worldstats.com/stats3.htm> (accessed 21 August 2011).

Jansen, J. (2010) 'The Better-Off Online', *Pew Research Center Publications*, Pew Internet & American Life Project, 24 November. Online. Available HTTP: <http://pewresearch.org/pubs/1809/internet-usage-higher-income-americans> (accessed 7 June 2011).

Jipguep, J. (1995) 'The Global Telecommunication Infrastructure and the Information Society', Proceedings ISOC INET '95. Online. Available HTTP: <http://www. isoc.org/inet95/proceedings/PLENARY/L1–6/html/paper.html> (accessed January 2010).

Joyce, M. (2007) 'The Citizen Journalism Web Site "OhmyNews" and the 2002 South Korean Presidential Election', Berkman Center for Internet and Society of Harvard University. Online. Available HTTP: <http://cyber.law.harvard.edu/sites/cyber.law.harvard.edu/files/Joyce_South_Korea_2007.pdf > (accessed 24 July 2011).

Juris, J. (2005) 'The New Digital Media and Activist Networking within Anti-Corporate Globalization Movements', *The Annals of the American Academy*, 597: 189–208.

Kalapese, C., Willersdorf, S. and Zwillenburg, P. (2010) *The Connected Kingdom*, Boston Consulting Group. Online. Available HTTP: <http://www.connectedkingdom.co.uk/downloads/bcg-the-connected-kingdom-oct-10.pdf> (accessed 14 August 2011).

Kalathil, S. and Boas, T. C. (2003) *Open Networks, Closed Regimes: The Impact of the Internet on Authoritarian Rule*, Washington: Carnegie Endowment for International Peace.

Kelly, K. (1999) 'The Roaring Zeros', *Wired*, September. Online. Available HTTP: <http://www.wired.com/wired/archive/7.09/zeros.html> (accessed 10 December 2010).

Kenyon, A. (2010) 'Investigating Chilling Effects: News Media and Public Speech in Malaysia, Singapore and Australia', *International Journal of Communication*, 4: 440–67.

Kim, E.-G. and Hamilton, J. (2006) 'Capitulation to Capital? OhmyNews as Alternative Media', *Media, Culture and Society*, 28 (4): 541–60.

Klotz, R. J. (2004) *The Politics of Internet Communication*, Lanham, MD: Rowman & Littlefield.

Lane, D. (2004) *Berlusconi's Shadow*, London: Allen Lane.

Lauria, J. (1999) 'American Online Frenzy Creates Overnight Billionaires', *Sunday Times*, 26 December.

Lee-Wright, P., Phillips, A. and Witschge, T. (2011) *Changing Journalism*, London: Routledge.

Lister, R. (2004) *Poverty*, Cambridge: Policy Press.

Livingstone, S. (2010) 'Interactive, Engaging but Unequal: Critical Conclusions from Internet Studies', in J. Curran (ed.) *Media and Society*, 5th edn, London: Bloomsbury Academic.

Mandel, M. J. and Kunii, I. M. (1999) 'The Internet Economy: The World's Next Growth Engine', *BusinessWeek Online*, 4 October. Online. Available HTTP: <http://www.businessweek.com/1999/99_40/b3649004.htm?scriptFramed> (accessed 2 February 2011).

Marquand, D. (2008) *Britain since 1918*, London: Phoenix.

Moos, J. (2011) 'The Top 5 News Sites in the United States are. ... ', Poynter Institute. Online. Available HTTP: <http://www.poynter.org/latest-news/romenesko/128994/the-top-5-news-sites-in-the-united-states-are/> (accessed 5 August 2011).

Morozov, E. (2011) *The Net Delusion*, London: Allen Lane.

Mosco, V. (2005) *The Digital Sublime*, Cambridge, MA: MIT Press.

Murdoch, R. (2006) 'Speech by Rupert Murdoch at the Annual Livery Lecture at the Worshipful Company of Stationers and Newspaper Makers', *News Corporation*, 3 March. Online. Available HTTP: <http://www.newscorp.com/news/news_285.html> (accessed 1 September 2010).

Negroponte, N. (1995; 1996) *Being Digital*, rev. edn, London: Hodder and Stoughton.

Nel, F. (2010) *Laid Off: What Do UK Journalists Do Next?* Preston: University of Central Lancashire. Online. Available HTTP: <http://www.journalism.co.uk/uploads/laidoffreport.pdf> (accessed 20 August 2011).

Nerone, J. (2009) 'The Death and Rebirth of Working-class Journalism', *Journalism*, 10 (3): 353–55.

Nielsen (2011) 'Media and Information Sites Thrive in Popularity as Consumers Seek the "Real World" on the Web', Nielsen Press Room. Online. Available HTTP: <http://www.nielsen.com/uk/en/insights/press-room/2011-news/media_and_information-sites-thrive.html> (accessed 2 August 2011).

Ofcom (2010a) 'Perceptions of, and Attitudes towards, Television: 2010', PSB Report 2010 – Information Pack H, 8 July. Online. Available HTTP: <http://stakeholders.ofcom.org.uk/binaries/broadcast/reviews-investigations/psb-review/psb2010/Perceptions.pdf> (accessed November 2010).

Ofcom (2010b) *International Communications Market Report*, London: Ofcom. Online. Available HTTP: <http://stakeholders.ofcom.org.uk/binaries/research/cmr/753567/icmr/ICMR_2010.pdf> (accessed 23 August 2011).

Office of Fair Trading (2009) *Review of the Local and Regional Media Merger Regime*. Online. Available HTTP: http://www.oft.gov.uk/news/press/2009/71–09 (accessed 23 December 2009).

Olmstead, K., Mitchell, A. and Rosenstiel, T. (2011) 'Navigating News Online', Pew Research Center, Project for Excellence in Journalism. Online. Available HTTP: <http://pewresearch.org/pubs/1986/navigating-digital-news-environment-audience> (accessed 20 August 2011).

ONS (2008) *Internet Access 2008: Households and Individuals*, London: Office of National Statistics.

Park, M.-Y., Kim, C.-N. and Sohn, R.-W. (2000) 'Modernization, Globalization and the Powerful State: The Korean Media', in J. Curran and M.-Y. Park (eds) *De-Westernising Media Studies*, London: Routledge.

Perry, B. and Olsson, P. (2009) 'Cyberhate: The Globalization of Hate', *Information & Communications Technology Law*, 18 (2): 185–199.

Pew (2009a) Pew Project for Excellence in Journalism, *State of the News Media 2009*, Pew Research Center Publications, 16 March. Online. Available HTTP: <http://www.stateofthemedia.org/2009/narrative_overview_intro.php?cat=0&media=1> (accessed 10 December 2009).

——(2009b) 'Trend Data', Pew Internet & American Life Project. Online. Available HTTP: <http://www.pewinternet.org/Static-Pages/Trend-Data/Online-Activities-Daily.aspx> (accessed 2 April 2010).

——(2011) 'The State of the News Media 2011: An Annual Report on American Journalism', Pew Research Center's Project for Excellence in Journalism. Online. Available HTTP: <http://stateofthemedia.org/2011/newspapers-essay/#fn-5162-39> (accessed 20 August 2011).

Pew Research Center for the People and the Press (2011) 'Internet Gains on Television as Public's Main News Source', 4 January. Online. Available HTTP: <http://pew research.org/pubs/1844/poll-main-source-national-international-news-internet-television-newspapers> (accessed 7 January 2011).

Porter, M. (2008a) *On Competition*, Boston: Harvard Business School Press.

——(2008b) 'The Five Competitive Forces that Shape Strategy', *Harvard Business Review*, January: 79–93.

Poster, M. (2001) *What's the Matter with the Internet*, Minneapolis: University of Minnesota Press.

Price, R. (1998) 'Reversing the Gun Sites: Transnational Civil Society Targets Land Mines', *International Organization*, 52 (3): 613–44.

Redden, J. and Witschge, T. (2010) 'A New News Order? Online News Content Examined', in N. Fenton (ed.) *New Media, Old News*, London: Sage.

Rodan, G. (2004) *Transparency and Authoritarian Rule in Southeast Asia*, London: RoutledgeCurzon.

Rohlinger, D. and Brown, J. (2008) 'Democracy, Action and the Internet after 9/11', *American Behavioral Scientist*, 53 (1): 133–50.

Ryan, J. (2010) *A History of the Internet and the Digital Future*, London: Reaktion Books.

Sani, A. (2009) *The Public Sphere and Media Politics in Malaysia*, Newcastle: Cambridge Scholars Publishing.

Schwartz, E. I. (1994) 'Power to the People: The Clinton Administration is Using the Net in a Pitched Effort to Perform an End Run Around the Media', *Wired*, 1 January. Online. Available HTTP: <http://www.wired.com/wired/archive/2.12/whitehouse_pr.html> (accessed 10 January 2010).

Scott, E. (2004) '"Big Media" Meets the "Bloggers": Coverage of Trent Lott's Remarks at Strom Thurmond's Birthday Party', Kennedy School of Government Case Study C14-04-1731.0, Cambridge, MA: John Kennedy School of Government, Harvard University.

Scott, T. D. (2008) 'Blogosphere: Presidential Campaign Stories that Failed to Ignite Mainstream Media', in M. Boler (ed.) *Digital Media and Democracy: Tactics in Hard Times*, Cambridge: MIT Press.

Simon Wiesenthal Centre (2011) '2011 Digital Terrorism and Hate Report Launched at Museum of Tolerance New York'. Online. Available HTTP: <http://www.wiesen thal.com/site/apps/nlnet/content2.aspx?c=lsKWLbPJLnF&b=4441467&ct=9141065> (accessed 8 July 2011).

Stiglitz, J. (2002) *Globalization and its Discontents*, London: Penguin.

Stratton, J. (1997) 'Cyberspace and the Globalization of Culture', in D. Porter (ed.) *Internet Culture*, London: Routledge, 253–76.

Sklair, L. (2002) *Globalization*, 3rd edn, Oxford: Oxford University Press.

Slevin, J. (2000) *The Internet and Society*, Cambridge: Polity.

Smith, A., Schlozman, L., Verba, S. and Brady, H. (2009) 'The Internet and Civic Engagment', Pew Internet & American Life Project, 1 September Online. Available HTTP: <http://www.pewinternet.org/Reports/2009/15–The-Internet-and-Civic-Engage ment.aspx> (accessed 10 May 2010).

Smith, P. and Smythe, E. (2004) 'Globalization, Citizenship and New Information Technologies: from the MAI to Seattle', in M. Anttiroiko and R. Savolainen (eds) *eTransformation in Governance*, Hershey, PA: IGI Publishing.

Solaria Sun (2011) 'Cisco Systems Financial Crisis', 4 August. Online. Available HTTP: <http://solariasun.com/3521/cisco-systems-financial-crisis/> (accessed 12 August 2011).

Solt, F. (2008) 'Economic Inequality and Democratic Political Engagement', *American Journal of Political Science*, 52 (1): 48–60.

Sutton, L., Smith, N., Deardon, C. and Middleton, S. (2007) 'A Child's-eye View of Social Difference', Joseph Rowntree Foundation: The Centre for Research in Social Policy (CRSP), Loughborough University. Online. Available: <http://www.jrf.org.uk/publications/childs-eye-view-social-difference> (accessed 10 January 2011).

Taubman, G. (1998) 'A Not-so World Wide Web: The Internet, China, and the Challenges to Nondemocratic Rule', *Political Communication*, 15: 255–72.

Thompson, D. (2010) 'The Tea Party Used the Internet to Defeat the Internet President', *The Atlantic*, 20 November. Online. Available HTTP: <http://www.theatlantic.com/business/archive/2010/11/the-tea-party-used-the-internet-to-defeat-the-first-internet-president/65589/> (accessed 22 August 2011).

Toffler, A. and Toffler, H. (1995) *Creating a New Civilization*, Atlanta: Turner.

Tomlinson, J. (1999) *Globalization and Culture*, Cambridge: Polity.

Torres, R. (2008) 'World of Work Report 2008: Income Inequalities in the Age of Financial Globalization', International Institute for Labour Studies, International Labour Office, Geneva. Online. Available HTTP: <http://www.ilo.org/public/english/bureau/inst/download/world08.pdf> (accessed 9 December 2010).

Turkle, S. (1995) *Life on the Screen*, New York: Simon and Schuster.

——(2011) *Alone Together*, New York: Basic Books.

Ugarteche, O. (2007) 'Transnationalizing the Public Sphere: A Critique of Fraser', *Theory, Culture and Society*, 24 (4): 65–69.

Valliere, D. and Peterson, R. (2004) 'Inflating the Bubble: Examining Investor Behaviour', *Venture Capital*, 4 (1): 1–22.

Van Dijk, J. (2005) *The Deepening Divide*, London: Sage.

Volkmer, I. (2003) 'The Global Network Society and the Global Public Sphere', *Development*, 46 (1): 9–16.

Wheale, P. R. and Amin, L. H. (2003) 'Bursting the Dot.com "Bubble": A Case Study in Investor Behaviour', *Technological Analysis*, 15 (1): 117–36.

Witschge, T., Fenton, N. and Freedman, D. (2010) *Protecting the News: Civil Society and the Media*, London: Carnegie UK. Online. Available HTTP: <http://www.carnegieuktrust.org.uk/getattachment/1598111d-7cbc-471e-98b4-dc4225f38e99/Protecting-the-News–Civil-Society-and-the-Media.aspx> (accessed 9 June 2011).

Woolcock, M. (2008) 'Global Poverty and Inequality: A Brief Retrospective and Prospective Analysis', *Political Quarterly*, 79 (1): 183–96.

Worthington, R. (2003) *Governance in Singapore*, London: RoutledgeCurzon.

Wunnava, P. V. and Leiter, D. B. (2009) 'Determinants of Intercountry Internet Diffusion Rates', *American Journal of Economics and Sociology*, 68 (2): 413–26.

Zickuhr, K. (2010) 'Generations 2010', Pew Internet and American Life Project. Washington: Pew Research Centre. Online. Available HTTP: <http://pewinternet.org/Reports/2010/Generations-2010.aspx> (accessed 20 August 2011).

Chapter 2

Rethinking internet history

James Curran

Introduction

When the internet expanded in the 1980s and early 1990s, it was cloaked in romance.[1] The internet's pioneer users developed a distinctive argot, introducing acronyms like MOO and MUD (which refer to adventure and role-playing games). To use the internet in this period was like belonging to a cult, with its own inner secrets, sub-cultural style and tough entry requirement of technical competence. Users were overwhelmingly young, and in the know.

Even when the internet entered the mainstream in the mid-1990s, it still retained something of its early exotic allure. Long articles appeared in the prestige press, explaining how the internet worked and what it could be used for. Words like 'cyberspace', derived from internet pioneers' romance with science fiction, became part of the general vocabulary. It was around this time that serious attempts to research the origins and development of the internet got under way. However, these early histories were conditioned by the awestruck period in which they were written, something that was reflected in the way they all spelt the internet with a capital 'I' (Abbate 2000; Gillies and Cailliau 2000; Berners-Lee 2000; Rheingold 2000).[2] Although illuminating, these accounts are laudatory. Their central theme is that utopian dreams, mutual reciprocity and pragmatic flexibility led to the building of a transformative technology that built a better world.

There is a clear parallel between the emergence of this historiography and pioneer Victorian histories of the British press, written in 1850–87, a period when liberals, in particular, invested enormous hope in the transformative power of popular newspapers mass produced by new print technology. As with early internet history, these studies genuflected before the altar of technology by capitalising the first letters of Newspaper Press (e.g. Hunt 1850: 178; Grant 1871–72: 453). They were also adulatory, associating the rise of the popular press with the march of reason, liberty and progress.

It was only later – when the lapse of time encouraged a greater critical distance and when negative trends in the press became too prominent to ignore – that the central themes of pioneer press history were challenged.[3] This revisionist moment has not yet arrived in internet history. While there are new illuminating specialist studies, general histories of the internet are stuck in the pioneer mould. They are celebratory chronicles of technology and progress (Flichy 2007; Banks 2008; Ryan 2010).[4]

This chapter will attempt to depart from this standard template in two ways. Most histories of the internet concentrate on its early heroic phase. By contrast, this account will give as much attention to the later as to the earlier period of internet development. This changes, as we shall see, the trajectory of internet history.

This account will also attempt to sketch in some aspects of the non-Western advance of the internet. Standard internet histories narrate the development of the internet as a Western phenomenon. This makes sense for the early phase because the internet was a Western invention. But the internet became global, and its history needs to be understood in these terms. As we shall see, de-Westernising internet history also leads to a more complicated story.

Technical development of the internet

The technical history of the internet can be briefly summarised. The internet began as a small, publicly owned computer network established in 1969 in the United States. This network expanded with the development of a shared computer language and set of protocols. E-mail (or network mail, as it was first called) was introduced in 1972. The term 'internet' emerged in 1974 as a simple abbreviation for *internetworking* between multiple computers.

The 1980s and 1990s saw the internationalisation of internet development that had previously been centred mainly in the US. A key moment of change came when CERN, the European Organization for Nuclear Research, adopted IP for its internal network of computers in 1985, and opened its first external IP connections in 1989. This was followed in 1991 by the creation of the world wide web – a user interface that provided a convenient method of organising and accessing distributed data across computer networks. This gave a strong fillip to global expansion. The internet reached Asia by the late 1980s, though it was not until 1995 that Africa established its first home-grown internet services. By 1998 the internet reached every populated country in the world.

The overlapping period of the 1990s and 2000s witnessed the rapid popularisation of the internet. This was greatly assisted by the development of the first graphical browser for the web in 1993, and the emergence of search engines and web directories that made the internet accessible to a much wider audience. The number of computers connected to the internet grew from 562 to more than 300 billion between 1983 and 2005 (Comer 2007). By 2010, there were an estimated two billion users worldwide, equating to more than a quarter of the world's population (ITU 2010).

Underpinning this remarkable development were certain key innovations. One was the transformation of the computer from a vast machine occupying an entire room, and requiring the attendance of a white-coated priesthood, into a powerful, easy-to-use artefact that can sit on a lap or be held in a hand. Another was the development of computer networking through the development of shared codes for transporting and addressing communications. A third was the transformation of connective software that facilitated the accessing, linking and storage of information (with the creation of the web constituting the key break-through). A fourth was the prior building of the international telephone system in a way that facilitated interoperability between countries. The internet was able to 'piggy back' on the international telephone network, facilitating its rapid global expansion.

However, the evolution of the internet was not simply a technological process determined by scientific innovation. It was also shaped by the objectives of the people who funded, created and fashioned it. These objectives were to clash, culminating in a battle for the 'soul' of the internet.

Military sponsorship

It is a much remarked-upon paradox that, although the internet can be viewed as an agency of peace, it was a product of the Cold War. When, in 1957, the Soviet Union launched a satellite orbiting the earth, it won the first lap of the 'space race'. This galvanised the Pentagon into setting up the Advanced Research Projects Agency (ARPA), whose many projects included a scheme to promote interactive computing through the creation of the world's first advanced computer network (ARPANET). Although the network was conceived originally as a way of sharing expensive computer time, it acquired another rationale. Computer networking would facilitate, it was argued, the development of a sophisticated military command and control system capable of withstanding a nuclear attack from the Soviet Union. This recasting of the project led to major public investment in networking technology and expansion (Edwards 1996; Norberg and O'Neil 1996).

It also resulted in the design of the early internet being influenced by military objectives, in a form that tends to be downplayed (e.g. Hafner and Lyon 2003). One overwhelming military concern was the creation of a computer network that would withstand Soviet attack. This led the military to sponsor a devolved system without a command centre that could be destroyed by the enemy. This was very different from the centralised, hierarchal data systems developed for American corporations by IBM. Its practical effect was the creation of a network that was difficult not only to 'take out' but also to control.

Military considerations also led to the development of network technology that would enable the system to function if parts of it were destroyed. A key military attraction of packet-switching (central to the development of the internet) was that it dispensed with vulnerable, open lines between sender and receiver. Instead, messages were disaggregated into units ('packages') before dispatch, sent through different routes depending on traffic and network conditions, and reassembled on arrival. Each packet was wrapped in a kind of digital envelope with transport and content specifications.

A further military concern was to have a networking system that could serve different, specialised military tasks. This encouraged the creation of a diverse system that allowed different networks to be incorporated, once minimum requirements had been met. It also led to the addition of satellite and wireless for internetworking, since these were well adapted to communication with jeeps, ships and aeroplanes.

The design of the internet thus bore the imprint of military objectives. This was because it was conceived as a strategic line of defence against the evil Soviet empire. The internet was a *Dr Strangelove* project, whose rationale resembled the subtitle of the satirical 1964 film: 'How I learned to stop worrying and love the Bomb'.

State sponsorship also assisted indirectly the building of the internet in other ways. The US defence budget funded the first American electronic digital computer in 1946, and subsidised the technical advance of the US computer industry (Edwards 1996). The American state also supported the American space programme, whose by-product – orbiting satellites – helped to carry the increased volume of internet communication. In effect, the American state underwrote a major part of the internet's research and development costs.

This was not something that the private sector was eager to do because computer networking linked to the defence programme did not seem a good commercial prospect. Indeed, in 1972 the telecommunication giant AT&T declined the government's offer to take over ARPANET, the forerunner of the modern internet, on the grounds that it would be unprofitable. Yet, after supporting research and development, and the cost of building a significant user base, the American state 'shepherded' the internet to market. In 1991, the ban on commercial use of the public internet was lifted, and in 1995 the public internet was privatised.

Values of scientists

The objectives of military sponsors of the internet were interpreted and mediated by computer scientists. A good working relationship was established between the two, helped by the fact that military and scientific aims overlapped. Thus, the military objective of survivability in the event of Soviet attack pointed towards the adoption of a decentralised network structure. But this also accorded with the desire of university departments, linked to the early internet, not to be subject to central network control.

Similarly, the internet's modular structure served the military need for flexibility. It also suited academics who wanted to enhance the internet's value as a research tool by incorporating more networks. The add-on nature of the internet thus met the concerns of both.

Mutual tact seems also to have prevented the raucous campus protests against the Vietnam War in the later 1960s and early 1970s from affecting the harmonious relationship between scientists and the military (Rosenzweig 1998). When a serious clash of priorities developed over the issue of security, this was resolved amicably through the division of the internet into military and civilian networks in 1983.

The mutual trust that developed between the military and scientists resulted in the latter having considerable autonomy. As a consequence, the values of academic science became the second formative influence on the development of the internet. The culture of science is committed to the public disclosure of research, collective dialogue and intellectual cooperation in order to further scientific advance. This cultural tradition gave rise to the cooperative development of networking protocols, and their open release. As a consequence, a tradition of openness and reciprocity became part of the founding tradition of the net.

However, the 'openness' championed by scientists took the form of expert disclosure and access rather than of opening up the internet to mass consumption. This was because the work of academic science – then as now – was usually addressed to people inside the relevant knowledge community, and took a technical, self-referential form. This exclusionary tradition was a feature of the early internet. Considerable computer expertise was needed to go online; and computer scientists initially showed little interest in changing this.

Countercultural values

If the military–scientific complex shaped the early internet, its subsequent development was strongly influenced in the 1980s by the American counterculture (and later by its European counterpart). This counterculture had different strands, although these were often intertwined. A communitarian strand aimed to promote togetherness through the fostering of mutual empathy and understanding. A hippy sub-culture sought individual self-realisation by breaking free from repressive convention, while a radical sub-culture hoped to transform society through the transfer of power to the people. These different currents within the counterculture influenced how the emerging internet was used.

In a strikingly original study, Fred Turner (2006) documents the way in which hip journalists and cultural entrepreneurs acted as brokers, bringing together two divergent groups, and sustaining a creative partnership between them. Their brokerage skill lay in flattering and awakening hope. They told computer scientists, accustomed to being viewed as nerds, that they were cool messiahs destined to transform the world; and they briefed activists in the counterculture – already in steep decline by the 1980s – that a technology existed that could make their fading dreams come true. Together, computer scientists and activists, these brokers proclaimed, could free the computer from its utilitarian purpose, and make it work for humanity.

Change was already in the air. During the 1980s, commercial online services had developed outside the public internet, offering the opportunity to shop and chat, though without much success. Even without countercultural input, the internet would have been put to new uses. However, a promethean partnership of scientists and activists played an important role in re-imagining the computer.

In the 1980s, its communard strand developed local area networks in California, usually funded as low-subscription-based services supported by volunteer labour. This was typified by the WELL (Whole Earth 'Lectronic Link), established in the San Francisco area in 1985, originally as a dial-up bulletin board system. It was the brainchild of Stewart Brand, then a radical rock concert impresario, and Larry Brilliant, a left-wing doctor and Third World campaigner. Brilliant enrolled numerous fellow former members of The Farm, a large, self-sufficient agricultural commune in Tennessee. They created an electronic commune that grew into 300 computer-mediated 'conferences' which brought together social and political activists, as well as enthusiasts of all kinds. One of the WELL's largest sub-groups was fans of the radical rock group the Grateful Dead. Deadheads (as they were disrespectfully called) spent hours online discussing the Grateful Dead's enigmatic lyrics and exchanging music recorded at live gigs – something that the rock group supported as part of its public stand *in favour* of the 'pirating' of its music. However, participation in the WELL declined after a few years. The electronic commune was bought in 1994 by a shoe manufacturer, Bruce Katz. The internecine conflict that followed the takeover led to steep decline (Rheingold 2000: 331–34).

Similar communal experiments occurred in Europe, typically with the local state acting as midwife. The best-known of these was Amsterdam's Digital City (called DDS in the Netherlands). This began as a pilot project sponsored by the local council in 1994, and was reconstituted in 1995 as a 'virtual city' with a Foundation grant. Different squares in the 'city' were given over to specific topics (such as politics, film and music), and in each of these cybercafés were created as meeting places. The experiment captured the imagination of squatting-movement activists, university students, workers in the creative industries, and others living in Amsterdam. At its height, the project involved thousands of people, facilitated popular access to online services and mobilised online voting on a range of issues. However, public involvement fell away in the later 1990s after the initial excitement wore off. The project was then weakened by internal conflicts, and failed to secure long-term funding.

More enduring were experiments that linked geographically dispersed grassroots networks, some influenced by radical American students (Hauben and Hauben 1997). These included Usenet (1979), BITNET (1981), FidoNet (1983) and PeaceNet (1985). Usenet newsgroups, built around the UNIX system, proved to be the most important of these networks. Set up initially to discuss issues to do with UNIX software and troubleshooting, they diversified to cover a wide spectrum of topics from abortion to Islam. Usenet newsgroup sites rose from just 3 in 1979 to 11,000 by 1988, and over 20,000 by 2000 (Naughton 2000: 181–82). This poor relation started as a dial-up service, was subsequently allowed to ride on the ARPA network, and was then carried by the internet.

Meanwhile the hippy strand of the counterculture helped to turn the computer into a playground. During the early 1990s, a cult was created around text-based adventure games in which participants could take on assumed identities and interact with others, freed from the visual markers of age, gender, ethnicity, class and disability. Celebrants hailed this as a space in which people could explore their real selves, break free from the constraints and prejudices of everyday life, attain greater empathy with others and build a better world based on liberated subjectivities (Turkle 1995). Others saw it as a liberating context in which people could have promiscuous, virtual sex (and pass themselves off as being younger and more svelte than they were in real life), freed from the conventions of the offline world (Ito 1997).

The counterculture also contributed to the emergence of hip computer capitalism. Thus, Steve Jobs and Steve Wozniak, who launched Apple in 1980, came out of the alternative movement. Jobs had travelled to India in a quest for personal enlightenment, while Wozniak was heavily involved in the radical rock scene. In 1982, Wozniak personally funded the organisation of a rock festival dedicated to the Information Age. At the festival, which attracted more people than Woodstock, there was a giant video screen on which was projected a simple message:

> There is an explosion of information dispersal in the technology and we think this information has to be shared. All great thinkers about democracy said that the key to democracy is access to information. And now we have a chance to get information into people's hands like never before.
>
> (Cited in Flichy 1999: 37)

The counterculture thus reconceived how the computer could be used in order to advance its vision of the future. Its activists transformed the internet from being a tool of a techno-elite into becoming the creator of virtual communities, a sub-cultural playground and agency of democracy.

European public service

The third formative influence shaping cyberspace was a European welfarist tradition that had created great public health and broadcasting systems. While the internet was born in the United States, the world wide web was created by Tim Berners-Lee in the publicly funded European Particle Physics Laboratory at CERN.

Tim Berners-Lee was inspired by two key ideas: that of opening up access to a public good (the storehouse of knowledge contained in the world's computer system) and that of bringing people into communion with each other. The son of two mathematicians, Berners-Lee found fulfilment in serving the community. While not automatically anti-market, he resented the exaltation of market values above all else. He is often asked, he says, in the United States (though less frequently in Europe) whether he regrets not making money out of the invention of the world wide web. His response reflects the values of public service:

What is maddening is the terrible notion [implied in this question] that a person's value depends on how important and financially successful they are, and that this is measured in terms of money. ... Core in my upbringing was a value system that put monetary gain well in its place.

(Berners-Lee 2000: 116)

Berners-Lee's desire not to promote the web through a private company was prompted by his conviction that it would trigger competition and lead to the subdivision of the web into private domains. This would subvert his conception of 'a universal medium for sharing information' and undermine the purpose of his project. He persuaded the management of his publicly funded agency to release the world wide web code in 1993 as a gift to the community. He subsequently became the head of the agency regulating the web (World Wide Web Consortium (W3C)) in order to 'think about what was best for the world, as opposed to what would be best for one commercial interest' (Berners-Lee 2000: 91).

Thus, the bequest of the web made freely available a vast cornucopia of knowledge and information. It was inspired by the ideal of serving society rather than self.

Commercialisation of the internet

The fourth influence shaping the development of cyberspace was the marketplace. The lifting of the commercial ban on use of the public internet in 1991 mentioned earlier had seemingly a wholly benign effect. It encouraged the launch of browsers and search engines that made the web user friendly. Their arrival, as Berners-Lee (2000: 90) acknowledges, 'was a very important step for the Web'.

In the mid-1990s, all aspects of the internet seemed enormously positive. Even if the internet was a product of a superpower war machine, its military legacy was terminated in 1990 when ARPANET handed over control of the public internet backbone to the National Science Foundation. A combination of academic, countercultural and public service values had created an open public space which was decentralised, diverse and interactive. The ways in which the internet could be used had been greatly extended. The growing influence of commerce seemed merely to extend the benefits of this new medium to more people by simplifying its technical aspects and promoting its use, without detracting from its fundamental nature.

The largely uncritical reception given to the commercialisation of the net during the mid-1990s accorded with the ethos of the time. This was a moment of triumphalism when democracy and capitalism had defeated communism (Fukuyama 1993). The period's mood music was reinforced by the outpourings of experts. The MIT guru Nicholas Negroponte set the tone in a celebrated book, published in 1995, which portrayed the internet as an integral part of a democratising digital revolution. The public, he predicted, will *pull* what it wants from the internet and digital media, rather than accept what is *pushed* at it by media giants. Media consumption, he continued, is becoming 'customised' according to individual taste, and 'the monolithic empires of mass media are dissolving into an army of cottage industries', making obsolete 'industrial-age cross-ownership laws' (Negroponte 1996: 57–58 and 85). Similarly Mark Poster (1995), another revered net expert, concluded that we are entering the 'second media age', in which monopoly would be replaced by diversity, the distinction between senders and receivers would be dissolved, and the ruled would become rulers. In these, and most other commentaries, the market was not viewed as a limitation on the emancipatory power of the net.

The coalition that had created the pre-market internet fractured during the 1990s. Some academic computer scientists set up internet companies and became millionaires. Others quietly acquiesced to software licensing restrictions, while university administrators looked for ways to make money out of their computer science departments. A new generation of computer industry leaders emerged, whose informality and populism seemed to set them apart from the stuffy corporate culture of their predecessors. In this changed environment, capitalism seemed hip: the way to make money, express individuality and avoid state control. The language used to discuss new communications technology changed. The metaphor of the 'information superhighway', with its 1950s association of statist modernism, gave way to the romantic image of 'cyberspace' (Streeter 2003). Everything seemed wondrous, transformative, positive.

Consequences of commercialisation

The commercialisation of the internet changed its character. The adoption in 1997 of a standard protocol for credit card transactions gave an important boost to online sales. The internet became in part a commercial mall, a place where virtual shops set up in business and where products and services were sold.

However, the *content* that proved easiest to sell was not the creative works of minority artists about which some analysts write so lyrically (e.g. Anderson 2006) but pornography and gaming (a category that includes both games and gambling). Although porn accounted for little more than 1 per cent of total web content (Zook 2007), it accounted for an estimated 17 per cent of all searches in 1997, and a still significant 4 per cent in 2004 (Spink, Patridge and Jansen 2006). Porn catered for a well-defined market, including large numbers of young men. Thus, among Canadian students, whose average age was 20, 72 per cent of men and 24 per cent of women said that they had visited porn sites in the previous 12 months (Boies 2002). Not only popular, porn was something that online users were willing to pay for. The adult entertainment industry in the US – in which net porn now plays an important part – made $2.8 billion in 2006 (Edelman 2009). Similarly, online gaming proved to be a great success, reaping an estimated $11.9 billion in worldwide revenue (DFC Intelligence 2010).

It took longer for general online shopping to take off, for a variety of reasons.[5] Thus, it was only in 2008 that a bare majority in Britain said that they had bought anything online (Office for National Statistics (ONS) 2008). Yet, by 2010, this had risen to 62 per cent (ONS 2010). All the indications are that online shopping will grow rapidly and will come to dominate the sale of certain products and services.

A side-effect of commercialisation was to promote net advertising in a form that could be intrusive. The advertising industry introduced first of all the banner advertisement (a horizontal strip, reminiscent of early press display advertisements). This was followed by advertisements of different shapes such as 'button', 'skyscraper' and pop-up 'interstitials' and by new types of advertisements that contain audio-visual elements (more like television commercials).

These developments were viewed by some as a portent of things to come. They indicated that what had once been a largely pre-market space in which content was freely distributed and available to all online could be transformed into a commodified space where selling and advertising became prominent, fees-only websites proliferated at the expense of the web's open access 'commons', and net neutrality was terminated in order to make way for the creation of a fast internet service for the affluent (and a slow one for budget citizens).

Advancing market influence had already introduced unobtrusive controls. Corporations asserted intellectual property rights over computer software in a way that threatened to undermine the open, collaborative tradition on which the internet had been built (Lessig 1999; Weber 2004). Corporate pressure was also brought to bear in the United States (and elsewhere) for intellectual property rights to be updated and given stronger protection. In 1976, the United States passed a Copyright Act which extended copyright to software. This was buttressed in 1998 by the Digital Millennium Act, which greatly strengthened legal provision against piracy that threatened digital media companies. Its effect, however, was to overprotect intellectual property rights at the expense of legitimate 'fair use' of web content (Lessig 2001).

Still more restrictive was the development of a commercial technology of surveillance from the 1990s onwards (Schiller 2007; Deibert et al. 2008; Zittrain 2008). One method entailed the monitoring of data and traffic over a network (for example Google searches) in a form that tracks users, gathers information about which websites are visited and what users do on these sites. Another method was to install software that monitored the activities of a specific computer and its user. This software had the potential to enter the 'backdoor' of other computers, enabling the monitoring of their activity. The third approach was to collate data from different sources to compile a social network analysis about the personal interests, friendships, affiliations and consumption habits of users.

Surveillance technology came to be deployed very extensively. In the United States, an estimated 92 per cent of commercial websites aggregated, sorted and used for economic purposes data about people's use of the net (Lessig 1999: 153). Most people made themselves vulnerable to this monitoring by waiving their rights of privacy in order to gain free access. Overriding 'human rights' protection of privacy was weak in the United States, though greater protection was available in Europe.

This technology, first originated for marketing and advertising purposes, came to be used in ways that had not been intended. According to a study released in 2000, 73 per cent of US firms routinely checked on their workforce's use of the net (Castells 2001: 74). More importantly, autocratic governments adopted – as we shall see – commercial surveillance software in order to monitor and censor the internet.

Commercialisation also established more subtle forms of control based on market power. The beguiling vision of boutiques, cottage industries and consumer-sovereigns that Nicholas Negroponte (1996) had proclaimed proved to be wide off the mark. By 2011, four giants had established a dominant position in different sectors of the internet. Indeed, they had a level of capitalisation that made them among the biggest companies in the world: Apple ($331bn), Microsoft ($220bn), Google ($196bn) and Oracle ($167bn) (Naughton 2011a). Their economic muscle could be flexed in ways that were restrictive. For example, Apple's beautifully designed iPhones and iPads in 2011 did not allow the addition of applications that had not been approved beforehand by Apple. Disobey the Apple Way, and your handheld computer was liable not to work. Underpinning this was a new layer of control, since smartphones are tethered to controlled mobile networks (in contrast to the way that freely programmable computers are connected via landline networks) (Naughton 2011b).

Leading media corporations also set about colonising cyberspace. They had back catalogues of content, large reserves of cash and expertise, close links with the advertising industry, brand visibility and cross-promotional muscle. They also bought up rival companies to boost their portfolios. By 1998, over three-quarters of the 31 most visited news and entertainment websites were affiliated with large media firms (McChesney 1999: 163). Some ten years later, leading news organisations dominated (as we saw in Chapter 1[6]) the most-visited news websites in both the UK and the USA. Media audience concentration became a marked feature of online consumption, just as it had offline (Baker 2007). If some players were new, the pattern of consolidation was the same. The effect of the media majors' incursions into cyberspace was also to raise the prevailing level of costs. Creating and maintaining multi-media, audience-pulling websites became an expensive business that made it more difficult for outsiders, with limited resources, to compete effectively.

It also became apparent that the rise of search engines was a mixed blessing. On the one hand, they offered enormous advantages in terms of navigating and making sense of the web. On the other, they structured the web in ways that tended to guide users to mainstream internet destinations (Miller 2000). Thus, in 2002, Yahoo! UK organised content in terms of 'channels' such as shopping, fun, business, personal and connect. Its directory headings were more varied by 2011, but still represented a simplifying and restrictive way of structuring web content. By contrast, Google adopted a more open-ended approach. However, the first ten items under specified topics were the ones that tended to be read, and these were listed on the basis of the net's equivalent of audience ratings. This had the effect of marginalising alternative sources (Hindman 2009), save for a minority of users adept at refining online searches.

In brief, commercialisation played an important part in popularising the internet and making it accessible to a wider public. However, commercialisation also introduced economic and metadata controls, and a new technology of surveillance, that curtailed the diversity and freedom of the internet.

Revolt of the nerds

When the progressive coalition which shaped the early internet fell apart, one group stood its ground and took practical steps to limit the commercialisation of the internet. This was an informal community of computer scientists who resisted the imposition of 'proprietary software' – programmes whose use was restricted by private patent or copyright.

The nerds' revolt began in 1984, when Richard Stallman, a radical programmer at MIT, set up the Free Software Foundation. He had been outraged when a colleague had refused to pass on a printer code on the grounds that it was now restricted by licence. This seemed to Stallman an enforced form of private self-ishness that violated the norm of cooperation on which his professional life had been based. His outrage turned to anger when AT&T announced its intention to license the widely used and previously unrestricted UNIX operating system. In his view, this amounted to the corporate capture, with the full authority of the law, of a program that had been produced communally.

Richard Stallman, a bearded, romantic figure with the appearance of an Apostle, gave up his secure job and set about building almost single-handedly a free alternative to the UNIX operating system. It was called GNU (standing for 'GNU is Not UNIX'). Between 1984 and 1988, Stallman designed an editor and compiler, which were hailed as masterpieces of skill and ingenuity. Then, Stallman's hands sustained repetitive strain injury, and he slowed down. The GNU project was still some way from completion. A then unknown Finnish student, Linus Torvalds, who had heard Stallman give a charismatic talk in Helsinki, filled the breach. With the help of his friends, Torvalds developed in 1990 the missing kernel of the GNU system. The computer community collectively improved the resulting GNU/Linux operating system, making it one of the most reliable in the world. Such was its sustained success that IBM decided in 1998 to hitch its wagon to the protest movement. It officially backed the Linux system, agreeing to invest money in its further development without seeking to exercise any form of proprietary control.

IBM also embraced, on the same terms, the Apache server. This derived from a program released freely by a publicly funded agency, the National Center for Supercomputing Applications (NCSA) at the University of Illinois. Initially full of bugs, it was transformed by the hacker community through cumulative improvements ('patches') and renamed Apache. It became a widely used free server – its success again accounting for its open source adoption by IBM.

This was followed by the launch of the freely available client software Mozilla Firefox, in 2003–4. By 2011, it had become the second most widely used web browser in the world. It played a key part in the so-called second browser war during the 2000s, when the dominance of Microsoft's Internet Explorer was weakened against all the odds. One of Mozilla Firefox's attractions was that it provided a way of blocking online advertising.

What partly underpinned the effectiveness of this concerted protest was that it enlisted the protection of the state (something that radical libertarians tend to ignore). The Free Software Foundation set up by Stallman released its projects under a General Public Licence (GPL). This contained a 'copyleft' clause (the wordplay is typical computer nerd humour) requiring any subsequent improvement in free software to be made available to the community, under the GPL. Contract and copyright law was thus deployed to prevent companies from modifying free software and then claiming the resulting version as their property. It was also used to ensure that future refinements in free software were 'gifted' back to the community.

The successful open source movement kept alive the tradition of the open disclosure of information. It perpetuated the cooperative norms of the scientific community in which people make improvements, or develop new applications (like the world wide web), on the basis of open access to information and then return the favour by making the basis of their discoveries freely available. It also kept faith with the values of academic science, with its belief in cooperation, freedom and open debate in pursuit of scientific advance. The result was the creation of a practical alternative to proprietary software.

The open source (OS) movement drew upon highly trained computer scientists at universities, research laboratories and in the computer industry, as well as skilled hackers. OS activists tended to have a shared belief that the power of the computer should be harnessed to the public good, and were inclined to view any form of authority with suspicion. While their motives were altruistic, they also gained satisfaction from the thrill of creativity and recognition from their peers (Levy 1994). The OS community was also guided by standards, rules, decision-making procedures and sanctioning mechanisms. It was partly this which made it so effective (Weber 2004).

User-generated content

The OS campaign had links to a concerted move to revive user participation. For example, Richard Stallman had been one of the people who had advocated in the 1990s the creation of a web-based online encyclopaedia that would be generated and revised collectively in much the way that OS code is produced. This dream was fulfilled when Jimmy Wales and Larry Sanger launched Wikipedia in 2001. The project proved to be an enormous success. By 2008, it had recruited

75,000 active contributors. In 2011, Wikpedia published some 19 million articles in over 200 languages, covering an enormous range of subjects. While this volume of output was inevitably uneven in quality, Wikipedia entries could attain a high standard supported by the self-correcting mechanism of collective revision, a shared norm of adhering to factual accuracy, unobtrusive safeguards, and an academic tail of hypertextual links (Benkler 2006; Zittrain 2008). Wikipedia's value was so widely recognised that in June 2011 it became the world's seventh most popular website.[7]

The rise of Wikipedia was accompanied by the meteoric growth of social media websites. Facebook was set up by Harvard students in 2004, took off as a young elite social networking site, and then grew exponentially when it became open to all in 2006. It enables users to publish in effect to their friends, while excluding unwanted attention. YouTube was created as a video-sharing website in 2005, and also became a rapid success. It offers a way in which users can circulate what they enjoy, and in the process provide an opportunity for marginalised performers and artists to connect to a wider public. Although these websites are mostly commercial (indeed YouTube was acquired by Google in 2006), they are free at the point of use, and are sustained by the collective talents and resources of the community they serve. They have successfully renewed the do-it-yourself, communal tradition initiated by experiments like WELL and Amsterdam's Digital City.

The radical strand of the early web also found expression in the founding of WikiLeaks in 2006. A small, non-profit organisation, it receives, processes and makes publicly available information supplied by whistleblowers and others. It caused a sensation in 2010 when it released footage of an American helicopter gunning down Iraqi civilians in Baghdad in 2007. This was followed by the mass leaking of US diplomatic cables, which, among other things, provided a revealing insight into America's informal empire. WikiLeaks overcame the potential problem of being buried in the web's vast emporium, and largely overlooked, by forming strategic alliances with leading media organisations. In effect, WikiLeaks turned the tables: governments rather than users were scrutinised through data stored on computers.

Recalcitrant users

The nerd revolt was effective partly because it was backed up by recalcitrant users. The pre-market internet had accustomed people to expect web content and software to be free. For this reason, it proved difficult to re-educate them into becoming paying consumers.

This is illustrated by early attempts to commercialise the web. In 1993, the publicly funded agency NCSA released free its pioneer browser, Mosaic, on the net. Within six months, a million or more copies were downloaded. Members of the Mosaic team then set up a private company and offered an improved, commercial version, Netscape, on a three-month, free-trial basis. However, demands for payment, after the free trial, were widely ignored. Netscape's management then had to decide whether to insist on payment or change tack. It opted to make its service free because it feared – probably rightly – that continued attempts to charge would cause people to migrate to a free alternative. Netscape turned instead to advertising and consultancy as its main source of revenue (Berners-Lee 2000: 107–8).

Companies which tried to charge website fees also ran into trouble. A large number failed during the 1990s (Schiller 2000; Sparks 2000). Not much greater success attended the selling of web content in the next two decades, outside of three specialist sectors – pornography, games and financial information. Even successful alternative websites found it difficult to persuade their users to part with money (Kim and Hamilton 2006; Curran and Witschge 2010). Faced with a growing economic crisis, a few newspaper publishers attempted to construct a new business model in 2010–11 by charging for content that they had previously made available free – with results that it is too early to assess. However, the music industry found, after a long and disastrous delay, a compromise solution to the online pirating of music: in effect, it opted for charging less for online tracks, with some success.

Initially, there was antipathy to net advertising. In 1994 the US law firm Canter and Siegel posted an advertisement for its immigration law advice service to thousands of newsgroups. The next day it was so inundated with abusive replies ('flames') that its internet service provider repeatedly crashed (Goggin 2000). In 1995, a survey found that two-thirds of Americans did not want any net advertising (McChesney 1999: 132). Subsequently, after software became available for filtering out e-mailed spam, online advertising became more accepted. Indeed, large numbers opted to visit advertising websites like Craigslist and Gumtree.

Looking back

The history of the Western internet is thus a chronicle of contradiction. In its predominantly pre-market phase, the internet was powerfully influenced by the values of academic science, American counterculture and European public service. Originating as a research tool linked to a military project, the internet acquired multiple new functions – as the creator of virtual communities, a playground for role-playing and as a platform for interactive political debate. The crowning culmination of this first phase was the gift of the web to the world, creating a storehouse of information freely available to all.

However, this early formation was overlaid by a new commercial regime. A determined attempt was made to charge for software that had previously been free. Major media organisations established well-resourced websites. Search engines, seeking to harvest advertising, signposted visitors to popular destinations. The growth of online entertainment tended to sideline political discourse. New commercial surveillance technology was developed to monitor user behaviour, accompanied by legislation strengthening intellectual property rights in cyberspace.

Yet the old order refused to surrender without a fight. Dissenting computer workers collectively developed and made available OS software. Users, conditioned by the norms of the early internet, often refused to pay for online content and shifted to sites that were free. The spirit that had re-imagined the computer and discovered new uses for it in the 1980s was powerfully renewed in the 2000s. It led to the creation of the user-generated Wikipedia, social media and the whistleblower website WikiLeaks.

The balance struck between the old and the new is inherently unstable. Already cyberspace is more commercialised in 2012 than it was 15 years ago. The internet could change very rapidly in favour of a market regime. Yet, a determined effort was made to sustain the founding traditions of the internet, and this has met so far with a significant degree of success.

However, if the main progressive effort in the West was to combat market censorship of the internet,[8] its counterpart in the East was mainly directed against state censorship. It is to this that we now turn, in a necessarily preliminary attempt to widen the scope of internet history.

March to democracy

It was widely predicted in the 1990s that the global diffusion of the internet would assist the march to democracy. The keyboard, we were told, would prove mightier than the secret police: dictatorships would fall like dominoes because the internet would inspire a clamour for freedom.[9]

This forecast is refuted by a recent comparative analysis of internet diffusion rates and measurements of democratic change in 72 countries between 1994 and 2003 (Groshek 2010). It found that 'Internet diffusion was not a specific causal mechanism of national democratic growth' (Groshek 2010: 142). Even in three instances (Croatia, Indonesia and Mexico) where the internet seems to have made a significant democratic input, the actual processes of causation are complex. The internet can be seen as a 'coincidental developmental condition', an aspect of larger social and political change that contributed to a nation's democratic development (Groshek 2010: 159).

One reason why the 'internet as the grave digger of dictatorship' thesis proved to be overblown was that it failed to appreciate that democracy is only one source of governmental legitimacy. Economic growth (Singapore), fear of a strong neighbour (pre-1996 Taiwan), nationalism (China), ethnic affiliation (Malaysia), God's will (Iraq) and identification with national liberation (Zimbabwe) are just some of the alternative sources of legitimation sustaining resilient authoritarian regimes. In addition to brute force, authoritarian governments have also deployed non-coercive strategies for sustaining their rule, such as co-opting powerful interests, developing clientelist systems of patronage that reward their supporters, and adopting a policy of divide and rule (Ghandi and Przeworski 2007;

Magaloni 2008). Above all, authoritarian governments can often count on pragmatic acceptance, underpinned by the struggle to make ends meet and an entertainment-centred popular culture.[10]

The second thing that the 'technology of freedom' thesis got wrong was that it mistakenly assumed that the internet is uncontrollable. It was widely argued in the 1990s that because the internet is a decentralised system in which information is transmitted via independent, variable pathways through dispersed computer power, it could not be controlled by location-bound government. Dissident communications, we were told, could be produced outside the jurisdictional control of national government and downloaded in the privacy of people's homes. Freedom would take wing because it could no longer be suppressed in the internet age.

In an eloquent debunking account, Evgeny Morozov (2011) summarises the various ways in which authoritarian regimes, around the world, have sought to censor the internet. To simplify, this boils down to seven things. Authoritarian governments can foster a general climate of fear by jailing, torturing or killing critics. They can require all domestic websites and internet service providers to be licensed, and withdraw these licences if they are in breach of restrictive laws. They can outsource censorship by requiring all internet service providers to filter out access to any URL on a government blacklist (irrespective of where in the world it originates from). They can monitor the internet behaviour of potential dissidents through surveillance software (by, for example, planting a malignant link to a critical petition). They can deploy automated software to identify 'harmful' internet communications, such as critical, anonymous posts, that need to be wiped. They can unleash programming to defeat evasion, including the identification of proxy sites, and disable critical sites through DOD (Distributed-Denial-of-Service) attacks. The ultimate weapon is to pull the plug – closing down internet communication in a region (China), suspending the texting of messages for a period (Cambodia) or stopping mobile phone coverage in a city (Iran) (Morozov 2011; cf. Deibert et al. 2008; Freedom House 2009).

Governments have also sought to make the internet a propaganda tool – what Morozov (2011: 113) calls 'spinternet' – not merely through the creation of official websites but through more sophisticated methods. For example, in Nigeria the government seeded support groups to proselytise online; in Russia, the principal internet entrepreneur, Kontantin Rykov, is a close government ally; and in China, some patriotic online computer games were state sponsored. In Iran, the arrest of dissidents facilitated – through gaining access to their e-mail and mobile phone contacts – the rapid round-up of networks of critical citizens in 2009–10. New technology proved, in this case, to be a more efficient method of identifying and apprehending enemies of the state than old-fashioned Soviet methods of bugging and trailing suspects.

The extent to which the internet was controlled in practice varied greatly across authoritarian countries. In part, this depended on the will and capability of governments. Some authoritarian regimes, like those in Iran, China and

Uzbekistan, became undisputed leaders in censoring the internet; others, like those in Ethiopia and Yemen, were dysfunctional; while others still, like the authorities in Malaysia and Morocco, chose to adopt relatively liberal internet regimes.[11]

How much control was exercised also depended on the wider context. Some authoritarian governments could rely on poverty as the ultimate censor (as in Burma) (OpenNet Initiative 2009). Other regimes, such as that in Singapore, controlled the internet as a consequence of the consensual support that they enjoyed.[12] By contrast, large-scale alienation (as in Iran) could produce activists adept at evading censorship.

In brief, those who predicted that the rise of the internet would lead to the fall of authoritarian regimes were confounded by the way most of these regimes survived in the internet era. Many authoritarian governments across the world had greater resources at their disposal, and were better able to censor the internet, than was appreciated in the cyber-utopian moment of the mid-1990s.

But there is a recent exception where, it is claimed, new communications technology inspired people to rise up against dictators. This claim has been repeated so often that it is worth looking at it more closely.[13]

Arab uprisings

On 18 December 2010, mass street protests took place in Tunisia. They were followed by tumultuous demonstrations, rallies and occupations that caused President Ben Ali to flee the country on 14 January, 2010. The contagion of discontent spread to Egypt, where popular protests forced, on 11 February, the resignation of President Hosni Mubarak after almost 30 years of rule. During January and February, popular protests occurred across much of the region. Some of these were placated by promises of liberalising reform, as in Jordan and Morocco. But in Bahrain mass protests were put down with the help of Saudi Arabian troops. Yemen descended into virtual civil war; the Gaddafi regime was deposed in Libya; and a rebellion took place in Syria. There were thus six 'insurgent' countries where the ruler departed, or was confronted by large-scale, sustained protests.

Since protests happened over so short a period, and were supported by digital technology, some have called them the 'Twitter' or 'Facebook' revolutions (e.g. Taylor 2011). Social media, it is claimed, enabled flash demonstrations to take place, and encouraged protests to spread across national frontiers. What made this situation unprecedented, it is argued, is that people could communicate with each other on a mass scale and gain strength from each other in ways that could not be controlled by the authorities. Typically, this analysis foregrounds the drama of the uprisings and the enabling role of communications technology, while paying little attention to the past or to the wider context of society (e.g. El-Naway 2011; Mullany 2011).

A closer examination suggests that these first drafts of history are seriously flawed. The Arab region was not especially primed by new communications technology to erupt. An analysis of 52 million Twitter users found that only

0.027 per cent identified their locations as Egypt, Yemen and Tunisia (Evans 2011). The Facebook penetration rate in the region's trouble spots is not high: a mere 1 per cent in Syria, 5 per cent in Libya, though it is 17 per cent in Tunisia (Dubai School of Government (DSG) 2011: 5, figure 6). Less than a quarter of the population in Egypt and Syria are internet users, a proportion that falls to 6 per cent in Libya (DSG 2011: 10, figure 12). This is much lower than in many authoritarian parts of Asia. In China, for example, 32 per cent of the population had internet access in 2010 (Internet World Stats 2011a). This suggests that it was not communications technology that made the Arab region especially combustible.

Out of the six 'insurgent' countries (Bahrain, Egypt, Tunisia, Libya, Syria and Yemen), Bahrain alone features in the top five ranking of Arab countries for Facebook user penetration or for internet use in 2010 (DSG 2011: 5, figure 6; and 12, figure 15). In other words, what the great bulk of insurgent countries have in common is that they are *not* part of the information communication technology vanguard in the Arab region.[14] Other countries with greater access to Facebook – for example Saudi Arabia and the UAE – did not turn on their dictators. This surely suggests that there were underlying causes specific to the insurgent countries that gave rise to popular revolt.

This is corroborated by the history of these countries. The Arab uprisings were the product not of Twitter and Facebook but of dissent fermented over decades (Wright 2008; Hamzawy 2009; Alexander 2010; Joshi 2011; Ottaway and Hamzawy 2011, among others). In Syria, the 2011 uprising had been preceded by the 1982 rebellion, which had been put down with enormous brutality. Yemen had a civil war in 1994, and was approaching the condition of a failed state by the time of the 2011 uprising. Bahrain, Egypt, Libya and Tunisia had recurrent protests in the 1980s, 1990s and 2000s. Ever since 1975, Bahrain had degenerated into a beleaguered police state, following its suspension of parliament. In Egypt, the Kefaya Movement had united disparate anti-government groups in 2004–5. In the first three months of 2008 alone, there had been some 600 protests in the country. A powder keg was waiting to blow.

Underlying this incendiary situation was a mixture of factors – some that were common to all insurgent Arab countries, and others that were country specific. One common factor was growing opposition to regimes that were viewed as corrupt and repressive. Resentment was particularly strong in those countries, like Tunisia and Libya, where it was felt that the benefits of economic development were funnelled towards those close to the regime (Durac and Cavatorta 2009).

Another factor common to most of the affected countries was high unemployment, compounded by rising expectations. Countries across the region expanded their higher education and post-15 education rates (Cassidy 2011; Barro and Lee 2010). But increasingly educated populations found that the labour market did not offer the opportunities that they had been educated for. The anger and disappointment this generated was a key driving force of the political turmoil that shook the Arab world (Campante and Chor 2011), in much the way that it had fuelled anti-colonial protests in the former British Empire.

There were also very specific economic causes. There was high unemployment and underemployment in all the affected countries, concentrated disproportionately among the young. In some states, neoliberal policies pursued earlier had led to the loss of public subsidies and jobs. In general, rising food prices added to discontent. Economic factors were especially important in generating opposition in Tunisia, where resistance began in the poorer areas, and in Egypt, where trade unions played a significant role.

In addition, intra-elite tensions, tribal conflicts and religious enmities was a contributory factor in the uprisings. Thus, there was strong Shia opposition to the Sunni ruling minority in Bahrain; bitter Sunni opposition to the secular regime in Syria; and fundamentalist opposition to the 'compromised' government in Yemen.

In brief, there was a common thread of active dissent toward regimes in all the insurgent countries, which extended back for decades. This dissent had deepseated economic, political and religious causes. The role of digital media was secondary.

However, it mattered that the authorities lost control over communications. In Tunisia, the two main TV channels initially played down both the unrest and civilian casualties, and then attempted to demonise the protesters as thugs and outlaws (Miladi 2011). The Tunisian government also jammed critical content on Facebook and blogs, and stepped up 'phishing' for personal information in order to disable dissident networks. In Egypt, the authorities attempted to pull the plug after mass demonstrations on 25 January 2011 by blocking Twitter, Facebook and mobile phone messages in quick succession, before shutting down the entire internet on 27 January. Similarly, a complete blackout of the internet was ordered in Libya. But in all three countries the authorities moved too late, and the clampdown was not fully effective.

The part played by *different* media in the uprisings is difficult to establish. But it would seem that the mobile phone was especially important in mobilising and coordinating protests. Those taking part also filmed the protests, and regularly sent the footage to the website of the popular satellite TV channel Al Jazeera, based in Qatar. This was broadcast in a professionally edited form across the region. In addition, footage was fed to Western television organisations, something that had domestic relevance because Western powers, and in particular the US, had close links to the military in Tunisia and Egypt, and to anti-Gaddafi rebels in Libya.

It would also seem that the ability of a small number of techie dissidents to outwit the authorities was strategically important. According to Harb (2011), 'Arab activists from across the regions started exchanging codes and software that allowed Egyptians to access the internet, despite government blockades'. Google stepped in, supplying new software in 2011 that enabled protesters to 'tweet' over the phone (Oreskovic 2011). Arab activists across the region also acted, over a long period, as informal publicists, translating content and relaying visual footage – functioning, in the words of the Tunisian blogger Sami bin Gharbia, as 'the echo chamber of the struggle on the street' (cited in

Ghannam 2011). This echo chamber was further amplified by tweeting sympathisers in the West.

In short, the uprisings had deep underlying causes and were prefigured by protests over many years, largely ignored in the West. But the emergence of new media – in particular the mobile phone, internet and pan-Arab satellite TV – contributed to the build-up of dissent, facilitated the actual organisation of protests, and disseminated news of the protests across the region and to the wider world. If the rise of digital communications technology did not cause the uprisings, it strengthened them.[15] However, it remains to be seen whether new technology strengthened them enough to secure not regime decapitation, but real regime change.

Advance of women

If one momentous historical change has been the faltering march to democracy, another has been the advance of women. Sharp inequalities persist between men and women in terms of income, life chances and public influence, but they have lessened over time – albeit in an uneven way – across the world (Hufton 1995; Rowbotham 1997; Kent 1999; Sakr 2004, among others). Underpinning this historic shift have been the rise of the service industries, rising female participation in the paid workforce, the decline of social ascription, improved education, better contraception, feminism and the erosion of gender theories legitimating inequality.

One way the development of the internet connected to this historic trend was to provide a tool for the *organised* woman's movement. In Islamic countries, the rise of leading Muslim reformers at the end of the nineteenth century encouraged the spread of more liberated perspectives (Hadj-Moussa 2009). By the 1980s, the women's movement had become a political force in the Middle East and North Africa (MENA) region. Feminists generated intense controversy by talking about taboo subjects such as domestic violence, sexual harassment, female genital mutilation and rape (Skalli 2006), and gained a growing influence, especially among young women from elite or educated backgrounds. But this was in a region where internet use among women was especially limited (Wheeler 2004: 139, table 9.1). It was also a context where female literacy was sometimes low.

Despite these obstacles, important gains were made. Thus, in Morocco, a new generation of women's organisations emerged in the 1980s that operated outside formal political circles. By the early 2000s they had incorporated the internet as a part of their campaigning activity, helped by the fact that Morocco had a higher internet penetration rate than its neighbours. The main target of the women's movement was the Moudawana, the family code governing marriage, divorce and child custody, which had previously provided women with few rights. In 2003 campaigners secured reform of the Moroccan family code in a way that outlawed many discriminatory practices, in addition to raising the minimum age of marriage from 15 to 18, removing the need for women to have a guardian's approval before marriage and giving women the right to divorce their husbands (Tavaana 2011).

This and other successes arose from a concerted campaign conducted through the full spectrum of the media across the region. This produced a sustained backlash that led to the murder of the female Kuwaiti editor Hedaya Al-Saleem by a policeman (subsequently convicted) and the killing of female journalists in Algeria (Skalli 2006: 41). This persecution encouraged a growing sense of cohesion among campaigners, extending across frontiers and supported by frequent online communication between Arab-speaking members of the women's movement.

However, the strongest outpost of the women's movement in MENA was the Persian-speaking theocracy of Iran. Between 1978 and 2005, the number of women's rights NGOs increased from 13 to 430. The growth of the women's movement found expression online partly because women accounted in 2003 for 49 per cent of internet users in Iran, a much higher proportion than in most of the region. The issues discussed on Iran's most popular feminist blogs included divorce, stoning, banning female participation in sporting events and discriminatory laws in general (Shirazi 2011). These were supplemented by other progressive blogs that engaged with personal politics, such as that written by the popular blogger Lady Sun (Sreberny and Khiabany 2010).

This portrayal of the net as an arm of the organised women's movement in the Middle East needs to be qualified in two ways. First, much web content was conditioned by patriarchal values, and was hostile to women's liberation. Second, only a small minority of women probably read online content originating directly from the women's movement. Feminist blogs and publications do not feature in Wheeler's (2007) small-scale study of young female Egyptian internet users in 2004. Her subjects, who often spent hours each week in internet cafés, emerge as quite instrumental – for example getting information for essays or seeking to improve their English in order to get a better job. It was primarily through their online interactions with other women – rather than through any link to an organised movement – that they derived support for negotiating the constraints of their conservative environment.

If one response to gender inequality was to try to change it through organised political action, another was to seek to advance in the world as a purposive individual and triumph against the odds. Youna Kim (2010) presents a vivid portrait of young Asian women with high expectations, encouraged by educational success and sometimes privileged backgrounds, encountering – or facing the prospect of entering – the male-dominated world of work in Korea, Japan or China. In this case study, their 'rebellion' took the form of flight to the West, postgraduate education and the search for new opportunities to realise their talents and ambitions. One inspiration for their flight was Hollywood images of independent women who took control of their lives. While respondents recognised that these were fictional idealisations, they also hoped that they were in part realistic. These images contributed to a utopian self-imagining in which respondents aspired to remake themselves, in a Western context, as autonomous women who placed themselves at 'the centre of [their] biography' (Kim 2010: 40).

An unrelated study provides a glimpse into how the internet features in this cultural dynamic. Yachien Huang (2008) found that university-educated women in Taiwan tended to watch the American TV series *Sex and the City* on their computer screens instead of on family television sets, which were often dominated by male surveillance and choice control. Internet bulletin boards also provided these women with an opportunity to discuss and debate aspects of this series. Its fascination for these young women arose partly from the transitional time in which they lived. Rising female consumer power and economic expectations in Taiwan had not been mirrored by a corresponding change in the traditionalist culture of Taiwanese society, with its expectation of demure female behaviour, duty, and self-sacrifice. The series, projecting a hedonistic world of independent, affluent women in Manhattan, provided a 'cultural resource' for Taiwanese women seeking to negotiate their obligation to be a 'good girl' with their desire to have more 'individualistic lifestyles and open sexuality' (Huang 2008: 199). It was an inspiration for 'their struggle for agency' in a male-dominated world, but one that tended to take a personal, individualised route. As one interviewee put it, the lesson of the series is 'choose what you want, and don't make yourself miserable' (Huang 2008: 196).

The history of the internet is thus bound up with the struggle for greater gender equality. The internet provided a tool for an organised campaign for women's liberation in the Middle East and elsewhere. It also distributed depictions of autonomous women that inspired the seeking of personal solutions to gender inequality.

Internet and individualism

This last response is one aspect of another important historical change. There has been a cumulative shift from values and beliefs that prioritise the collective good of the community, and of groups within it, to ones that give priority to the satisfaction of the needs, desires and aspirations of the individual. This has been encouraged by, among other things, the rise of the market system, increasing mobility, the weakening of custom and tradition, and the declining influence of the family and collective organisations (Beck and Beck-Gernsheim 2001).

Some see the internet as encouraging this more individual-centred orientation because this is supposedly wired into the internet's DNA. According to Barry Wellman and associates (2003):

> The development of personalization, wireless portability, and ubiquitous connectivity of the Internet all facilitate networked individualism as the basis of community. Because connections are to people and not to places, the technology affords shifting of work and community ties from linking people-in-places to linking people at any place. Computer-supported

communication is *everywhere*, but it is situated *nowhere*. It is I-alone that is reachable wherever I am: at a home, hotel, office, highway, or shopping center. The person has become the portal.

(Wellman et al. 2003)

Wellman and associates conclude that the internet has reinforced 'networked individualism' at the expense of 'group or local solidarities'. This is a variant of the standard argument that, by annihilating distance, the internet has eroded group affiliations based on workplace or proximity, and enabled individuals to connect with other like-minded individuals regardless of place (Cairncross 1997).

Plausible though it sounds, this orthodoxy overlooks the way that communalism in the real world can shape online experience. Thus, Miller and Slater (2000) found that strong nationalist sentiment in Trinidad gave rise to nationalist web content. Even chat rooms celebrated a sense of being 'Trini' through the display of 'ole talk' and 'liming' – the ability to communicate, to be expressive and warm, and to be witty about everyday things – that was viewed as being part of the island's distinctive national culture. Online encounters with foreigners also led some Trinidadians to feel that they should act as informal national ambassadors. Strong national consciousness thus infused Trinidadians' online experience in ways that supported their sense of communal identity. Underlying this intense sense of national belonging, argue Miller and Slater, was the historical experience of slavery, migration and social dislocation.

Similarly, Madhavi Mallapragada's study of expatriate and diasporic Indians (2000) concluded that the internet was widely used to stay connected to a distant homeland. Her subjects sought out web content that displayed India's rich cultural heritage; some discussed how to deal with their assimilating children, who were turning their backs on their Indian identity; and a minority even used the net to facilitate arranged marriages between members of their family and people living in India. Likewise, Larry Gross (2003) argues that the internet provides emotional support, practical advice and a sense of belonging among gay men encountering persecution or prejudice in different parts of the world. In both these instances, the internet supported 'group or local solidarities': to call it 'networked individualism' is to miss the point that it was a collective identity that was being sought and affirmed.

Similarly, the collectivist culture of Japan generated the distinctive Nico Nico Dougwa (NND) video-sharing website in which comments are overlaid on the screen rather than written beneath it. The comments are pithy, often witty and limited to ten. Any user can delete a comment and replace it with another. This creates an atmosphere of live, collective viewing not unlike watching a football match, with spontaneous comments from the crowd.

The website developed a mass following, with some 5 million regular users in 2008. Its acolytes developed a culture of 'kuuki' – 'the shared atmosphere of appreciation that one needs to catch, if one wants to comment appropriately and to understand the joy of being a Nico Chuu [fan]' (Bachmann 2008a: 2). This group togetherness is reinforced by the anonymity of those making comments, in which even a pseudonymous tag is omitted. However, if a distinctive style is recognised, the group may bestow the honour of conferring a nickname.

Nico Nico Dougwa is very obviously the product of a group-centred culture. Yet 'tag wars', reflecting divergent responses to a video, can sometimes occur, causing group cohesion to break down. Online anonymity can also provide a cover for expressing controversial views that would not be acceptable in the off-line world. This is a more pronounced feature, notes Bachmann (2008b), of the Japanese internet forum 2channel. His overall conclusion is that the online experiences in Japan which he studied both reflect and reaffirm group togetherness, while also sometimes giving expression to a desire to escape group control.

The unifying thread of these case studies, mostly located outside the West, is that strongly communal life in the real world can penetrate the online experience, and result in the internet offering support – though sometimes in a complex or contradictory way – for the maintenance of communal identities. The implication of this is that the social impact of the internet is likely to have been different in the collectivist East than in the more individual-centred West.

However, the dynamic of change is towards greater individualism, even in the East. The internet can provide a space for the expression of individual identity even in collectivist societies. Thus, a study of Japanese students' use of advanced mobile phones concludes that it reinforces individualism and strengthens interiority in three distinct ways (McVeigh 2003). Phones as artefacts enable students to express their individuality through choice of colour, functions, ring tones and phone accessories (such as colourful figurines hung from phone straps). Mobile phones make it easier to express private feelings, primarily through texting and e-mail. Above all, mobile phones increase 'personalized individualization' by providing students with a sense of personal space. In Japan, living areas are often cramped, and there is a high level of surveillance by employers and educators. Students repeatedly stressed that their mobile phones enabled them to communicate privately with friends and create 'their own world' (McVeigh 2003: 47–48). However, there may be more ambiguity in this outcome than this Western author perhaps acknowledges. Students were expressing themselves as individuals within the strongly group-conditioned context of being a Tokyo University student.

Sima and Pugsley's study of blogs and bloggers in China (2010) also argues that the internet enables the showcasing of individuality, and a public process of self-reflection and self-discovery. They contend that this both reflects and expresses the greater individualism of China's 'Generation Y', who are growing up at a time of increasing consumerism and the one-child family rule that encourages a greater emphasis on the self among the young. However, the internal evidence of their article suggests that individual voices can sometimes be presented as a collective voice – that of China's new generation (Sima and Pugsley 2010: 301).

In general, the rise of the internet as a medium of self-communication has enabled greater self-expression, and probably strengthened the trend towards individualism. This would seem to be the case in the West (Castells 2009), and there is some evidence that the internet has also reinforced the trend towards greater individualism in Asia. But communal identities remain strong in many parts of the world, influencing use of the internet.

Retrospect

Historians of the internet have tended to concentrate on the early, Edenic phase of Western internet development. This revised history has emphasised, by contrast, the way in which commercialisation subsequently distorted the internet in the West, while state censorship, in particular, muzzled the internet in the East. Growing corporate influence, the development of online audience concentration, the introduction of commercial surveillance technology and the strengthening of intellectual property law all entailed the superimposition of a new set of constraints on the internet as a consequence of advancing market influence. Likewise the introduction of restrictive internet licensing, the outsourcing of state censorship to internet service providers and the adaptation of commercial surveillance technology to state snooping imposed a further set of controls when the internet developed outside its north-western cradle. In brief, the rise of the internet was accompanied by the decline of its freedom.

However, this trend was resisted in both East and West. The rise of the open source movement, people's continued reluctance to pay for web content, and the revival of the user-generated tradition all represented an attempt to arrest the commercial transformation of the internet. Likewise the heroic dissident hackers, who outwitted authoritarian governments in Egypt and elsewhere, were keeping alive the conception of a free internet. The founders of Wikipedia and numerous hackers in Cairo, were both part of the same project: in different ways, they were renewing the founding tradition and vision of the internet.

If one task of rethinking internet history is to take full account of the later period, another task is to narrate the history of the internet as a global rather than Western phenomenon. This preliminary reconnaissance, which necessarily leaves out large parts of the world, concludes that the internet was less effective in destabilising authoritarian regimes than was widely anticipated. The internet also contributed to the advance of women by providing a tool for the organised women's movement and by distributing the sometimes pirated products of Hollywood feminism. More contentiously, internet self-communication seems to have promoted the expression and assertion of self, though the evidence also points to the way in which strongly communal cultures could result in the internet supporting communal identities.

The interaction between the internet and society is complex. This is under-scored by this chapter, which indicates that this relationship has varied both in time and space. Yet, even allowing for this complexity, the weight of evidence points to one firm conclusion: society exerts, in general, a greater influence on the internet than the other way around. That is why many of the prophecies about the impact of the internet – surveyed in the first chapter and encountered again in this chapter – have not been fulfilled.

This is not a novel insight into the influence of new communications technology. It is one that dawned on idealistic liberals in Britain after 1880 when they realised that the popular press had not become, as they anticipated, an autonomous agency of rational and moral instruction but broadly reflected the people who controlled and read popular papers (Hampton 2004). Wiser and more sceptical, they stopped capitalising the 'Newspaper Press'. Perhaps we should do the same in relation to the 'Internet'.

Notes

1 My thanks go again to Joanna Redden, and to Justin Schlosberg for his valuable research assistance centred on this chapter.
2 Naughton (2000) broke free from this historians' pack by adding a brief last chapter that identified commercialism as a threat to the future of the internet. This reflected the originality of this fine book, which even now offers the best account of the technological development of the internet, and powerfully conveys the excitement of doing computer science.
3 This challenge came from different directions, summarised in terms of historiography by Curran (2002 and 2011), and in terms of contemporary thought by Hampton (2004).
4 Their continuing awe is reflected in their capitalisation of the 'Internet'.
5 See Chapter 1, pages 6–7.
6 See pages 19–20.
7 These uncorroborated figures are derived from Wikipedia (2009 and 2011).
8 The Western internet was not free, however, of government, and allied, censorship. For attempts to muzzle WikiLeaks, see Chapter 4.
9 Morozov (2011), and Mosco (2005) cite numerous politicians, public officials, journalists and academics who predicted that the rise of the internet would undermine dictatorships. For a more guarded and scholarly legatee of this tradition, see Howard (2011), who argues that the internet is a key 'ingredient' of the 'recipe' for democratisation.
10 An example of this de-politicisation is provided by Morozov (2011: 58), who notes that among the most-searched websites in Russia is one about 'how to lose weight' but not one about the abuse of human rights.
11 The OpenNet Initiative (2011), based on a collaborative partnership between four leading academic institutions, provides a very useful summary of censorship by country, from which this has been derived.
12 See Chapter 1.
13 This examination excludes the protests in Iran since these are discussed in Chapter 5.
14 For example, in 2011, 24% of Egyptians were internet users, compared with 41% of Moroccans, 44% of Saudi Arabians and 69% of those living in UAE (Internet World Stats 2011b).
15 A recent study (Alexander 2011) illuminates the role of the internet and satellite TV in contributing to the uprising in Egypt. However, it plays down the underlying causes of the revolt.

References

Abbate, J. (2000) *Inventing the Internet*, Cambridge, MA: MIT Press.
Alexander, A. (2010) 'Leadership and Collective Action in the Egyptian Trade Unions', *Work Employment Society*, 24: 241–59.

Alexander, J. (2011) *Performative Revolution in Egypt*, London: Bloomsbury.

Anderson, C. (2006) *The Long Tail*, London: Business Books.

Bachmann, G. (2008a) 'Wunderbar! Nico Nico Douga Goes German – and Some Hesitant Reflections on Japaneseness', London: Goldsmiths Leverhulme Media Research Centre. Online. Available HTTP: <http://www.gold.ac.uk/media-research-centre/project2/project2-outputs/> (accessed 20 June 2011).

——(2008b) 'The Force of Affirmative Metadata', paper presented at the Force of Metadata Symposium, Goldsmiths, University of London, November.

Baker, C. E. (2007) *Media Concentration and Democracy*, New York: Cambridge University Press.

Banks, M. (2008) *On the Way to the Web*, Berkeley, CA: Apress.

Barro, R. and Lee, J.-W. (2010) 'A New Data Set of Educational Attainment in the World, 1950–2010', NBER Working Paper No. 15902 the National Bureau of Economic Research. Online. Available HTTP: <http://www.nber.org/papers/w15902> (accessed 12 February 2011).

Beck, U. and Beck-Gernsheim, E. (2001) *Individualization*, London: Sage.

Benkler, Y. (2006) *The Wealth of Nations*, New Haven: Yale University Press.

Berners-Lee, T. (2000) *Weaving the Web*, London: Orion.

Boies, S. C. (2002) 'University Students' Uses of and Reactions to Online Sexual Information and Entertainment: Links to Online and Offline Sexual Behaviour', *Canadian Journal of Human Sexuality*, 11 (2): 77–89.

Cairncross, F. (1997) *The Death of Distance*, Boston, MA: Harvard Business School Press.

Campante, F. R. and Chor, D. (2011) '"The People Want the Fall of the Regime": Schooling, Political Protest, and the Economy', Faculty Research Working Paper Series. Harvard Kennedy School. Online. Available HTTP: <http://jrnetsolserver.shor enseteincente.netdna-cdn.com/wp-content/uploads/2011/07/RWP11–018_Campante_ Chor.pdf> (accessed 2 July 2011).

Cassidy, J. (2011) 'Prophet Motive', *New Yorker*, 28 February: 32–35.

Castells, M. (2001) *The Internet Galaxy*, Oxford: Oxford University Press.

——(2009) *Communication Power*, Oxford: Oxford University Press.

Comer, D. (2007) *The Internet Book*, London: Pearson Education.

Curran, J. (2002) *Media and Power*, London: Routledge.

——(2011) *Media and Democracy*, London: Routledge.

Curran, J. and Witschge, T. (2010) 'Liberal Dreams and the Internet', in N. Fenton (ed.) *New Media, Old News: Journalism and Democracy in the Digital Age*, London: Sage.

Deibert, R., Palfrey, J., Rohozinski, J. and Zittrain, J. (eds) (2008) *Access Denied: The Practice and Policy of Global Internet Filtering*, Cambridge, MA: MIT Press. Online. Available HTTP: <http://opennet.net/accessdenied> (accessed 15 May 2011).

DFC Intelligence (2010) 'Tracking the Growth of Online Game Usage and Distribution', 8 October. Online. Available HTTP: <http://www.dfcint.com/wp/?p=292> (accessed 19 February 2011).

DSG (Dubai School of Government) (2011) *Arab Social Media Report, 2*. Online. Available HTTP: <http://www.dsg.ae/portals/0/ASMR2.pdf> (accessed 25 June 2011).

Durac, V. and Cavatorta, F. (2009) 'Strengthening Authoritarian Rule through Democracy Promotion? Examining the Paradox of the US and EU Security Strategies: The Case of Bin Ali's Tunisia', *British Journal of Middle Eastern Studies*, 36 (1): 3–19.

Edelman, B. (2009) 'Red Light States: Who Buys Online Adult Entertainment?', *Journal of Economic Perspectives*, 23 (1): 209–20.

Edwards, P. (1996) *The Closed World*, Cambridge, MA: MIT Press.

El-Naway, M. (2011) *Sunday Mirror*, 20 February, p. 8.

Evans, M. (2011) 'Egypt Crisis: The Revolution Will Not Be Tweeted', *Sysomos Blog*. Online. Available HTTP: <http://blog.sysomos.com/2011/01/31/egyptian-crisis-twitte/> (accessed 25 June 2011).

Flichy, P. (1999) 'The Construction of New Digital Media', *New Media and Society*, 1 (1): 33–39.

——(2006) 'New Media History', in L. Lievrouw and S. Livingstone (eds) *The Handbook of New Media*, rev. edn, London: Sage.

——(2007) *The Internet Imaginaire*, Cambridge, MA: MIT Press.

Freedom House (2009) 'Freedom on the net: a Global Assessment of Internet and Digital Media'. Online. Available HTTP: <http://freedomhouse.org/uploads/specialreports/NetFreedom2009/FreedomOnTheNet_FullReport.pdf> (accessed 2 August 2011).

Fukuyama, F. (1993) *The End of History and the Last Man*, Harmondsworth: Penguin.

George, C. (2005) 'The Internet's Political Impact and the Penetration/Participation Paradox in Malaysia and Singapore', *Media, Culture and Society*, 27 (6): 903–20.

Ghandi, J. and Przeworski, A. (2007) 'Authoritarian Institutions and the Survival of Autocrats', *Comparative Political Studies*, 40 (11): 1279–1301.

Ghannam, J. (2011) 'Social Media in the Arab World: Leading up to the Uprisings of 2011', Centre for International Media Assistance, CIMA: Washington, DC.

Gillies, J. and Cailliau, R. (2000) *How the Web Was Born*, Oxford: Oxford University Press.

Goggin, G. (2000) 'Pay per Browse? The Web's Commercial Future', in D. Gauntlett (ed.) *Web Studies*, London: Arnold.

Grant, J. (1871–72) *The Newspaper Press*, 3 vols, London: Tinsley Brothers.

Groshek, J. (2010) 'A Time-series, Multinational Analysis of Democratic Forecasts and Internet Diffusion', *International Journal of Communication*, 4: 142–74.

Gross, L. (2003) 'The Gay Global Village in Cyberspace', in N. Couldry and J. Curran (eds) *Contesting Media Power*, Boulder, CO: Rowman and Littlefield.

Hadj-Moussa, R. (2009) 'Arab Women: Beyond Politics', in P. Essed, D. Goldberg and A. Kobayashi (eds) *A Companion to Gender Studies*, Malden, MA: Blackwell.

Hafner, K. and Lyon, M. (2003) *Where Wizards Stay up Late*, London: Pocket Books.

Hampton, M. (2004) *Visions of the Press in Britain, 1850–1950*, Urbana: University of Illinois Press.

Hamzawy, A. (2009) 'Rising Social Distress: the Case of Morocco, Egypt, and Jordan', *International Economic Bulletin*, Carnegie Endowment for International Peace. Online. Available HTTP: <http://www.carnegieendowment.org/ieb/?fa=view&id=23290> (accessed 15 June 2011).

Harb, Z. (2011) 'Arab Revolutions and the Social Media Effect', *M/C Journal*, 14 (2). Online. Available HTTP: <http://journal.media-culture.org.au/index.php/mcjournal/article/viewArticle/364> (accessed 23 October 2011).

Hauben, M. and Hauben, R. (1997) *Netizens*, New York: Columbia University Press.

Hindman, M. (2009) *The Myth of Digital Democracy*, Princeton: Princeton University Press.

Howard, P. (2011) *The Digital Origins of Dictatorship and Democracy*, New York: Oxford University Press.

Huang, Y. (2008) 'Consuming Sex and the City: Young Taiwanese Women Contesting Sexuality', in Y. Kim (ed.) *Media Consumption and Everyday Life in Asia*, Milton Park: Routledge.

Hufton, O. (1995) *The Prospect before Her*, London: HarperCollins.

Hunt, F. K. (1850) *The Fourth Estate: Contributions towards a History of Newspapers and the Liberty of the Press*, London: David Bogue.

Internet World Stats (2011a) 'Usage and Population Statistics: China', Miniwatts Marketing Group. Online. Available HTTP: http://www.internetworldstats.com/asia/cn.htm (accessed 3 August 2011).

Internet World Stats (2011b) 'Usage and Population Statistics: Mid East', Miniwatts Marketing Group. Online. Available HTTP: http://www.internetworldstats.com/stats5.htm (accessed 4 December 2011).

Ito, M. (1997) 'Virtually Embodied: The Reality of Fantasy in a Multi-User Dungeon', in D. Porter (ed.) *Internet Culture*, New York: Routledge.

ITU (2010) *Measuring the Information Society*, Geneva: International Telecommunication Union. Online. Available HTTP: <http://www.itu.int/ITU-D/ict/publications/idi/2010/Material/MIS_2010_without_annex_4-e.pdf> (last accessed 19 April 2011).

Joshi, S. (2011) 'Reflections on the Arab Revolutions: Order, Democracy and Western Policy', *Rusi Journal*, 156 (2): 60–66.

Kent, S. K. (1999) *Gender and Power in Britain, 1640–1990*, London: Routledge.

Kim, E. and Hamilton, J. (2006) 'Capitulation to Capital? OhmyNews as Alternative Media', *Media, Culture and Society*, 28 (4): 541–60.

Kim, Y. (2010) 'Female Individualization? Transnational Mobility and Media Consumption of Asian Women', *Media, Culture and Society*, 32: 25–43.

Lessig, L. (1999) *Code and Other Laws of Cyberspace*, New York: Basic Books.

——(2001) *The Future of Ideas*, New York: Random House.

Levy, S. (1994) *Hackers*, London: Penguin.

McChesney, R. (1999) *Rich Media, Poor Democracy*, Urbana: University of Illinois Press.

McVeigh, Brian J. (2003) 'Individualization, Individuality, Interiority, and the Internet: Japanese University Students and E-mail', in N. Gottlieb and M. McLelland (eds) *Japanese Cybercultures*, New York: Routledge.

Magaloni, B. (2008) 'Credible Power-sharing and the Longevity of Authoritarian Rule', *Comparative Political Studies*, 41(4/5): 715–41.

Mallapragada, M. (2000) 'The Indian Diaspora in the USA and around the World', in D. Gauntlett (ed.) *Web Studies*, London: Arnold.

Miladi, N. (2011) 'Tunisia – a Media Led Revolution', *Aljazeera.net*. Online. Available HTTP: <http://english.aljazeera.net/indepth/opinion/2011/01/201111161423174986 66.html> (accessed 24 June 2011).

Miller, D. and Slater, D. (2000) *The Internet*, Oxford: Berg.

Miller, V. (2000) 'Search Engines, Portals and Global Capitalism', in D. Gauntlett (ed.) *Web Studies*, London: Arnold.

Morozov, E. (2011) *The Net Delusion*, London: Allen Lane.

Mosco, V. (2005) *The Digital Sublime*, Cambridge, MA: MIT Press.

Mullany, A. (2011) 'Egyptian Uprising Plays out on Social Media Sites Despite Government's Internet Restrictions', *New York Daily News*, 29 January. Online. Available HTTP: <http://articles.nydailynews.com/2011-01-29/news/27738202_1_election-protests-anti-government-protests-social-media> (accessed 20 August 2011).

Naughton, J. (2000) *A Brief History of the Future*, London: Phoenix.

——(2011a) 'Forget Google – It's Apple that Is Turning into the Evil Empire', *Observer*, 6 March.

——(2011b) 'Smartphones Could Mean the End of the Web as We Know It', *Observer*, 17 July.

Negroponte, N. (1996; 1995) *Being Digital*, rev. edn, London: Hodder and Stoughton.

Norberg, A. and O'Neil, J. (1996) *Transforming Computer Technology*, Baltimore, MD: Johns Hopkins University Press.

ONS (Office for National Statistics) (2007) 'Consumer Durables', London: Office for National Statistics. Online. Available HTTP: <http://www.statistics.gov.uk/cci/nugget.asp?id=868> (accessed 14 February 2008).

——(2008) *Internet Access 2008*, London: Office for National Statistics. Online. Available HTTP: <http://www.statistics.gov.uk/pdfdir/iahi0808.pdf > (accessed 14 February 2009).

——(2010) *Internet Access*, London: Office for National Statistics. Online. Available HTTP: <http://www.statistics.gov.uk/cci/nugget.asp?id=8> (accessed 21 August 2011).

OpenNet Initiative (2009) 'Country Profiles: Burma'. Online. Available: HTTP: <http://opennet.net/research/profiles/burma> (accessed 19 April 2009).

——(2011) 'Country Profiles'. Online. Available: <http://opennet.net/research> (accessed 10 July 2011).

Oreskovic, A. (2011) 'Google Inc Launched a Special Service ... ', Reuters. Online. Available HTTP: <http://www.reuters.com/article/2011/02/01/us-egypt-protest-google-idUSTRE71005F20110201> (accessed 25 June 2011).

Ottaway, M. and Hamzawy, A. (2011) 'Protest Movements and Political Change in the Arab world', Carnegie Endowment for International Peace, Policy Outlook. Online. Available HTTP: <http://carnegieendowment.org/files/OttawayHamzawy_Outlook_Jan11_ProtestMovements.pdf> (accessed 20 June 2011).

Poster, M. (1995) *The Second Media Age*, Cambridge: Polity.

Rheingold, H. (2000) *The Virtual Community*, rev. edn, Cambridge, MA: MIT Press.

Rodan, G. (2004) *Transparency and Authoritarian Rule in Southeast Asia*, London: Curzon Routledge.

Rosenzweig, R. (1998) 'Wizards, Bureaucrats, Warriors, and Hackers: Writing the History of the Internet', *American History Review*, December: 1530–52.

Rowbotham, S. (1997) *A Century of Women*, London: Viking.

Ryan, J. (2010) *A History of the Internet and the Digital Future*, London: Reaktion Books.

Sakr, N. (ed.) (2004) *Women and Media in the Middle East*, London: I. B. Tauris.

Schiller, D. (2000) *Digital Capitalism*, Cambridge, MA: MIT Press.

——(2007) *How to Think About Information*, Urbana: University of Illinois Press.

Shirazi, F. (2011) 'Information and Communication Technology and Women Empowerment in Iran', *Telematics and Informatics* (article in press). Online. Available HTTP: <http://www.mendeley.com/research/information-communication-technology-women-empowerment-iran/> (accessed 20 June 2011).

Sima, Y. and Pugsley, P. (2010) 'The Rise of a "Me Culture" in Postsocialist China', *The International Communication Gazette*, 72 (3): 287–306.

Skalli, L. (2006) 'Communicating Gender in the Public Sphere: Women and Information Technologies in the MENA Region', *Journal of Middle East Women's Studies*, 2 (2): 35-59.

Sparks, C. (2000) 'From Dead Trees to Live Wires: the Internet's Challenge to the Traditional Newspaper', in J. Curran and M. Gurevitch (eds) *Mass Media and Society*, 3rd edn, London: Arnold.

Spink, A., Partridge, H. and Jansen, B. (2006) 'Sexual and Pornographic Web Searching: Trends Analysis', *First Monday*, 11 (9). Online. Available HTTP: <http://firstmonday.org/htbin/cgiwrap/bin/ojs/index.php/fm/article/view/1391/1309> (accessed 23 October 2011).

Sreberny, A. and Khiabany, G. (2010) *Blogistan*, London: I. B. Tauris.

Streeter, T. (2003) 'Does Capitalism Need Irrational Exuberance? Business Culture and the Internet in the 1990s', in A. Calabrese and C. Sparks (eds) *Toward a Political Economy of Culture*, Boulder, CO: Rowman and Littlefield.

Tavaana (2011) 'Moudawana: A Peaceful Revolution for Moroccan Women'. Online. Available HTTP: <http://www.tavaana.org/nu_upload/Moudawana_En_PDF. pdf> (accessed 21 June 2011).

Taylor, C. (2011) 'Why Not Call It a Facebook Revolution', *CNN*, 24 February. Online. Available HTTP: <hhtp://articles.cnn.com/2011-02-24/tech/facebook.revolution_1_ facebook-wael-ghonim-social-media?_s=PM:TECH> (accessed 2 March 2011).

Turkle, S. (1995) *Life on the Screen*, New York: Simon and Schuster.

Turner, F. (2006) *From Counterculture to Cyberculture*, Chicago: University of Chicago Press, 2006.

Weber, S. (2004) *The Success of Open Source*, Cambridge, MA: Harvard University Press.

Wellman, B., Quan-Haase, A., Boase, J., Chen, W., Hampton, K., de Diaz, I. I. and Miyata, K. (2003) 'The Social Affordances of the Internet for Networked Individualism', *Journal of Computer-Mediated Communication*, 8 (3). Online. Available HTTP: <http:// onlinelibrary.wiley.com/doi/10.1111/j.1083-6101.2003.tb00216.x/full> (accessed 23 October 2011).

Wheeler, D. (2004) 'Blessings and Curses: Women and the Internet Revolution in the Arab World', in N. Sakr (ed.) *Women and Media in the Middle East*, London: I. B. Tauris.

——(2007) 'Empowerment Zones? Women, Internet Cafes, and Life Transformations in Egypt', *Information Technologies and International Development*, 4 (2): 89–104.

Wikipedia (2009) 'Wikipedia: About'. Online. Available HTTP: <http://en.wikipedia. org/wiki.wikpedia:About> (accessed 20 February 2009).

——(2011) 'History of Wikipedia'. Online. Available HTTP: <http://en.wikipedia.org/ wiki/History_of_Wikipedia> (accessed 30 July 2011).

Williams, S. (2002) *Free as in Freedom*, Sebastopol, CA: O'Reilly.

Wright, S. (2008) 'Fixing the Kingdom: Political Evolution and Socio Economic Challenges in Bahrain', *CIRS Occasional Papers*, No. 3, Georgetown University.

Zittrain, J. (2008) *The Future of the Internet and How to Stop It*, London: Allen Lane.

Zook, M. (2007) 'Report on the Location of the Internet Adult Industry', in K. Jacobs, M. Janssen and M. Pasquinelli (eds) *C'lickme: A Netporn Studies Reader*, Amsterdam: Institute of Network Cultures.

Part II

Political economy of the internet

Chapter 3

Web 2.0 and the death of the blockbuster economy

Des Freedman

Introduction: a new mode of production?

Every era has its own *zeitgeist* titles and the current one, based on the transformative power of the web, is no exception. Enter (physically or virtually) any bookstore and you will be dazzled by *The Wisdom of Crowds*; *Crowdsourcing: Why the Power of the Crowd is Driving the Future of Business*; *Wikinomics: How Mass Collaboration Changes Everything*; *We-Think*; *Here Comes Everybody: The Power of Organizing without Organizations*; and *The Art of Community: Building the New Age of Participation*. These titles are premised on the idea that social media, online platforms, digital technologies and collaborative networks have fundamentally changed the ways in which we socialise, amuse ourselves, learn about the world, conduct public affairs and, above all, do business. They are the popular economics literature of the Web 2.0 world in the same way that, a decade earlier, *The Death of Distance*; *The Weightless World*; *Living on Thin Air*; and *Being Digital* epitomised the heady optimism of the 'new economy' that was said to be emerging in the 1990s (before the millennial dotcom crash).

This chapter examines this literature and explores the claims that the internet facilitates a media economy based on niches and not mass markets, on flexibility and not on standardisation, on abundance and not scarcity, and on entrepreneurial start-ups and not on the industrial corporations that dominated the twentieth century. Online logic is conceived by theorists such as Chris Anderson (2009a, 2009b), Larry Downes (2009), Jeff Jarvis (2009), Charles Leadbeater (2009), Clay Shirky (2008) and Don Tapscott and Anthony Williams (2008) as adhering to a totally different set of operating principles in which the internet (based on bits and not atoms) will put an end to the rule of monopolies and inspire more decentralised and customised networks of media flows. We will no longer have media concentration but media dispersion, where access to niche markets and endless back catalogues will satiate the public's desire for individuality and unlimited choice. Back in 1996 the MIT technologist Nicholas Negroponte predicted that '[w]holly new content will emerge from being digital, as will new players, new economic models, and a likely cottage industry of information and entertainment providers' (1996: 18). A decade later, Chris

Anderson, editor of *Wired* magazine, the chronicler of the web revolution, now saw fit to highlight 'the economics of abundance – what happens when the bottlenecks that stand between supply and demand in our culture start to disappear' (2009a: 11).

These trends are, however, by no means confined to the media or entertainment sectors but are now seen to be forces impacting on the wider economy: lowering transaction costs, stimulating innovation, collapsing barriers between producers and consumers and indeed handing a much more productive and integral role to what were previously seen as rather passive customers. For Jeff Jarvis (2009), Google provides by far the best role model for *any* company operating in the new, digitally enhanced business era: it has changed 'the fundamental architecture of societies and industries the way steel girders and rails changed how cities and nations were built and how they operated' (2009: 27). For Tapscott and Williams (2008), the online encyclopaedia Wikipedia best encapsulates the possibilities and relationships offered by 'new models of production based on community, collaboration, and self-organisation rather than on hierarchy and control' (2008: 1). Whatever their respective conceptual starting-points and political objectives, many Web 2.0 commentators coalesce around the notion that web culture is ushering in a far more efficient, creative, smoother, democratic and participatory form of capitalism: 'A new mode of production is in the making' (Tapscott and Williams 2008: ix).

This chapter assesses the underlying dynamics of a new digital mode of production and interrogates the technological and economic principles on which it is based. Inspired by more critical accounts of the internet's recent history (for example Fuchs 2009; Sylvain 2008; Zittrain 2008), it examines the economics of abundance in the light of current trends in online distribution and consumption and considers whether the theorising of a 'niche economy' can account for residual patterns of conglomeration and concentration in the online world. In acknowledging the contradictory trends towards diversification and massification and towards specialisation and generalisation in the emerging online media economy, the chapter attempts to integrate the hugely significant developments of the online era into an older account of capitalism as a system in which innovation, creativity and, indeed, everyday economic performance are structurally subordinated to the needs of the most powerful interests operating in the marketplace. The pipes may be increasingly digital, but the piper is still being paid and looking to make a profit.

The death of the blockbuster economy and other themes

Contemporary proponents of Wikinomics and Crowdsourcing are the most recent embodiments of an evolving information society discourse that originally sought to theorise the salience of information and knowledge in post-industrial societies (Bell 1973; Machlup 1962; Porat 1977; Toffler 1980; Touraine 1971). These titles focused on the changing economic and occupational structures of late twentieth-century capitalism and identified symbolic goods and the service sector as the motors of the economy. Information, not oil or electricity, had become the central ingredient of a post-industrial age; knowledge workers, not coal miners, were its most productive citizens and innovation, not production, its 'axial' principle. In the 1990s, a second generation of writers then attempted to popularise and update these ideas for a world increasingly subject to the twin forces of globalisation and information technology. Notably, a huddle of business correspondents such as Cairncross (1997), Coyle (1997) and Leadbeater (1999) focused on processes of de-territorialisation and de-materialisation that were said to be transforming the foundational principles of Western economies. According to its most passionate political advocate, then British prime minister Tony Blair, this 'new economy' is 'radically different. Service, knowledge, skills and small enterprises are its cornerstones. Most of its output cannot be weighed, touched or measured. Its most valuable assets are knowledge and creativity' (Blair 1998: 8).

Despite many critiques of the 'new economy' (see, for example, Madrick 2001 and Smith 2000) and the uncertainties in relation to the internet following the dotcom crash in 2000 (assessed by Cassidy 2002), many of these ideas remain entrenched in current economic thinking and, indeed, have been intensified by the huge consumer take-up of online services since the crash. The success of Web 2.0 in terms of both revenues and users has led a number of influential commentators to formulate a series of rules, tendencies and predictions in relation to the potential of the web to democratise production, equalise distribution and liberate labour. These commentators may have different political and strategic positions vis-à-vis the direction and regulation of the internet but there is a consensus concerning those economic features that have allegedly made it such a revolutionary tool for collaboration and disruption. These features are first summarised and then, in the second part of the chapter, critiqued and contextualised.

The economy of abundance

Thanks to the increasing capacity and falling price of microprocessors and semiconductors, vast amounts of computing power are now available to consumers for a fraction of the price they once were. Furthermore, digital technology has solved the problem of limited bandwidth that plagued the analogue universe: media systems based around a handful of broadcast channels and print titles have been superseded by communications environments that feature essentially unlimited storage space. Billions of web pages, digital compression technology and low entry costs to production and distribution (for example a mobile phone and a broadband connection) have massively expanded choice (in quantitative terms) and put an end to the notion that media products are a scarce resource. 'The Internet', as Jarvis so elegantly puts it, 'kills scarcity and creates opportunities in abundance' (2009: 59); 'scarcity', according to Larry Downes (2009: 122), 'has been replaced by abundance'.

The editor of *Wired* magazine, Chris Anderson, named by *Time* magazine in 2007 as the twelfth most influential thinker in the world, has written two books (Anderson 2009a, 2009b) that reflect on the implications of this economy of abundance and map out the shape of media markets in the digital world. Instead of focusing on the few, lucrative hits that are churned out by giant media corporations, he argues that we should turn our attention from the 'head' to the 'long tail' of media markets, where millions upon millions of low-volume transactions are now set to be more lucrative than the increasingly unpredictable number of blockbusters. The power of the Top Ten has been usurped by the economics of the Next Thousand: 'If the twentieth century entertainment industry was about *hits*, the twenty-first will be equally about *niches*', insists Anderson (2009a: 16). Abundant storage space means that online shops can offer an inventory that vastly exceeds their offline competitors and more adequately satisfies the full range of consumer taste. According to Anderson (2009a: 23), for example, 45 per cent of the sales of Rhapsody, a digital music seller, are for tracks not carried by Wal-Mart, 30 per cent of Amazon's titles won't be found in any Barnes and Noble store, while 25 per cent of Netflix's titles are not available in any Blockbuster shop. The long tail, however, is both efficient *and* democratic: 'Bringing niches within reach reveals latent demand for non-commercial content' (2009a: 26), and thus exposes consumers to a far more diverse range of content than the traditional media economy ever did. This changes the balance of power inside decision-making processes in the cultural industries away from hierarchical elites and down to 'us', the new gatekeepers of popular (and niche) taste. 'The ants', he states (2009a: 99), 'have megaphones'.

Technologies of abundance have had an impact on media industries in another decisive way: digitisation and the web's unlimited storage capacity have helped to lower transaction and distribution costs to such an extent (see Downes 2009: 38–40) that it is now possible to make money by giving things away for free. Google is enormously profitable but provides its search engine to users at no cost; Craigslist allows users to search its classified ads without paying a penny; there is an increasing number of games, songs, news, entertainment and software online, much of which is available for free. This is less about a culture of piracy than, as Chris Anderson puts it (2009b: 12), 'an entirely new economic model': of 'Free'.

> The Web has become the land of the free, not because of ideology but because of economics. Price has fallen to the marginal cost, and the marginal cost of everything online is close enough to zero that it pays to round down.
>
> (Anderson 2009b: 92)

This is precisely the phenomenon that is proving to be so traumatic for existing record companies, newspapers and magazines, which are seeing sales and revenues decline in the face of vicious price competition from their online rivals.

Both Jarvis ('Free is impossible to compete against' [2009: 76]) and Anderson ('Free' refers to 'the hole where the price should be, the void at the till' [2009b: 34]) endow this 'radical' new form of pricing with a mysterious and irrepressible power. They do not claim that 'Free' ignores or transcends the rules of free-market economics – after all, it is based on lucrative advertising subsidies – but, rather, that the market will, in the end, simply bow to its allure. 'In the digital realm', Anderson argues (2009b: 241), 'you can try to keep Free at bay with laws and locks, but eventually the force of economic gravity will win'. Indeed, 'Free' redistributes value often in a more 'democratic' way than traditional market transactions – benefiting small companies who advertise on Google or the hundreds of thousands of advertisers on Craigslist, where the 'value in the classifieds was simply transferred from the few to the many' (2009b: 129). The abundant media economy has, therefore, not only carved up the market into a series of interlocking niches but reconfigured the power relationships within this economy by challenging the ability of the 'old media' to charge exorbitant prices for its products. As Anderson puts it (2009b: 127): 'You can't charge scarcity prices in an abundant market.'

Boulders versus pebbles

If it is true, as Anderson suggests, that a market of niches is replacing the old 'blockbuster economy', then what is likely to happen to the organisations that have traditionally relied on the distribution of hits to mass audiences? 'Big media', the twentieth-century icons of industrial production, had a significant role to play when attention was abundant but outlets were scarce. They spent millions on production and marketing, developed efficient business models for reaching large numbers of consumers and dominated the markets in which they participated. In a situation of digital abundance, however, the blockbuster strategy is doomed. According to the influential *Harvard Business Review* blogger Umair Haque (2005: 106), the Web 2.0 environment is structured along the lines of 'coordination', not command, economies and of 'distributed', not centralised, economies of scale. The 'product strategies' required to profit from niche markets are, therefore, 'openness, intelligence, decentralization and connectedness' (2005: 106), precisely the qualities lacking in the 'old media', with their proprietorial instincts and hierarchical structures. We are set to witness the decline in effectiveness of 'competition-killing strategies' and the emergence of 'a truly competitive market' (Anderson 2009b: 175).

This means that those companies most likely to thrive in a digital cornucopia are those that have understood the implications of abundance and the fact that '[o]wning pipelines, people, products, or even intellectual property is no longer the key to success. Openness is' (Jarvis 2009: 4). For Jarvis, this effectively means Google, which he describes as 'the first post-media company' (2009: 4). By realising that networked power is accrued by those who focus their activities on *linking* rather than *owning*, Google demonstrates by far the best example of a company that understands internet logic. 'If Google thought like an old-media company ... it would have controlled content, built a wall around it, and tried to keep us inside' (2009: 28). Instead, Google benefits from dominating search traffic on *open* networks, in contrast to the proprietorial behaviour of companies like Sony and Apple, who have imposed a 'closed architecture' (Tapscott and Williams 2008: 134) on their respective PSPs and iPods. This mirrors the pre-digital attitudes of the major record labels, who, in response to the growth of a fan-led remix culture, have sought to assert their ownership rights and have clamped down on the resulting 'mashups'. Google logic would suggest that the labels should instead link these fans together, putting the labels' content at the centre of this relationship, rather than threatening to sue them. 'Customer value, not control', according to Tapscott and Williams (2008: 143), 'is the answer in the digital economy'.

Google's success, together with the decline of the blockbuster economy, demonstrates to many of the latest generation of 'new economy' theorists that the institutional architecture of the media has shifted radically. The old, vertically integrated conglomerates have wilted under the pressure of Web 2.0 and are being challenged by start-ups who are lighter on their feet, less wedded to centralised control and more open to collaborative possibilities. Charles Leadbeater describes this as a 'new organizational landscape' (2009: xxi) in which the mass media 'boulders' that dominated the pre-digital age 'have been drowned by a rising tide of pebbles' (2009: xix) dropped by individual users. The most successful new media companies are those that are able to organise the 'pebbles', whether that is Wikipedia in terms of information, Flickr for photographs, Amazon for books, YouTube for video, Twitter for snippets of conversation or Facebook for social interaction. Google, of course, catalogues the whole beach. Whether you are a 'boulder' or a 'pebble' is not merely a matter of size (Google, after all, is a rather large collection of pebbles) but of composition. 'Boulders' are highly dense and concentrated on the inside, while 'pebbles' are light and more transparent. 'There is relatively little inside a pebble compared [to] a boulder. That is why pebbles tend be more outward looking' (2009: xxii) and far more suited to the dynamics of a networked economy. The cottage industry of media organisations that Negroponte predicted in 1996 (see page 69) has, it seems, finally arrived.

The culture of sharing

The 'outward looking' perspective of digital actors relates to another central feature of the new media economy: that the competitive instinct of the large corporation is being challenged by the collaborative urge of the individual user. The internet, through its vast number of nodes 'connecting people with information, action, and each other' (Jarvis 2009: 28), lends itself to horizontal, peer-to-peer exchanges in a way that previous mass broadcast systems did not. It is stubbornly, or perhaps fundamentally, *social* in its wiring and thus invites its users to aggregate their skills and knowledge in the interests of all. For Leadbeater (2009: 7), the web's 'underlying culture of sharing, decentralization and democracy' has led to a situation he describes as 'We-Think', a revolution in 'how we think, play, work and create, together, *en masse*' (2008: 19). This is not an Orwellian form of 'Groupthink' but an opportunity to use technology to harvest the ideas and creativity of millions of ordinary people. In the pre-digital age, innovation largely took place within the walls of the company and inside the laboratory; the web allows for collective forms of innovation that originate in garages, bedrooms, studies and living rooms. According to Tapscott and Williams (2008: 15): 'Mass collaboration across borders, disciplines and cultures is at once economical and enjoyable. We can peer produce an operating system [like Linux], an encyclopedia [like Wikipedia], the media, a mutual fund ... We are becoming an economy unto ourselves.'

This new, 'grass roots' economy has a curious dynamic. It is an economy of niches produced by a mass of collaborators; it is highly specialised, but organised on collective principles that profit from the 'wisdom of crowds' (Surowiecki 2004). From this perspective, the internet is facilitating a form of mass participation in which immobile 'boulders', with their hierarchical structures and bureaucratic procedures, are being outmanoeuvred by 'flatter' and more adaptable institutional structures. 'To be organised', argues Leadbeater (2009: 24), 'we no longer always need an organization, certainly not one with a formal hierarchy'. For Tapscott and Williams (2008: 15), 'firms that cultivate nimble, trust-based relationships with external collaborators are positioned to form vibrant business ecosystems that create value more effectively than hierarchically organized businesses'. For example, *Diggnation*, the web TV programme based on the collaborative news aggregator Digg, attracts an audience of some 250,000 people a week and gathers up to $4 million in advertising per year – 'Not bad for two guys on a couch', argues Jarvis (2009: 134). When society is run according to principles of mutuality and grass-roots entrepreneurialism, and when the source of value is the many and not the few (or 'everybody', as opposed to an elite [Shirky 2008]), there are some notable implications both for the structural transformation of the media industries and the democratic possibilities that are said to follow.

First, the flattening of hierarchies and spread of point-to-point communication that has occurred because of the polycentric nature of the internet has shrunk the space in which gatekeepers traditionally used to operate. When the web allows buyers to communicate directly with sellers, fans with bands and readers with writers, there is little need for an intermediary – an estate agent, a record company, a second-hand car dealer or even a newspaper that brings you out-of-date classified advertising. Instead, we have Craigslist for classifieds, MySpace for music, Rightmove for house sales and Auto Trader for vehicles. This process of disintermediation, or the fact that '[m]iddlemen are doomed', as Jarvis puts it (2009: 73), has long been noted by scholars (see Sparks 2000 in relation to newspapers). However, as crowds mobilised by the internet increasingly provide each other with the information and resources necessary to make informed decisions about everyday life, and as the internet facilitates far more direct transactional relationships than previously, gatekeepers are revealed as the 'proprietors of inefficient marketplaces' (Jarvis 2009: 76). How can the traditional ad agency possibly compete with the startling efficiencies of Google's algorithm-based approach to customised advertising?

Second, digital technologies are alleged to have contributed to a huge democratisation of the media production process, placing creative tools in the hands of a far greater number of users. Given the falling price of camcorders, editing software, broadband subscriptions and mobile phone rates, content creation is also increasingly in the hands of the 'crowd'. Pew research shows that 38 per cent of US teenagers, for example, regularly share content online, while 21 per cent remix original content and a further 14 per cent contribute to blogs (Purcell 2010: 4). According to Leadbeater (2009: 211), 'while old-style industrial media consigned us to mainly watching and reading, the web vastly extends the range of people who can join public debate and expands the range of the ideas they can propose'. The television commercials for Doritos crisps made by 'amateurs' exemplify the democratising possibilities of 'crowdsourced' production. Instead of hiring expensive ad agencies, user-generated content (costing anywhere from £6.50 for a commercial shown on British television to $2,000 for one shown during the Superbowl) is seen to be a hallmark of a more collaborative approach to creativity, one that is 'bringing back to life an older, folk culture, which is extinguished by the mass-produced, industrial culture of the record and film industry of the 20th century' (Leadbeater 2009: 56).

This idea of the blurring of distinctions between producers and consumers is finally realising the predictions of Toffler (1980) about the rise of the 'prosumer' and of Fiske (1987) about the emergence of a 'semiotic democracy' engineered by a media-literate 'active audience'. For Tapscott and Williams, however, the rise of 'prosumption' amounts to an *economic* revolution: 'You can participate in the economy as an equal, cocreating value with your peers and favorite companies to meet your very personal needs, to engage in fulfilling communities, to change the world, or just to have fun!' (Tapscott and Williams, 2008: 150). Indeed, so revolutionary is the possibility of 'prosumption' that Anderson actually compares the creation of user-generated content today with Marx's vision of unalienated labour in the *German Ideology*, where he imagines a communist society in which ordinary people, freed from the constraints of wage labour, would be able to 'hunt in the morning, fish in the afternoon, rear cattle in the evening, criticize after dinner' (quoted in Anderson 2009a: 62).

This idea of creative and enjoyable production relates to another significant shift in the social relations of the contemporary world, concerning the character of labour in a digital economy. For many of the current 'new economy' theorists, the collaborative principles that are hard-wired into the internet are being carried across into the most far-sighted workplaces. Where labour used to be alienating and where workers were often excluded from decision making, the 'Wiki Workplace (Unleashing the Power of Us)' (Tapscott and Williams 2008: 239–67), one based on using digital technologies to share knowledge, exchange ideas and co-create, now offers opportunities for employee participation, fulfilling work and, of course, a more efficient use of labour. Tapscott and Williams's book is filled with examples of companies that have blossomed by listening to their customers and employees, by involving them in decision making and by giving them a degree of autonomy that is more likely to stimulate innovative thinking. The result is, they argue (2008: 240), that we are 'shifting from closed and hierarchical workplaces with rigid employment relationships to increasingly self-organized, distributed, and collaborative human capital networks that draw knowledge and resources from inside and outside the firm'.

The best example of this, according to the literature, is Google, the most dynamic and forward-thinking example of a 'wiki workplace'. Employees are fed for free (the chef having a particularly important role to play in many accounts of the company [for example Vise 2008: 192–203]), transported on free, Wi-Fi-enabled buses to the Googleplex and, perhaps most famously, given one day off a week to work on their own projects. This '20 per cent rule' provided the time and space from which both Google News and Google Product Search emanated (Vise 2008: 130–40). Google's 'Don't Be Evil' slogan, presumably, applies as much to its own workplace as to Google products not because of any intrinsic benevolence on the part of its founders but because 'the costs of evil are starting to outweigh the benefits ... When people can openly talk with, about, and around you, screwing them is no longer a valid business strategy' (Jarvis 2009: 102). Work, freed from the opacity and isolation of the pre-digital era, can finally be enjoyed as an activity that rewards both the worker and the company.

Disrupting capitalism

In the literature described thus far, the mode of social organisation through which the benefits of the web can best be realised is the free market. There are some rare exceptions. Leadbeater criticises the market fundamentalism of libertarian cheerleaders like Chris Anderson and describes himself, along with Clay Shirky and Yochai Benkler, as 'communitarian optimists' (2009: xxviii) who are inspired by the non-commercial possibilities of social production and peer networks. Leadbeater condemns the way in which private property has been assumed to be the foundation of all productive activity and argues that the 'spread of the web invites us to look at the future from a different vantage point' (2009: 6) in which proprietorial and non-proprietorial forces coexist. Leadbeater envisages public and private goods as complementary and calls for a mixed economy where market transactions are tamed by the collaborative spirit and structure of the web. He is explicitly *not* calling to replace market relations with the 'idealistic commune capitalism of open-source and We-Think' (2009: 121), but for the principles of the 'commons' to inform and ameliorate private capitalism.

In general, however, there is a common assumption that Web 2.0 provides the most fantastic opportunities for the renewal and intensification of *private* enterprise. The literature is filled with talk of the efficiencies, cost-benefits and strategic possibilities offered by digital technologies. The internet challenges firms to adapt to this new environment or lose out to their competitors: it is the classic case of a 'disruptive' technology that shakes up the status quo and paves the way for a glorious future. This is the approach adopted by legal scholar Larry Downes, who argues that the internet, like railroads in the nineteenth century, is a 'disruptive' technology, a force of Schumpterian 'creative destruction' that 'ultimately demand[s] dramatic transformation' (2009: 3). Instead of looking for a 'killer app' on the internet, Downes (2009: 10) argues that the internet *is* the 'killer app': 'a technological innovation whose introduction disrupts long-standing rules of markets or even whole societies'. Despite the recent battering suffered by financial markets, Downes insists that 'markets generally work better than traditional forms of government in establishing rules for disruptive technologies' (2009: 4). Left to itself, the innate capacity of disruptive technologies, in this case the tenacity of the internet in exposing the inefficiencies of analogue forms of business and driving down production and transaction costs, will force companies increasingly to integrate 'Google logic' into their business plans.

Indeed, this is viewed as one of the beauties of a social system in which, from time to time, individuals who are first to identify the benefits of a new technology and who are not afraid to upset the corporate apple-cart, burst onto the scene and make us look at the world in a different way. These are what Downes (2009: 220) refers to as 'rebels' and what Jarvis calls 'disruptive capitalists' (2009: 4): people like Sergey Brin and Larry Page of Google, Craig Newmark of Craigslist and Jeff Bezos, founder of Amazon, who embody the original frontier spirit of nineteenth-century capitalism. These fearless pioneers take 'decisions that make no sense under old rules of old industries that are now blown apart thanks to these new ways and new thinkers' (Jarvis 2009: 4). They are the outsiders, attacked by entrenched business interests and treated with suspicion by governments. Of course, this is precisely the image welcomed by the pioneers themselves. For example, when challenged by European and US regulators as well as its more established competitors, Google has repeatedly fallen back on this narrative. 'Every government sort of has some group that's busy trying to figure out what we're up to', argues Google's Executive Chairman, Eric Schmidt. 'We're quite disruptive, and in the course of that disruption we tend to create enemies' (quoted in Oreskovic 2010). This nurtures a rather romantic image of capitalism in which the rebels take all the risks and in which technology instils social change that, despite the resulting turbulence, uncertainty and opposition, lays the foundation for a more productive future. This latest incarnation, based on the collaborative spirit of Web 2.0, is ushering in a new era that, if we are to believe Tapscott and Williams (2008: 15), is 'on par with the Italian Renaissance or the rise of Athenian democracy ... A new economic democracy is emerging in which we all have a lead role'. This is the promise of the digital media economy.

Capitalism bites back

While the new business literature contains an enormous amount of empirical data, a passionate commitment to the participatory possibilities of the web and a justifiable suspicion of traditional management economics, much of it is nevertheless based on a series of unsubstantiated claims, profound misunderstandings and puzzling absences that render it incapable of providing a rigorous account of the dynamics of the Web 2.0 environment. In general, it is so steeped in a business-minded mode of address that it is hard to read the titles as anything other than paeans to market entrepreneurialism aimed at a particular stratum of Western CEOs, investors and politicians.

There is an entirely different approach to evaluating claims of a new digital economy: one that is based on a Marxist critique that combines recognition of the revolutionary achievements of capitalism with an analysis of why capitalism is systematically unable to make available the full potential of these achievements to its subjects. Indeed Marx and Engels's tribute to capitalism in the *Communist Manifesto* is almost as glowing as Jarvis's or Anderson's are to Google some 160 years later (although obviously with a sting at the end). They famously write that the capitalist class has played a 'most revolutionary part' in human history: 'It has been the first to show what man's activity can bring about. It has accomplished wonders far surpassing Egyptian pyramids, Roman aqueducts, and Gothic cathedrals' (Marx and Engels 1975 [1848]: 36). It has done this, not because of the 'genius' of individual scientists and technologists or the bravery of pioneering entrepreneurs, but because it is a system based on a structural need to innovate and move forward.

> The bourgeoisie cannot exist without constantly revolutionising the instruments of production, and thereby the relations of production, and with them the whole relations of society. Conservation of the old modes of production in unaltered form, was, on the contrary, the first condition of existence for all earlier industrial classes. Constant revolutionising of production, uninterrupted disturbance of all social conditions, everlasting uncertainty and agitation distinguish the bourgeois epoch from all earlier ones.
>
> (Marx and Engels 1975: 36)

Yet, just as Marx was captivated by capitalism's innovations, he was horrified by the means by which it seeks to reproduce itself. First, he notes that, as opposed to earlier societies where any surplus was consumed by the ruling elite, capitalists need to re-invest this surplus in order to compete more effectively in a market. Capital, understood by Marx as any accumulation of value that acts to increase its own value, 'exists and can only exist as many capitals' (Marx 1973: 414). Competition, as embodied in the modern free market, is the DNA of this new social system, and innovation is therefore required in order to step up productivity, reduce labour costs, identify new markets and increase the rate of profit. Capitalists then become wedded to the further competitive accumulation of capital in order to be able most effectively to achieve these aims: 'Accumulate, accumulate! That is Moses and the prophets' (Marx 1918: 606). This means that capitalists will do everything they can to extract more value from the production process; that labour, once an essential part of human subjectivity, becomes something over which the labourer has less and less control; that objects which were previously enjoyed for their immediate qualities instead become valued mainly for their ability to be exchanged in a market transaction; and finally, that, due to the lack of coordination in the economy, there will be a tendency towards crises of overproduction that will wipe out weaker capitals. These processes of exploitation, alienation, commodification and concentration are, according to Marx, the terrible price to be paid by the majority of people for the wonderful technological advances experienced under capitalism: for the development of railroads, electricity, vaccination programmes, broadcasting and, of course, the internet.

The central issue for this chapter is the extent to which informational goods and processes in particular are subject to these same tendencies or whether, as much of the literature discussed earlier suggests, the internet's privileging of collaboration and transparency insulates it from these dangers and somehow removes the *digital* economy from the endemic flaws of a crisis-ridden capitalism. One response to this question is to stress, as Larry Downes does (2009: 3), 'the unique properties of information' that render it distinct from other commodity forms. This is an argument used not simply by market economists but by, for example, the Marxist academic Christian Fuchs, who acknowledges that the particularities of information – its intangibility, its ease of duplication, its rate of diffusion and its striving for connections (2009: 76) – lead to a significant contradiction. 'Information networks both extend and undermine capital accumulation. Information networks aggravate the capitalist contradiction between the collective production and the individual appropriation of goods' (2009: 77). The social character of information is bound to collide with the privatised organisation of the market.

Nicholas Garnham's valuable study of *Capitalism and Communication* (Garnham 1990) provides one way of navigating this contradiction. Reflecting on the specific characteristics of cultural commodities – that they are non-rivalrous, that costs of production vastly outweigh costs of distribution and that they seek novelty – Garnham argues that 'it has been difficult to establish the scarcity on which price is based' (1990: 160). However, he shrugs off the idea that cultural products are immune from rules of the marketplace and identifies the particular strategies that have been applied to media commodities precisely in order to bring them within the scope of market disciplines. Given that distribution costs are marginal in comparison with production costs, there is first a drive towards securing the largest audiences in order to maximise profits (1990: 160). Second, there is a structural need artificially to re-introduce scarcity in order to regain control over pricing through such means as setting up monopolistic channels of distribution, providing free content as a loss-leader for expensive hardware and turning audiences into commodities to be sold to advertisers (1990: 161). Finally, in order to deal with the uncertainties of popular taste, there is a tendency to produce not isolated goods but a 'cultural repertoire across which the risks can be spread' (1990: 161).

Some of these approaches appear to be utterly incompatible with the new digital media economy described earlier. Anderson's 'long tail' thesis directly negates the urge to maximise ratings, focus on hits and produce a repertoire, while attempts to introduce scarcity and monopolise distribution channels would seem to be futile in an economy of abundance. The rest of this chapter, therefore, reflects on the extent to which strategies like these are relevant to informational networks in the Web 2.0 world and considers Olivier Sylvain's argument that 'the constitutive practices of the "networked information economy" are not actually immune to the undemocratic problems of concentration, centralization, and surveillance. To the contrary, those problems too are constitutive of the new media' (Sylvain 2008: 8).

Commodification in the new digital economy

One of the great attractions of the internet is that it consists, to a great extent, of enthusiastic participants who contribute their time and energy – their labour – for no reward other than individual fulfilment and mutual gain. Contributors to, for example, Wikipedia, Linux, Digg, review sites and blogs all play a crucial role in what appears to be a thriving gift economy. Vast areas of the web have no paywalls, no box office, no subscriptions and no rental fees, none of the price mechanisms that usually apply to the circulation of commodities. There is no immediate point of purchase when a user visits Google, Facebook, MySpace and YouTube. Indeed, Anderson describes the free supply of books, music, software, news, computer games and even the use of bicycles in the digital world as evidence of 'a nonmonetary production economy' (2009b: 189).

There are two immediate problems with Anderson's argument that 'Free' is, as the title of his book (Anderson 2009b) puts it, a 'radical price'. First, it is not always clear what is meant by 'free'. Free content online is, of course, dependent on the purchase or rental of a computer or mobile device, together with access to the web (neither of which is free) and, for example in the case of news, is simply paid for at a different point in the chain: through advertising, print sales and, in the case of the BBC, a licence fee. Content, in other words, always has to be subsidised, whether by the individual user donating their time or the firm wishing to make its services available across different platforms. This is very similar to 'free' admission to London museums, which is subsidised by the taxpayer to the tune of £18.06 per visitor to the Victoria & Albert Museum and £13.87 per visitor to the Natural History Museum (*Guardian* 2010: 17). Indeed, just as 'Free' is a rather ambiguous concept, Anderson's claim that marginal costs in a digital economy are effectively zero (see p. 5) underestimates the costs of marketing and production that are necessary to offer some goods and services for 'free'.

Second, even where content is provided for 'free' at the direct point of contact, there is nevertheless a tendency within a market system to find, wherever possible, a non-zero price. This is what lies behind the very risky decision by the owners of, for example, the *New York Times* and the London *Times* to start charging for content. 'Paywalls' may or not work for more generalist audiences (in contrast to specialist business users, who have already demonstrated a willingness to pay for premium content), but the fact that leading media moguls like Rupert Murdoch feel they have no choice but to introduce them is indicative of their need to generate revenue, despite the resulting uncertainty. For rights holders (though of course not for aggregators who do not have to worry about paying for content), the current structure of 'Free' is a particularly difficult concept on which to build a sustainable business. 'I like the competition that markets bring', argues Patience Wheatcroft, the editor-in-chief of the *Wall Street Journal Europe*. 'It's difficult to have a market if you're giving things away. Paid for is something we should aim to keep' (quoted in Armstrong 2009: 5). 'Free', while having obvious benefits for consumers in the short term, is not likely, *in the context of a capitalist market*, to generate the revenues needed to pay journalists, writers, directors and casts that are required to produce original and high-quality content.

Yet, whether something is 'free' or not has little to do with any meaningful understanding of commodification. It is not the fixing of a price (even if that price is zero) that turns a good into a commodity, but its general incorporation into a system of market exchange. As Marx puts it, 'objects of utility' become commodities 'only by means of the relations which the act of *exchange* establishes directly between the products, and directly, through them, between the producers' (Marx 1918: 44, emphasis added).

So while we pay nothing to search on Google, to publicise ourselves on LinkedIn or to watch a video on YouTube, others are nevertheless paying for the ability to reach *us*. What is being sold here is our profile, our consumption habits and our search history in precisely the way that Garnham argued that the main commodity in the cultural industries is the audience as it is sold, over and over again, to advertisers. Far from relationships being 'the one thing you can't commoditize' as Tapscott and Williams claim (2008: 44), Facebook achieves just this objective as 'friendship' becomes the currency that drives the network. Similarly, LinkedIn also functions by transforming professional profiles into objects of exchange to attract advertisers. Relationships do not just 'matter' on LinkedIn but are quantified and monetised as a market of biographies.

Indeed, to the extent that much of the labour online is carried out by highly active 'prosumers' (Tapscott and Williams 2008: 124–50), this makes for an incredibly efficient way of gathering, filtering and analysing data that can be sold on to advertisers. Google and Facebook, with their 'instant personalisation' facilities, are vast storage containers of personal information that users 'freely' provide. Despite concerns over safety and privacy, this data is then mined for its commercial value, leading Vincent Mosco to argue that digital technologies, far from challenging the logic of commodification, 'are now used to refine the process of delivering audiences of viewers, listeners, readers, movie fans, telephone and computer users, to advertisers' (Mosco 2009: 137). User-generated content, therefore, has as dual character: it is suggestive of a more participatory form of creativity and yet simultaneously very cost-effective as a means of generating free content that helps advertisers and marketers more precisely to identify and target desirable audiences.

For writers like Jarvis this is by no means an unwelcome process. When he writes that 'Google has turned commodification into a business strategy' (Jarvis 2009: 67), he is referring to mainstream economists' understanding of a commodity as a generic good, like sugar, steel or oil. By matching advertisers with consumers on the basis of algorithms rather than reputation, everything becomes commodified, even the mass of niches that makes up the contemporary audience. All Google ads look the same, whatever the marketing budget of the respective company, while users are measured by their 'clicks', not their backgrounds: 'There's little that distinguishes one of us from another – not age, income, gender, education, interest, all the things advertisers historically paid for. Everybody's just like everybody else. We're just users. We might as well be pork bellies' (2009: 68). Jarvis's argument is that, while this may be difficult for traditional brands, it is an efficient and potentially equalising development in the marketplace. But for many people who have no wish for their friendships to be privatised via Facebook or for their personal data to be surveilled and sold on by Google, this is a form of commodification in which their very labour, their own creative self-activity, is repackaged and turned into an object to be exchanged, at a price, on the open market.

Surely, however, Wikipedia, Linux, the majority of blogs and those peer-to-peer networks with an explicitly non-commercial character demonstrate that the internet is composed of two distinct spheres: a commodified and a non-commodified part, one section that operates like a capitalist marketplace and one that operates as a 'commons' (Benkler 2006, Leadbeater 2009, Lessig 2002)? Zittrain's concern that the internet's earlier 'generativity', its openness and unpredictability, is becoming tethered and 'appliancized' (2008: 8) and Benkler's worry about the information commons being threatened by increasing online concentration (2006: 240) are further evidence of a bifurcated internet, predicated on the idea that we need to protect and nurture the non-commodified zones in order to fend off the destructive, anti-democratic features of the commercial sector. According to this logic, the open source environment is the antithesis of proprietary production and constitutes a clear challenge to the principles of private accumulation.

In reality, it is becoming increasingly hard to separate the two parts of the internet and, far from one sector being insulated from the other, they are in constant tension. Peer-to-peer and open source may be seen by some as a progressive alternative to market structures and by others, including many rights holders, as a mortal threat to profits and investment, but capitalism, as we have already identified, is a dynamic and expansive system that attempts to deploy any technological innovation that may increase its profitability and efficiency. Indeed the whole premise of 'wikinomics' as developed by Tapscott and Williams (2008) is to use the principles of open source in order to invigorate and renew market institutions. 'Without the commons', they argue (2008: 91), 'there could be no private enterprise'. Their book, along with Anderson (2009b),

Downes (2009) and Jarvis (2009), is filled with examples of how major corporations, including IBM, Sun and Nokia, have sought to integrate the efficiencies of open source into their own corporate practices. Instead of arguing that open source is a competitive threat to capital accumulation, wikinomics suggests that the 'greatest risk is not that peer production communities will undermine an existing business model, but that a firm will prove unable to respond to the threat in time' (Tapscott and Williams 2008: 96). Companies, in other words, are being encouraged to learn how to apply the collaborative principles of open source to their specific business sector in order to increase productivity and achieve higher rates of growth.

In this situation, capitalism's ability to use, to its own advantage, even those technological developments that appear to challenge its commitment to proprietary principles provides a rebuttal to those who see 'We-Think' (Leadbeater 2009) as an intrinsically non-commodified set of practices. Instead, we should see the relationship between non-commercial and commercial spheres of the web as a fundamentally dialectical one where, as Christian Fuchs puts it (2009: 80), the parts 'are not only separated and different, they are entangled and meshed'. Crucially, however, in the context of a market economy, 'this means that the gift form is subsumed under the commodity form and can even be used directly for achieving profit' (2009: 80). This is no accident, but relates to the structural need of capitalism to monetise, and incorporate within a system of market exchange, even those practices – like blogging, commenting and reviewing – that spring from non-commercial urges. Wikipedia, Linux and Mozilla are crucial in demonstrating the collaborative potential of the internet, but they are illustrative less of the emancipatory power of the web than of the profound 'antagonism between information commodities and information gifts' (2009: 81) at the heart of the digital economy. Moreover, this specific form of commodification is not confined to core media or informational industries but, in contrast, 'thoroughly integrates the media industries into the total capitalist economy ... by producing audiences, *en masse*, and in specific demographically desirable forms, for advertisers' (Mosco 2009: 137). Commodification, according to this perspective, is not easily avoided or thrown off like a Weberian 'light cloak', but is a fundamental process through which capitalism is organised and reproduced, online just as much as offline.

Accumulation strategies

We might expect the organising principles of a 'new economy' and a 'digital mode of production' to behave in ways that are different to the competitive strategies adopted by twentieth-century industrial corporations. This was a model that frowned on collaboration and sought to concentrate all its expertise in-house, that operated as a bureaucracy with strict hierarchies and centralised decision making, and that fiercely protected its own intellectual property. 'New economy' proponents argue that one of the reasons for the success of the most prosperous Web 2.0 companies lies in their determination to avoid a 'command and control' mentality and to instil a more collaborative approach within corporate culture. According to Jarvis (2009: 69):

> In Google's economy, companies will no longer grow to critical mass by borrowing massive capital to make massive acquisitions ... Instead, they need to learn from Google and grow by building platforms to help others prosper. Indeed, growth will come less from owning assets inside one company and amassing risk there than from enabling others in a network to build their own value.

Success in the digital age, it appears, is more likely to be guaranteed for those companies who eschew proprietorial controls and Fordist accumulation measures and focus on the innovation necessary to make its services and products available to the greatest number of people.

However, even a cursory glance at Google's own history points to a rather different narrative. First, the company was launched on the basis of a $25 million investment in 1999 by two California-based venture capital groups who insisted that the founders, Sergey Brin and Larry Page, hire an experienced CEO 'to help them transform their search engine into a profitable business' (Vise 2008: 67). Although Brin and Page pioneered the technique that allowed them to catalogue billions of web pages, revenues only took off when they adopted the pay-per-click advertising model of a *rival* search engine, GoTo, into Google's now highly lucrative AdWords system (Battelle 2005: 125). In order to smooth the way for the transformation of Google into a public company in 2004, Google then handed Yahoo!, the new owners of GoTo (now called Overture), some 2.7 million shares worth hundreds of millions of dollars in order to settle its patent dispute with Yahoo! out of court. Furthermore, although the initial public offering (IPO) was vastly oversubscribed and presented as a model of shareholder democracy, the two owners insisted on a dual class structure in which their operational control of the company would be consolidated and protected. According to Google's IPO document, the executive triumvirate of Brin, Page and CEO Eric Schmidt was to control 37.6 per cent of the company, leaving new investors, in the words of Larry Page, with 'little ability to influence its strategic decisions through their voting rights' (Google 2004). Ironically, while acknowledging that this was unusual for technology companies, Page noted that the New York Times Company, the Washington Post Company and Dow Jones, all of them the most traditional of 'old media' firms, had similar structures that asserted the right of a handful of executives to retain overall strategic control (Google 2004) for the good of the company.

Google has long combined a determination to secure first-mover advantage in new and innovative markets with a rather more old-fashioned commitment to undermining its competitors, in particular Apple and Microsoft (see Vise 2008: 282–91), and to acquire firms that improve both its service and its market share.

In its short history it has bought, at the time of writing, over 100 companies –
including Blogger, Picasa, the satellite imaging service Keyhole, Doubleclick
and, most famously, YouTube – at a total cost of nearly $20 *billion*. Not bad for
a company that has *not* had to rely, in Jarvis's words, on making 'massive acquisitions'. It has also been heavily reliant on the traditional legal protections given to
firms by the state and, far from being amenable to sharing its intellectual property (IP), recognises that securing its IP is at the core of the company's ability to
generate revenue. According to Google's 2010 filing to the US Securities and
Exchange Commission:

> We rely on a combination of patent, trademark, copyright, and trade secret
> laws in the U.S. and other jurisdictions as well as confidentiality procedures
> and contractual provisions to protect our proprietary technology and our
> brand. We also enter into confidentiality and invention assignment agreements
> with our employees and consultants ... and we rigorously control access to
> proprietary technology.
>
> (Google 2010: 16)

The fact that Google requires its employees to sign confidentiality agreements
clashes somewhat with Jarvis's assertion that 'Google rewards – and more and
more, we expect – openness' (2009: 236), but, more significantly, it is a stark
reminder that there are firm restrictions on the autonomy of labour in a company
famous for its free lunches, staff perks and generous conditions. Once again, this
can be explained in terms not of Google's exceptionalism but of the opposite:
its status as a large firm operating in an emerging market. For example, consider
Google's celebrated '20 per cent rule', which stipulates that its software programmers should spend at least one day a week on their own projects. This is, as
Tapscott and Williams put it (2008: 260), evidence of the company's belief in
'collaboration and encouraging self-organization'. It has also been highly productive: Google News, the product search engine Froogle and social networking
service Orkut all originated from this seemingly enlightened corporate policy.
Yet should this be seen as 'time off', or as an effective incentive for research and
development, the results of which are wholly appropriated by Google and not by
the employee? Similarly, the provision by the company of high-quality free
lunches was a 'perk with a purpose. It would keep people near one another and
their desks; prevent them from developing poor eating habits that would
diminish productivity; eliminate the time they would otherwise spend going out
to lunch ... and create a sense of togetherness' (Vise 2008: 194). Even the
company's supply of Wi-Fi-enabled buses to take employees to and from its
Mountain View headquarters is an effective way of lengthening the working day
for staff, virtually all of whom would have laptops.

None of these strategies for maximising the exploitation of staff and accumulation
of capital should come as a surprise when reflecting on a public company with a
market valuation of approximately $160 billion and annual revenues of over

$20 billion. Google is simply following in the path of many previous market leaders by making shrewd acquisitions that enhance and make more efficient its offer, by thinking creatively about the ways in which it can extract full value from a highly skilled workforce and by constantly innovating in order to remain one step ahead of its rivals (should it not be able to buy them). Google's offices may be open plan but, as a company, it is hardly open source; indeed the company is not structured horizontally but, as we have seen, with operational power and strategic control concentrated at the top. 'Openness' and 'connectedness' are not the principles on which it is organised so much as the products that it sells. Indeed this is precisely what Google's then CEO, Eric Schmidt, admitted in a 2005 speech to Wall Street financial analysts:

> We are not quite as unconventional as we actually say all the time. The things that we do are unique in the way that products are created, but much of the rest of the business is run in all the normal ways and very much at the state-of-the-art but in a traditional way. We actually do care about objectives. Every quarter we go through, 'How are we doing?'
>
> (Quoted in Vise 2008: 256)

The digital economy depends, therefore, on the exploitation of paid creative labour and, in the context of uncertain business models and a highly unstable economy, we can expect an intensification of this exploitation. Consider, for example, the decision in 2010 by leading consumer magazine publisher Bauer – whose music titles include *Kerrang*, *Q* and *Mojo* – to impose an 'all rights' contract that secures its ownership of freelance content across all platforms but makes the freelancer 'liable for all damages and costs in the event of legal action' (Armstrong 2010). The 'new economy', however, also profits from the increasing amount of unpaid labour, otherwise known as 'user generated content' (UGC), facilitated by the falling costs of digital media technologies. As we have already noted, UGC has a contradictory character: expressive of the generative possibilities of the internet but all too easily used as 'free' content by media and information companies who, in previous years, would have expected to pay for such content. So while newspapers eagerly reproduce Twitter feeds about election debates and TV news bulletins gratefully broadcast 'witness videos' of bomb blasts and train crashes, UGC is actively sought by a range of companies wishing to reduce marketing costs and to associate themselves with the 'semiotic democracy' of consumer-made content. The 'new economy' literature is filled with examples of this 'participant consumerism' (Leadbeater 2009: 105): from the Canadian music label that organised a remix contest in which hundreds of DJs willingly sent in their entries (Tapscott and Williams 2008: 280) and saved the company tens of thousands of dollars, to the interactive web ads made for Chevrolet (Anderson 2009a: 226) and the celebrated case of the home-produced television commercials for Doritos transmitted during the hugely expensive ad breaks in the Superbowl (Leadbeater 2009: 105).

Tapscott and Williams argue that this kind of co-creation, enabled by the decentralised and interactive features of the internet, has resulted in a more engaged and active citizenry and the phenomenon of the 'prosumer' revolution (see p. 76). Yet, far from signalling a democratisation of media production and distribution, 'prosumption' is all too often incorporated within a system of commodity exchange controlled by existing elites who either *call* for user-generated material or *cull* material from already existing sites. In both cases, the imaginative labour of ordinary people is appropriated for the benefits that accrue to those companies, like Facebook, YouTube and MySpace, who hope to sell the personalised content generated by users to advertisers and marketers. As Fuchs argues, the more time that users spend online 'producing, consuming and exchanging content, communicating with others, the higher the value of the prosumer commodity they produce will become, the higher the advertisement prices will rise and the higher the profits of the specific Internet corporations will be' (2009: 82). It is a further example of the commodification and drive to accumulation that lies at the heart of the market economy, whether it is one based on Fordist assembly lines or digital networks.

Concentration in the digital media economy

Back in the heady days before the millennium, when the web was expanding rapidly and when fresh new upstarts were challenging traditional IT and media companies for hegemony over the internet, Oxford economist Andrew Graham (1998) pursued a rather unfashionable argument. He argued that, despite the capacity of the internet to operate on near-zero marginal costs, a digital media economy still required significant resources for the production and marketing of high-quality content. He predicted, therefore, an intensification of economies of both scale (to offset costs) and scope (due to convergence and cross-promotion) and the emergence of new types of scarcity (not of spectrum but of talent) and further concentration (as opposed to a 'world of free competition') because of the economic benefits of being in a network (1998: 33). Over ten years later, to what extent have Graham's predictions of the consequences of 'network effects' been proved right, or are we seeing an environment dominated by a plethora of information-age 'pebbles' rather than a concentration of corporate 'boulders' (see p. 73)?

Headline figures certainly appear to support Graham's analysis and to challenge the notion that bottlenecks are disappearing in crucial areas of the digital economy like search, advertising and entertainment. For example, figures from the internet rankings agency Hitwise (www.hitwise.com) reveal that Google dominates 92 per cent of search volume in New Zealand, 90.5 per cent in the UK, 88 per cent in Australia and 80 per cent in Singapore. Clear patterns of concentration are also visible in online advertising, where, in 2007, the top four companies (Google, MSN, Yahoo! and AOL) attracted 85 per cent of gross revenue in the US. According to the chairman of respected consultancy group

Marketspace, Jeffrey Rayport, we are witnessing the emergence of an online advertising oligopoly: 'Despite the promise of democratization of the Web, with nearly 120 million active sites last month, there is nothing that favors the little guy (or even most of the big guys) when it comes to online ad dollars' (Rayport 2007).

Far from digital networks leading to a dissolution of monopolistic behaviour, we are looking at some highly concentrated market sectors, particularly in the US, where iTunes controls 70 per cent of the music download market, Google 70 per cent of search, YouTube 73 per cent of online video, while Facebook accounts for 52 per cent of social networking traffic. Staggeringly, given the claims made about the internet's facilitating a more competitive environment, in 2009 Amazon controlled 18.2 per cent of the *entire* US e-commerce market, well above Wal-Mart's approximately 11 per cent share of the US retail market as a whole (*Internet Retailer* 2010). Combined, Google, Facebook and Yahoo! sites account for 31.5 per cent of *all* internet traffic in Hong Kong, nearly 28 per cent in the US, 23 per cent in Australia, 22.5 per cent in Singapore, 21.4 per cent in the UK and 20 per cent in New Zealand (www.hitwise.com). While these figures are likely to fluctuate over the next few years, they are nevertheless comparable to those same 'old media' markets that were held to be examples of the lack of competition that the web would supersede. It is, perhaps, not surprising that Google continues to be closely monitored for antitrust activity by the US Department of Justice and the Federal Trade Commission in relation to its latest acquisitions and innovations (for example Helft 2010).

Online news markets also demonstrate similar levels of concentration as well as a close relationship to their offline counterparts. According to the Project for Excellence in Journalism (PEJ 2010), the top 7 per cent of US online news sites attract 80 per cent of overall traffic, while the top ten single outlets are either traditional news providers or major online portals that account for over 25 per cent of total market share. Far from the internet guaranteeing the amplification of new voices, its analysis finds that 'the websites of legacy news organizations – especially cable stations and newspapers – dominate the online space in traffic in loyalty' (PEJ 2010). While there is an extremely long tail consisting of thousands of individual points of access to the news environment, the PEJ argues that traffic is concentrated amongst the top few sites and that 'a majority of online news consumers graze on the internet, but not very far, regularly visiting between two to five sites' (PEJ 2010), with the highest proportion of time spent on the most popular destinations.

The point is that although the internet is facilitating an enormous increase in content as well as the means of distributing this content, it is doing so on the basis of economic and consumer trends that are not that dissimilar to those of the past. Indeed, there remains not simply a pattern of oligopolistic markets but an incentive for companies to produce 'blockbusters' and an apparent willingness on the part of audiences to consume them. In an empirical investigation of Anderson's 'long tail' thesis (see pp. 72–73), Harvard Business School professor Anita Elberse found that the top 10 per cent of songs on the digital download service Rhapsody accounted for 78 per cent of all plays and that the top 1 per cent account for nearly one-third of all plays: a result that demonstrates 'a high level of concentration' (2008: 2). The 'tail' is certainly getting longer, i.e. there is now a vast amount of content that is accessible even if there is no demonstrable mass market for it, but it is also getting flatter and is, in general, 'a diversion for consumers whose appetite for true blockbusters continues to grow' (2008: 9). If this is correct, then Anderson's 'long tail' thesis is evidence not so much of an equalisation of power in the cultural marketplace but of the internet's capacity to act as a much more efficient and expansive storage system.

Elberse's conclusion that the companies that are set to gain most from the digital economy are not those that supply the 'tail' but those that are 'most capable of capitalizing on individual best sellers' (2008: 9) is a direct contradiction of the 'new economy' theorists who emphasise the power of niche culture. These theorists insist that, as the old 'mass market' fragments, we will inevitably see the 'shattering of the mainstream into a zillion different cultural shards' (Anderson 2009a: 5) and the emergence of a de-massified market. This is partly an empirical matter. There may be 'zillions' of tweets, blogs and uploaded videos, but there is little evidence to suggest that they are likely to replace traditional content providers as the most likely source of revenue or even news. The Project for Excellence in Journalism, for example, found in its analysis of online news that niche sites are less 'sticky' than generalist ones, with users returning far more often to and spending twice as long on sites with national and international profiles (PEJ 2010). Yet, even if it were true that there was no demand or incentive to produce blockbuster goods, there is little evidence that the circulation of niche goods is predicated on a *different* market logic, one that is *not* based on the tendency towards concentration and the need for accumulation. When Jarvis argues, in a section headed 'The mass market is dead – long live the mass of niches' (2009: 63), that 'Google figured out how to navigate the universe of niches and profit from it' (2009: 66), he is correctly identifying the extent to which even the smallest demographic may be commodified and used as a source of value.

But Anderson's and Jarvis's belief in the democratic benefits of a niche economy also appears to be based on a misunderstanding of the relationship between the 'mass' and 'niche', where the former is seen as an outmoded form of top-down control and the latter as a rather romantic expression of individuality. Both cite the celebrated aphorism of Marxist sociologist Raymond Williams, that '[t]here are no masses; there are only ways of seeing people as masses' (quoted in Anderson 2009a: 185; Jarvis 2009: 63), as proof of the welcome decline of the mass market. But Williams was saying no such thing: he was instead commenting on the power of elite institutions to organise the representation of ordinary people as an unruly 'mob' in order better to regulate them. He was condemning not the ability of citizens to act collectively but the use of the word 'masses' by industry leaders and politicians to commodify large groups of people. 'This is the trouble with phrases like "the masses" and "the great British people", which lead us to think not of actual people, living and growing in different ways, but of some large, many-headed thing with fixed habits' (Williams 1968: 93). Just as there ought to be nothing intrinsically threatening about 'masses', there is nothing automatically democratic about 'niches'.

Ironically, the growth of niches has contributed to another area of concentrated activity: the need for 'gatekeepers' to structure access to increasingly populated and complex markets. Record labels that were theorised out of existence by proponents of disintermediation (see p. 75) are starting to increase their share of digital revenues, while ad agencies, supposedly squeezed out by Google, are re-entering the field as the 'space between advertiser and publisher has become jam-packed over the last decade, with literally hundreds of ad networks, data companies, yield managers, ad servers and exchanges all purporting to serve advertisers or publishers in some unique way' (Learmonth 2010). Electronic book publishing, an area where the internet has transformed the possibilities of self-publishing, is instead the site of a vicious struggle between a handful of large publishers and manufacturers of e-readers like Amazon and Apple. According to Ken Auletta (2010), Amazon buys e-books from publishers for $13 but decided to retail them for $10 in order to increase sales of its Kindle device – the classic 'loss leader' device identified by Garnham (see p. 80). However, Auletta claims that Apple, when launching its rival iPad technology, intervened in this arrangement by selling its e-books for $15, a move that led publishers to force Amazon to raise its price or risk the publishers withholding their titles from Amazon. Far from publishers losing all their influence in this new market, they have retained their gatekeeping power as owners of the intellectual property that is most likely to generate revenue despite the increase in user-generated content and the emergence of disintermediating technologies. This is, however, precisely the type of market distortion that ought not to be possible in a technologically conceived economy of 'abundance' where 'creating artificial scarcity kills orthodox business dead' (Haque 2009). Instead, it is a reminder that traditional mechanisms for ensuring the viability of cultural commodities in a capitalist market – of oligopolies, bottlenecks and manufactured scarcity – are as relevant to the new digital economy as they were to the one it has allegedly replaced.

Conclusion

The accounts of the collaborative possibilities of the Web 2.0 world provided by Anderson, Downes, Jarvis and Tapscott and Williams are powerful reminders of the tremendous impact that the internet has had on many areas of creative and cultural life. Yet, for all their insider knowledge and cutting-edge perspectives, these books articulate a deterministic vision of a frictionless capitalism in which questions of property have been side-lined, profit making naturalised and exploitation minimised. The dynamics of the free market have been abstracted from their daily iteration and replaced with a technologically induced vision of an economic system based on an innate tendency to equalise and make transparent the social relations on which capitalism rests.

The problem is that even a digital capitalism is still subject to the same episodic crises of supply and demand and the same periods of speculation that affect other varieties of capitalism. Google may not have been as badly damaged by the recession as were, for example, house builders and steel makers, but it was nevertheless still affected by a decline in overall economic activity. 'Despite claims to the contrary', argues Mike Wayne (2003: 59), 'there is no new paradigm by which the economics of capitalism transcends its absolutely fundamental tendency towards overproduction and hence crisis'. Many of the factors that were symptomatic of the 'mass' media economy – especially its propensity towards monopolisation, commodification and accumulation – are central to the dynamics of a new media economy shaped by the contradictory forces of the internet that promise dispersion but reward concentration and that fetishise openness but encourage proprietary behaviour. The digital sphere is not a parallel economy but one that accentuates the tensions between the creativity and collaboration of a generative system and the hierarchies and polarisation prioritised by a system that rests, above all else, on the pursuit of profit.

References

Anderson, C. (2009a [2006]) *The Longer Long Tail: How Endless Choice Is Creating Unlimited Demand* (first published in the US as *The Long Tail*), London: Random House Business Books.

——(2009b) *Free: The Future of a Radical Price*, London: Random House Business Books.

Armstrong, S. (2009) 'It's Very Dangerous to Go Free', *Media Guardian*, 16 November.

——(2010) 'Bauer's Freelancers up in Arms over New Contracts', guardian.co.uk, 19 April. Online. Available HTTP: <http://www.guardian.co.uk/media/2010/apr/19/bauer-freelance contracts-row> (accessed 7 May 2010).

Auletta, K. (2010) 'Publish or Perish', *New Yorker*, 26 April. Online. Available HTTP: <http://www.newyorker.com/reporting/2010/04/26/100426fa_fact_auletta> (accessed 24 October 2011).

Battelle, J. (2005) *The Search: How Google and Its Rivals Rewrote the Rules of Business and Transformed Our Culture*, London: Nicholas Brealey.

Bell, D. (1973) *The Coming of Post-industrial Society: A Venture in Social Forecasting*, New York: Basic Books.

Benkler, Y. (2006) *The Wealth of Networks: How Social Production Transforms Markets and Freedom*, New Haven: Yale University Press.

Blair, T. (1998) *The Third Way: New Politics for the New Century*, Fabian Pamphlet 588, London: Fabian Society.

Cairncross, F. (1997) *The Death of Distance: How the Communications Revolution Will Change Our Lives*, London: Orion.

Cassidy, J. (2002) *dot.con*, London: Allen Lane.

Coyle, D. (1997) *The Weightless World: Strategies for Managing the Digital Economy*, Oxford: Capstone.

Downes, L. (2009) *The Laws of Disruption: Harnessing the New Forces that Govern Life and Business in the Digital Age*, New York: Basic Books.

Elberse, A. (2008) 'Should You Invest in the Long Tail?', *Harvard Business Review*, July–August, 1–11.

Fiske, J. (1987) *Television Culture*, London: Methuen.

Fuchs, C. (2009) 'Information and Communication Technologies and Society: A Contribution to the Critique of the Political Economy of the Internet', *European Journal of Communication*, 24 (1): 69–87.

Garnham, N. (1990) *Capitalism and Communication*, London: Sage.

Google (2004) *2004 Founders' IPO Letter*. Online. Available HTTP: <http://investor. google.com/corporate/2004/ipo-founders-letter.html> (accessed 24 October 2011).

——(2010) *10-K Report*. Online. Available HTTP: <http://investor.google.com/docu-ments/20101231_google_10K.html> (accessed 24 October 2011).

Graham, A. (1998) 'Broadcasting Policy and the Digital Revolution', *Political Quarterly*, 69 (B): 30–42.

Guardian (2010) 'Factfile UK: Education, Sport and Culture', *Guardian*, 27 April.

Haque, U. (2005) 'The New Economics of Media', www.bubblegeneration.com. Online. Available HTTP: <http://www.scribd.com/doc/12177741/Media-Economics-The-New-Economics-of-Media-Umair-Haque> (accessed 20 April 2010).

——(2009) 'The New Economics of Business (Or, the Case for Going Great-to-Good)', HBR Blog Network, 9 April. Online. Available HTTP: <http://blogs.hbr.org/haque/2009/11/why_news_corps_antigoogle_coun.html> (accessed 24 October 2011).

Helft, M. (2010) 'Justice Dept. Criticizes Latest Google Book Deal', *New York Times*, 4 February. Online. Available HTTP: <http://www.nytimes.com/2010/02/05/technol-ogy/internet/05publish.html> (accessed 10 May 2010).

Internet Retailer (2010) 'The Top 10 Retailers Are Big and Getting Bigger', *Internet Retailer*, 5 May. Online. Available HTTP: <http://www.internetretailer.com/dailyNews.asp?id=34738> (accessed 7 May 2010).

Jarvis, J. (2009) *What Would Google Do?*, New York: Collins Business.

Leadbeater, C. (1999) *Living on Thin Air*, London: Viking.

——(2009) *We-Think*, London: Profile Books.

Learmonth, M. (2010) 'Web Publishers Left with Little after Middlemen Split Ad Spoils', *Advertising Age*, 1 March. Online. Available HTTP: <http://adage.com/digital/article?article_id=142332> (accessed 3 April 2010).

Lessig, L. (2002) *The Future of Ideas: The Fate of the Commons in a Connected World*, New York: Vintage.

Machlup, F. (1962) *The Production and Distribution of Knowledge in the United States*, Princeton: Princeton University Press.

Madrick, J. (2001) 'The Business Media and the New Economy', Research Paper R-24, Harvard University, John F. Kennedy School of Government.

Marx, K. (1918) *Capital: A Critical Analysis of Capitalist Production, Volume One*, London: William Glaisher.

——(1973) *Grundrisse: Foundations of the Critique of Political Economy*, New York: Vintage.

Marx, K. and Engels, F. (1975) [1848] *Manifesto of the Communist Party*, Peking: Foreign Languages Press.

Mosco, V. (2009) *The Political Economy of Communication*, 2nd edn, London: Sage.

Negroponte, N. (1996) *Being Digital*, London: Coronet.

Oreskovic, A. (2010) 'Google CEO Says Company Tends to Create Enemies', Reuters. com, 13 April. Online. Available HTTP: http://uk.reuters.com/article/idUK TRE63C0AM20100413 (accessed 7 May 2010).

PEJ (Project for Excellence in Journalism) and the Pew Internet & American Life Project (2010) *The State of the News Media: An Annual Report on American Journalism*. Online. Available HTTP: <http://www.stateofthemedia.org/2010/online_nielsen.php> (accessed 9 April 2010).

Porat, M. (1977) *The Information Economy*, Ann Arbor, MI: University Microfilms.

Purcell, K. (2010) 'Teens and the Internet: The Future of Digital Diversity', Pew Research Centre. Online. Available HTTP: <http://www.pewinternet.org/~/media//Files/Presentations/2010/Mar/FredRogersSlidespdf.pdf> (accessed 23 April 2010).

Rayport, J. (2007) 'Advertising's Death Is Greatly Exaggerated', *Market Watch*, 8 June. Online. Available HTTP: <http://www.marketwatch.com/story/advertisings-death-is-greatly-exaggerated?dist=> (accessed 7 May 2010).

Shirky, C. (2008) *Here Comes Everybody: the Power of Organizations without Organization*, London: Allen Lane.

Smith, T. (2000) *Technology and Capital in the Age of Lean Production*, Albany, NY: SUNY Press.

Sparks, C. (2000) 'From Dead Trees to Live Wires: The Internet's Challenge to the Traditional Newspaper', in J. Curran and M. Gurevitch (eds) *Mass Media and Society*, 3rd edn, London: Arnold, 268–92.

Surowiecki, J. (2004) *The Wisdom of Crowds*, New York: Doubleday.

Sylvain, O. (2008) 'Contingency and the "Networked Information Economy": A Critique of *The Wealth of Networks*', *International Journal of Technology, Knowledge, and Society*, 4 (3): 203–10.

Tapscott, D. and Williams, A. (2008) *Wikinomics: How Mass Collaboration Changes Everything*, London: Atlantic Books.

Toffler, A. (1980) *The Third Wave*, London: Pan Books.

Touraine, A. (1971) *The Post-industrial Society: Classes, Conflicts and Culture in the Programmed Society*, London: Wildwood House.

Vise, D. (2008) *The Google Story*, London: Pan Books.

Wayne, M. (2003) *Marxism and Media Studies*, London: Pluto Press.

Williams, R. (1968) [1962] *Communications*, Harmondsworth: Penguin.

Zittrain, J. (2008) *The Future of the Internet*, London: Penguin.

Chapter 4

Outsourcing internet regulation

Des Freedman

Introduction: leave us alone

On 8 February 1996, President Bill Clinton signed into law a major piece of legislation, the Telecommunications Act, the first comprehensive overhaul of US communications since the 1934 Communications Act. Broadly deregulatory in spirit, it contained within it one especially controversial section, the Communications Decency Act (CDA), which sought to regulate indecency and obscenity on a relatively new part of the world's communications infrastructure, the internet, and to criminalise the circulation of pornographic content to people under 18 years of age. Later that day, many thousands of miles away on a mountaintop in Switzerland, the former Grateful Dead lyricist and internet freedom activist John Perry Barlow published a call to arms that combined righteous indignation with libertarian passion. Barlow argued that the CDA 'attempts to place more restrictive constraints on the conversation in Cyberspace than presently exist in the Senate cafeteria, where I have dined and heard colorful indecencies spoken by United States senators on every occasion I did' (Barlow 1996). His considered reaction: 'Well, fuck them.'

There then followed a manifesto for an open and unregulated internet that resonates in the online world to this day.

> Governments of the Industrial World, you weary giants of flesh and steel, I come from Cyberspace, the new home of Mind. On behalf of the future, I ask you of the past to leave us alone. You are not welcome among us. You have no sovereignty where we gather. We have no elected government, nor are we likely to have one, so I address you with no greater authority than that with which liberty itself always speaks. I declare the global social space we are building to be naturally independent of the tyrannies you seek to impose on us. You have no moral right to rule us nor do you possess any methods of enforcement we have true reason to fear.
>
> (Barlow 1996)

Interestingly, Barlow published his declaration from Davos, home of the World Economic Forum, the annual summit of business and political leaders who spend one week each year strategising and brainstorming about how best to preserve the spirit of the free market and to minimise government interference in the running of industry. Not for the first (or the last) time, a fierce declaration of support for the independence of the internet coincided with an equally robust defence of the principles of an unfettered capitalism.

Barlow's homage to the liberal principles of the US Constitution and the freedom of cyberspace were echoed by many internet activists. Nicholas Negroponte, the founder of MIT's Media Lab, wrote in his celebrated guide to the online world, *Being Digital* (Negroponte 1996), of the difference, in relation to regulation, between analogue atoms and digital 'bits'. 'Most laws were conceived in and for a world of atoms, not bits. I think the law is an early-warning system telling us "This is a big one." National law has no place in cyberlaw' (1996: 237). Negroponte's argument was twofold. First, he insisted, following much contemporary globalisation theory (see, for example, Ohmae 1995), that the traditional nation-state had lost its privileged position as the repository of symbolic and political power. Nations are 'not small enough to be local and they are not large enough to be global' (Negroponte 1996: 238). Second, he highlighted what he saw as an inevitable restructuring of the media world, away from the domination of large bureaucracies and towards the emergence of a new, decentralised layer of 'cottage industries'. The consequence for Negroponte is that just as 'media have gotten bigger and smaller at the same time, so must world governance' (1996: 239).

For many influential enthusiasts of the new internet environment, this translated into a consensus that government intervention would only stifle the creativity and innovation that was a hallmark of cyberspace. The people best placed to shape the development of the internet were not public policy experts, let alone meddling bureaucrats, but the engineers and programmers who designed the internet in the first place as a series of networks that were intrinsically hostile to outside interference: as reflected in its military origins, 'the Net interprets censorship as damage and routes around it' (Gilmore 1993). According to Kevin Kelly, former executive editor of *Wired*, the in-house magazine of the online world, the result of this was that:

> No one controls the Net, no one is in charge. The U.S. government, which indirectly subsidizes the Net, woke up one day to find that a Net had spun itself, without much administration or oversight, among the terminals of the techno-elite. The Internet is, as its users are proud to boast, the largest functioning anarchy in the world.
>
> (Kelly 1995: 598)

For Esther Dyson, the founding chair of the domain-naming organisation ICANN, government's role in relation to the internet was, necessarily, extremely limited. 'The question is how to focus the public's imagination on a better solution – not government regulation or even industry self-regulation, but an environment where consumers themselves can exercise their power and control their own information' (Dyson 1998: 6).

It is important to stress that these were voices reflecting a particular form of US libertarianism that is not necessarily illustrative of all political cultures but, nevertheless, they were (indeed, *are*) not marginal figures but individuals playing a decisive role in the popularisation of the internet across the globe. They reflected a passionately held view that, finally, here was a communication medium that could circumvent and potentially usurp the power of traditional gatekeepers – notably, 'old' media giants and all forms of government – and restore power to ordinary users. Despite the actual history of the internet, state power in its current form was viewed, not without reason, as we shall later see, as inimical to the free (in both monetary and political terms) and open development of networks that were characterised by principles of non-discrimination, decentralisation and connectivity.

This is hardly ancient history, but, given the developments on which this chapter focuses, it does appear that such libertarian narratives are emblematic of a very different period: when the internet was in its 'infancy', as opposed to the rather more mature stage of development in which it finds itself today. There is now a broad acceptance that, as with any large-scale communication medium with such vital economic and social significance, there needs to be at least a minimal system of rules to ensure its smooth functioning, safety and security. Of course, there is far less agreement concerning the forms that this regulation will take, together with the staffing, control and direction of the regulatory process in different countries. The situation is made massively more complicated by the ways in which the internet itself, as a technology predicated on facilitating abundance, interoperability and a lack of respect for national borders, has problematised and undermined traditional structures of regulation. As legal scholars Johnson and Post argued in a celebrated article concerning the inadequacy of existing legal regimes, the internet 'radically subverts a system of rule-making based on borders between physical spaces, at least with respect to the claim that cyberspace should naturally be governed by territorially defined rules' (Johnson and Post 1996: 1368).

This chapter, therefore, attempts to address key dynamics of the regulatory process as it has developed over the last decade. Instead of simply trying to describe and list the various locations in and mechanisms through which this regulation takes place, it focuses on the most significant literature and mobilising ideas that have helped to shape what we now understand as 'internet regulation'. It highlights the turn towards 'governance' and code-based regulation, but also discusses the continuities between 'networked' and more established forms of communication regulation. The chapter also considers how, despite different inflections in different countries, the internet is implicated in a fundamental neo-liberal transformation of the power relations inside the regulatory process, and poses the question: who are the regulators now? In asking this question, it suggests that, far from abandoning the idea of the state as a possible agent of robust and democratic regulation, we need to devise regulatory systems that are independent from both commercial *and* governmental interests and operate instead as guarantors of the public good. The internet is itself a creature of public policy and it is entirely legitimate to propose that fully democratic states – and not outsourced private interests, partisan administrations, authoritarian governments or opaque supranational bodies – should regulate the internet as a public utility that is accessible and accountable to all their citizens.

The non-governmentalisation of internet regulation

The anti-statist ideas that dominated the thinking of many internet advocates in the 1990s have morphed into a new consensus that the internet is best governed, wherever possible, by users and experts rather than by politicians and governments. Thomas Friedman, in his best-selling account of the possibilities unleashed by capitalist globalisation, *The Lexus and the Olive Tree* (Friedman 2000), makes an explicit distinction between what he sees as desirable 'governance' and undesirable 'government', where the latter is viewed as a 'global cop'. Coercion, for Friedman, is generally more of a last resort in the pursuit of democracy and free markets: 'when you are the shaper of a coalition in support of a certain human value, you would be amazed at what you can do without global government to create better global governance' (2000: 206). In relation to a technological innovation that relies on open standards, coercive forms of control will be at best counter-productive and at worst destructive. Indeed, the reason why the internet is so dynamic, according to Friedman, is precisely because of an openness in which the 'best solutions win out quickly and the dead are removed from the battlefield quickly' (2000: 226).

Governance, unlike more top-down forms of government-induced regulation, refers to a dispersed and flexible form of organisation and is seen 'to imply a network form of control, to refer primarily to a process and to have associated with it diverse agents' (Daly 2003: 115–16). For internet governance theorist Milton Mueller, 'it denotes the coordination and regulation of interdependent actors in the *absence* of an overarching political authority' (2010: 8). According to the UN Working Group on Internet Governance (WGIG), 'governance is the development and application by Governments, the private sector and civil society, in their respective roles, of shared principles, norms, rules, decision-making procedures and programmes that shape the evolution and use of the Internet' (quoted in de Bossey 2005: 4). Governance is, therefore, a more expansive and fluid concept than government, which 'refers not only to formal and binding rules, but also to numerous informal mechanisms, internal and external to the media, by which they are "steered" towards multiple (and often inconsistent) objectives' (McQuail 2005: 234). Rules are designed and protocols agreed on less by national governments operating in isolation than by specialist standards-setting organisations, like the Internet Engineering Task Force (IETF), the Internet Society and the World Wide Web Consortium (W3C), which have a normative, rather than a legal, power (Benkler 2006: 394). In a similar vein, the allocation of domain names is not a statutory exercise but one enforced by a private, non-profit company, the Internet Corporation for Assigned Names and Numbers (ICANN), which has taken over duties previously carried out by the US government.

These organisations are emblematic of what supporters view as a more independent and meritocratic approach to regulation that mirrors directly the decentralised structure and participatory potential of the internet. For A. Michael Froomkin (2003), a standards-setting body like the IETF is perhaps the best institutional expression of a Habermasian commitment to discourse ethics and an operational public sphere. Froomkin argues that the IETF exhibits a 'high degree of openness and transparency' as well as 'a surprising degree of self-consciousness, or reflexivity, in that IETF participants have a common story that explains how the IETF came to be and why its outputs are legitimate' (2003: 799). Indeed, it is the commitment on behalf of IETF participants to the 'emancipatory potential of communication' that ends up being of 'instrumental value in enhancing both democracy and commerce' (2003: 810). Yes, it is highly specialist, male dominated and monolingual (meetings are conducted in English), but in its single-minded purpose to preserve open standards it is 'inherently communitarian' (2003: 816) and the best inspiration we have with which to pursue common agreement about the infrastructure of the internet.

Even ICANN, which has generated an enormous amount of criticism for failing to act in a transparent or democratic fashion (see p. 111), was initially greeted by some commentators as a potential harbinger of 'good' governance. According to Manuel Castells, writing in 2001, 'its by-laws embody the spirit of openness ... decentralization, consensus-building and autonomy that characterized the *ad hoc* governance of the Internet over thirty years' (Castells 2001: 31). Whatever its actual shortcomings, Castells insisted that it was nevertheless very revealing that, in order to gain legitimacy, new bodies with oversight of the internet, such as ICANN, had to be set up 'on the tradition of meritocratic consensus-building that characterized the origins of the Internet' (2001: 33).

There has been a similar development at the international level. As a direct response to the internet's reluctance passively to yield to fixed, geographic borders, we have seen the emergence of a supranational governance regime that cannot be contained within traditional national systems of regulation. This includes both state-based supranational bodies like the World Trade Organization (WTO) and the World International Property Organization (WIPO), as well as ones with more civil society involvement like the World Summit on the Information Society, which met in 2003 and 2005 to discuss how best to overcome the digital divide, and the subsequent Internet Governance Forum. The internet has contributed, therefore, to the rise of a network of organisations that has led theorists to pronounce the emergence of a system of 'global media governance' (Ó Siochrú et al. 2002) composed primarily, but not exclusively, of intergovernmental agencies organised around the United Nations. According to Franklin, this is evidence of a decline in the power of nation-based policy structures and the re-spatialisation of ICT regulation: 'Translocal, transnational and supraterritorial trajectories and alliances overlay domestic–international demarcation lines as multilateral institutions broker "multi-stakeholder" meetings' (Franklin 2009: 223). A range of non-state actors from both the private sector and civil society are now central to the development and enforcement of contemporary information policies.

Governments and other stakeholders, however, are not only reaching up to a supranational level but reaching down to establish independent or quasi-autonomous regulatory agencies within their national jurisdiction. This points to a willingness to outsource a range of responsibilities that were previously carried out by the state but that have now been subcontracted to non-state organisations. The monitoring of content, allocation of domain names and the protection of privacy are all areas where the state (at least in some countries) has relinquished its role as sole arbiter of what is permissible or not. The preferred mechanisms of contemporary governance regimes are increasingly self-regulation, where industry modifies its behaviour in response to a set of agreed codes, and co-regulation, where industry works in partnership with the state to design and enforce adherence to rules (see Tambini et al. 2007 for an extensive discussion of modes of self-regulation of the internet). The European Commission's Audiovisual Media Services Directive, for example, explicitly advocates the use of self- and co-regulation to help deliver public policy objectives (EC 2010: 5).

Why should this be the case? Freedman (2008: 126) argues that the increasing appeal of self-regulation *across* the communications industry is a result, at least in part, of the desire by neoliberal actors to secure a more lightly regulated environment in order to pursue their own aims. However, there is little doubt that it is the characteristics of the internet itself that has galvanised the drive to self-regulation over statutory methods. For Ang (2008: 309–10), self-regulation can claim to be more appropriate for the online world, firstly, because, in the context of such a dynamic system, *informal* processes will be more adaptable to change and less likely to inhibit innovation and, secondly, because those in the best position to understand and then enforce any rules are unlikely to be judges or politicians, but entrepreneurs and software engineers. But there is another reason for the confluence of self-regulation with the online world. As Thomas Friedman puts it (2000: 471), 'precisely because the Internet is such a neutral, free, open and unregulated vehicle for commerce, education and communication, personal judgment and responsibility are critical when using this technology'. Self-regulation, in other words, appears to fit an environment in which content is freely extracted by the consumer and is not imposed by the broadcaster; it is suitable not only technologically but also culturally, as the individual user is credited with more agency than in analogue forms of media consumption. Self-regulation, to misquote Stanley Baldwin, aims to give the consumer both power *and* responsibility.

For example, illegal internet content in the UK is overseen not by a government department but by an industry-funded body, the Internet Watch Foundation

(IWF), set up by a group of internet service providers (ISPs) in 1996; the same is true in Spain, where the Internet Quality Agency (IQUA) was established in 2002, and in France, where the Internet Rights Forum was set up in 2001 precisely on the basis of the 'irrelevance of a top-down approach' (Falque-Pierrotin and Baup 2007: 164). The IWF argues that, as most illegal material, for example images of child sexual abuse and violent pornography, is hosted outside the UK and thus not accountable to UK obscenity or child protection laws, a new approach is needed. While it presses similar bodies in other countries to warn authorities about the existence of this material, it focuses its activity on passing on individual complaints to UK ISPs concerning the existence of illegal content on their networks and encourages them to remove it as quickly as possible: the policy of 'notice and takedown'. According to Peter Robbins, chief executive of the IWF, the system works on 'consensus': 'It's a corporate social responsibility of many of the companies that fund us to try and do something to make a difference to the type of content that we deal with' (Robbins 2009: 9).

UK law, in accordance with European e-commerce regulations, exempts ISPs and other online intermediaries from any liability for content where they can establish their status as 'mere conduits', in other words, where they can demonstrate that they have not knowingly circulated illegal material. Liability in this case rests with the original author or poster of the material. While early case law in the UK tended to rule against such 'innocent distribution' defences, recent cases have been more sympathetic to ISPs, proving perhaps the increasing effectiveness of self-regulation. Indeed, Zittrain (2009) argues that the 'notice and takedown' approach is a useful balance between copyright protection and amateur expression that operates on a reactive, rather than a proactive, model that better suits the permissive environment of the internet: 'a preemptive intervention to preclude some particular behaviour actually disempowers the people who might complain about it to decide that they are willing, after all, to tolerate it' (2009: 120). For Zittrain, this reflects the 'generative' nature of a technology where accessibility, unpredictability and 'unanticipated change' are at the heart of its appeal (2009: 70) and, therefore, where 'top-down' regulation is best minimised.

The growing tension between the 'generative' and the 'non-generative' in relation to regulation is most powerfully expressed by Yochai Benkler, who argues in *The Wealth of Networks* (Benkler 2006) that new, commons-based forms of information production are challenging incumbent, centralised and hierarchical information flows. Nowhere is this battle between the old and the new more visible than in the sphere of law and regulation, where battles over, for example, copyright, patents and the shape of social production are constantly being waged. For Benkler, this suggests a twenty-first-century 'clash of civilizations' where 'political and judicial pressures to form an institutional ecology that is decidedly in favor of proprietary business models are running headlong into the emerging social practices described throughout this book' (2006: 470). Regulation, however, does not appear to constitute a neutral process in the midst of this battle. Given how often the law has been used in a 'reactive and reactionary' (2006: 393) fashion to protect the interests of industrial actors and to contain the possibilities of the emerging social sharing media, regulation, for Benkler, seems to be expressive of an outdated information ecology. While he acknowledges that intervention may be necessary in limited circumstances, for example to open up a market using antitrust measures, what the 'emerging networked information economy therefore needs, in almost all cases, is not regulatory protection, but regulatory abstinence' (2006: 393).

Governmentalisation of internet regulation

Yet there is an alternative history to the formation of an idiosyncratic govern-ance regime for the internet, perhaps best expressed by Mueller's rather under-stated comment that, referring to the classic statement of cyber-libertarianism, 'Barlow's declaration hasn't aged well' (Mueller 2002: 266). There is instead another narrative that stresses that, despite globalisation processes, national governments continue to play key roles in shaping, populating and enforcing the various agencies and mechanisms involved in the regulation of online networks. From the US Digital Millennium Copyright Act of 1998, which sought to impose a heavily proprietorial intellectual property regime on the new digital environment through the mandating of anti-circumvention devices (Benkler 2006: 413–18), to the UK's Digital Economy Act of 2010, which sanctions the dis-connection of users persistently engaging in unlicensed downloads (see Doctorow 2010 for a critical view); from the Clinton administration's critical role in setting up ICANN in 1998 to the Chinese government's continuing control of access to the internet; from state support for the extension of copyright in both Europe and the US to increasing state supervision of cybersecurity measures across the world – the imprint of government is rarely absent from internet governance schemes. Indeed, to the extent that the state power over the internet *had* started to slip with the emergence of multilateral bodies and self-regulatory agencies, Mueller (2010: 4) asserts that states have more recently fought back in what he describes as a 'counter-revolution'. While there will be different inflec-tions of regulatory intervention in different countries, state coordination of the internet is increasingly significant.

The most celebrated account of and justification for the continuing role of nation-state-based regulation of the internet was developed by Goldsmith and Wu (2006) in their book subtitled 'Illusions of a Borderless World'. Goldsmith and Wu argue that not only are national borders and territorial governments still meaningful in a globalised world, but governments, at least the representative ones, are actually best placed to protect democratic institutions and spaces: 'With an open and free press, regular elections and an independent judiciary, democratic governments are the best system that human beings have ever devised for aggregating the varied interests and desires of a sovereign people into a workable governing order' (2006: 142). Supranational or hyperlocal assemblies may serve a purpose, but ultimately, while one can 'criticize traditional territorial government and bemoan its many failures, there is no reasonable prospect of any better system of governmental organization' (2006: 153).

Drawing on a traditional Weberian conception of states in relation to their monopoly of coercive power, Goldsmith and Wu insist that those people who thought the internet was outside the jurisdiction of nation-state-based forms of law were, quite simply, wrong: 'the last ten years have shown that national governments have an array of techniques for controlling offshore Internet communications, and thus enforcing their laws, by exercising coercion within their borders' (2006: viii). Castells, for example, argues that the need for the regulation of online spaces started to be taken seriously in 2000, when governments realised the threat posed by cybercrime (2001: 177). In an attempt to restore order and win back control of the regulatory arena, 'it became necessary for the most important governments to act together, creating a new global space of policing ... a network of regulatory and policing agencies' (2001: 178). Castells identifies the emergence of a new architecture, built on commercialisation and surveillance, that becomes 'the fundamental tool of control, making it possible to exercise regulation and policing by traditional forms of state power' (2001: 179).

This policing was most dramatically illustrated by the reaction of a series of nation-states to the publication in 2010 of some 250,000 US embassy cables by the whistleblowing website WikiLeaks. The cables revealed embarrassing details of diplomatic missives concerning the international community, including Anglo-American doubts about the security of the Pakistani nuclear industry, allegations of corruption involving the US-backed Afghan government and evidence of the Saudi regime's call to bomb Iran. Many countries adopted a distinctly non-libertarian stance to the circulation of the cables: China, Pakistan, Thailand (and the US Air Force) blocked access to some or all of the material, while the US Army and the White House warned employees against accessing classified material (IFEX 2010). The US Department of Justice then issued a subpoena demanding that Twitter hand over details of its users in relation to an ongoing investigation of the leaks, while Mastercard, Visa and PayPal all severed links with WikiLeaks after pressure from senior figures in Washington, DC (Hals 2010). WikiLeaks itself leaked an intelligence report by the Cyber Counterintelligence Assessments Branch on the dangers posed by the organisation that contained the following recommendation: 'The identification, exposure, or termination of employment of or legal actions against current or former insiders, leakers, or whistleblowers could damage or destroy this center of gravity and deter others from using Wikileaks.org to make such information public' (Army Counterintelligence Center 2008: 3).

In general, however, regulation in liberal democracies occurs less via direct control (or censorship) of decentralised users than by constraining intermediaries like content providers, ISPs and financial services companies through the creation of self-regulatory schemes. This achieves, in the words of Goldsmith and Wu, 'extraterritorial control through local intermediaries' (2006: 68). Self-regulation, in this context, suggests not the autonomous or peer-dominated process that we discussed in the previous section but one in which both agenda-setting as well as 'backstop' (enforcement) power rests largely with the state.

For example, a workshop organised by the Organisation for Economic Co-operation and Development (OECD) on the 'role of Internet intermediaries in advancing public policy objectives' agreed that, while restricting the liability of intermediaries had helped the internet to grow, there is nevertheless 'increasing national and international pressure from governments, intellectual property rights-holders, and some consumer groups, to enlist the help of Internet intermediaries to control copyright infringement, child pornography, improve cyber security etc.' (OECD 2010: 3). In other words, intermediaries are seen to offer a more effective regulatory mechanism to establish secure and operable networks than direct, coercive action. The key for government is to find the right regulatory balance between stimulating economically desirable activities and protecting individual rights to privacy and safety. Indeed, the US ambassador to the OECD gave the opening keynote to the workshop, in which she highlighted 'the increasing challenges for policy makers to maintain such "hands-off" policies in a rapidly changing environment characterized by increasing data flows across borders, heightened censorship and privacy concerns' (2010: 7). Intermediaries, in other words, are the key institutions through which governments are increasingly likely to maintain overall strategic oversight of the internet environment whilst delegating day-to-day operational control to private operators 'in the field'.

From a neoliberal perspective, state power is required to correct the 'increasingly Hobbesian' (Lewis 2010: 63) nature of the internet, to treat the online world as a 'failed state', much in the same way that military intervention has been justified to restore US-style democracy to physical territories such as Iraq and Afghanistan. James Lewis of the Center for Strategic and International Studies argues that while self-regulation has deep roots in an American political culture that has privileged scientific approaches and a discourse of 'engineering efficiency' (2010: 61), a hands-off approach is no longer sufficient to allow the state to maintain control. The idea that a functioning rule of law would spontaneously emerge to preside over the internet has been disproved and, instead, 'passive sovereignty is evolving into a more active assertion of the rights of national governments to exert their control' (2010: 63). This is a particularly urgent task for the US government because it is already being challenged by other regions and sovereign states, most notably China, who are starting to assert their own power over the internet. 'In this new phase of administering and securing the internet', Lewis concludes, 'governments will lead, not private actors' (2010: 64).

Such a statement, however, implies a false dichotomy between government and the private sector, given the fact that the US government (and it is by no means the only one) has long adopted a pro-business approach to the internet. This is best described by Ira Magaziner, President Clinton's adviser on technology matters and a key individual in the Clinton administration's team that sought to regulate the internet in the 1990s. It is worth quoting him at length as he confirms the US government's commitment to a

> market driven approach to the development of the internet. We felt that it was a bottom up kind of medium that should not be over-regulated, and we felt that we wanted to preserve the organic nature of the internet, but to set in motion a series of predictable rules that would allow commerce to take place because commerce requires a certain amount of predictability. So we advocated creation of uniform commercial code to govern transactions, market oriented approach to digital signatures; we opposed censorship of the internet, felt that that should be free content on the internet, that you wanted to evolve the government's mechanism to one that would gain global acceptance but that would still be market-driven and not heavy regulation. We advocated not having taxes on the internet, getting agreement for internet commerce to be free of tariffs across borders, and also to avoid internet taxation. At that time there were proposals floating around to tax bits. We proposed leaving, not having the FCC or ITU regulate the internet the way they did telecom, to keep the packet-switch networks out of FCC regulation.
>
> (quoted in Lewis 2010: 65)

Far from the government's retreating from the desire to control the online environment, Magaziner's comments make it clear that the Clinton administration – and there is no reason to believe that later administrations have behaved any differently (see the Federal Communication Commission's 2005 *Internet Policy Statement* [FCC 2005]) – sought to micro-manage the evolution of the internet and to secure an online space that was safe for business, reliable for consumers and acceptable to government. 'Light-touch' regulation, but regulation nonetheless, was, and remains, the preferred approach.

The codification of internet regulation

Yet the debate on internet regulation remains mired in a conceptual impasse between claims that cyberspace can or cannot easily be regulated, that any regulation that does occur should be subject to statutory or voluntary oversight, that regulation should be supervised by national or supranational regimes. Perhaps the most effective answer to this conundrum is provided by Stanford law professor Lawrence Lessig, who rejects the notion that regulation is somehow external to or imposed on technological systems like the internet. Instead, he argues in his celebrated account of the internet that 'cyberspace is regulated by its code' (Lessig 2006: 79). The programmes, protocols and platforms that make up the internet are not separate *from* but the very stuff *of* regulation. Software and hardware constitute the architectural foundation of cyberspace – its code – and this is what essentially structures online spaces. Code, according to Lessig, refers to 'the instructions embedded in the software or hardware that make cyberspace what it is. This code is the "built environment" of social life in cyberspace. It is its "architecture"' (2006: 121), which then embeds particular values into the technology and facilitates certain possibilities or, of course, presents certain constraints for the user. So just as open networks allow for unfiltered conversations, paywalls are designed to shut people out; while open source software encourages experimentation and remediation, 'tethered' devices like the iPad and iTouch try to stop you from leaving their space. So it is not enough to say that the internet is regulated by external forces, as networks themselves act to regulate their own environments, to induce certain forms of behaviour and to clamp down on others.

Crucially, Lessig works with a very expansive notion of regulation that goes way beyond the mere implementation of particular legal provisions or guiding principles. Regulation is 'produced' by the interaction of four 'modalities': the law, social norms, the market and architecture (2006: 123). The first three are not that contentious: we control our behaviour in the face of what the law may throw at us, with a regard to what is seen as 'acceptable' or not and also in the context of what the market makes available. Indeed, we have also long been regulated by physical architecture – witness Foucault's analysis of the self-regulatory impact of the Panopticon (Foucault 1977) – but, in the intersection of these four 'modalities', power in and over the online world is rapidly shifting towards those who design the hardware or who write the software. According to Lessig, 'code writers are increasingly lawmakers. They determine what the defaults of the Internet will be; whether privacy will be protected; the degree to which anonymity will be allowed; the extent to which access will be guaranteed' (2006: 79).

Lessig actually distinguishes between two types of code. 'Open code', such as that which drives peer-to-peer networks and free software, and fosters a kind of transparency in networked behaviour (2006: 153); 'closed code', on the other hand, is designed, above all, for proprietorial purposes and, while being far more opaque, now plays a central role in a market-driven internet space. After a period of collaboration and experimentation, commercial interests are increasingly defining the architecture of the online world: code becomes a vital commodity and, as such, enters the orbit of government's desire to foster a rule-bound and lucrative market for code-based services and products. According to Lessig, 'as code writing becomes commercial – as it becomes the product of a smaller number of companies – the government's ability to regulate it increases' (2006: 71), to the detriment of the 'open code' that has a far more democratic and inclusive flavour.

Lessig's account of code as regulation may smack of determinism – in the sense that code seems intrinsically to prescribe certain forms of behaviour – and it is certainly open to co-option by pro-state forces who recognise the power of internet architectures. Regulation by code, according to Goldsmith and Wu, for example, is essential and part of 'an underlying system of territorial government and physical coercion' (2006: 181), while for Lewis (2010: 63), 'those who set the standards, manufacture the hardware and write the code have a deep degree of control'. Lessig's point, however, is actually quite different. He is keen to stress that the internet, like any built environment, is always open to intervention and to re-coding. As Zittrain (2009: 197) warns, 'code is law, and commerce and government can work together to change the code'. Although everyday regulation of the internet may occur through small-scale actions – Lessig deploys the notion of 'bovinity', where '[t]iny controls, consistently enforced, are enough to direct very large animals' (2006: 73) – he is scathing about those who fail to see the bigger picture and who refuse to act to stop the imminent enclosure of the internet by commercial code. The failure to act, he argues, 'will produce not no regulation at all, but regulation by the most powerful of special interests' (2006: 337–38). The struggle for open code is no less than a struggle for democracy and against the potential abuse of state power: 'open code is a foundation for an open society' (2006: 153).

Libertarian ideas have not disappeared off the face of the earth

Lessig describes the complacency of those who continue to sit back in the face of the increasing circulation of 'closed code' as evidence of 'libertarian failure' (2006: 337). But surely, given the emergence of the governance regimes described in previous sections, libertarianism – the belief that individual freedom is best guaranteed by a lack of state intrusion into private matters – poses little threat in contrast to government or market failure. It is true that the passionate conviction of Barlow, Negroponte and others in the 1990s, that the internet is fundamentally hostile to and distorted by formal regulation, has been superseded by events. There remains, however, a powerful libertarian undercurrent in arguments that propose, if not the complete abolition of any kind of public oversight of the internet, only *minimal* levels of interference into the operation of a self-correcting organism such as the internet that is, according to this perspective, best served by market competition.

One factor that underpins the continuing attraction of libertarian ideas is the resilience of technologically determinist approaches to the internet, including the notion that the internet is, due to its DNA, fundamentally dealigned from existing systems of regulation. While there have been powerful critiques of determinism in the social sciences more broadly (see, for example, Williams 1974 and Webster 2006), Sonia Livingstone is right to suggest that 'it remains the assumption behind much public policy associated with social uses of the internet' (Livingstone 2010: 125). We can see this in the notion that digitalisation, simply by facilitating duplication, increasing scale and lowering costs of entry, is said to undermine traditional approaches to the enforcement of copyright, the protection of minors and the regulation of content. According to Emily Bell in an opinion piece for the *Guardian* (headed 'Digital media cannot be contained by the ana-logue rulebook'), 'once something is digitized, the ability over time to control it, charge for it, regulate it or contain it exponentially decreases' (Bell 2009: 4). This is very different to Lessig's proposition that, while code may enhance or constrain specific forms of online behaviour, it is not at all the case that code makes regulation impossible.

Second, we have the continuing hegemony of neoliberalism in which a combination of anti-state triumphalism and market economics 'permeates substantive broadband policymaking' (Sylvain 2010: 250). For Sylvain, the rather romantic libertarian ideas of 1990s internet pioneers, based on what he describes as 'engineering' principles of decentralisation, interoperability and consumer sovereignty, continue to motivate many in the policy community although, in practice, these ideas 'amount to little more than a policy of administrative deference to engineers, programmers, and entrepreneurs – not positive law per se' (2010: 224). In 2002, for example, Vint Cerf, one of the founders of the internet and chairman of ICANN, declared in a much-quoted statement for the Internet Society that the 'Internet is for everyone – but it won't be if Governments restrict access to it, so we must dedicate ourselves to keeping the network unrestricted, unfettered and unregulated' (Cerf 2002). The former CEO of Google, Eric Schmidt, made precisely the same point some years later when he bemoaned the impact of state intervention into the online world and, in particular, threats to regulate Google itself: 'When markets get regulated, creative innovation is slowed ... A much better outcome is for us to use good judgement. We take what we see as the consumer interest as our guiding principle' (quoted in Palmer 2009).

The association of deregulation with dynamism, and of intervention with illiberalism, is present in many key internet policy debates. When European politicians discussed whether to incorporate new 'non-linear' services into the European Union's Television without Frontiers Directive in 2006, Shaun Woodward, then UK communications minister, warned that 'the extension of scope will create huge new regulatory burdens, expensive and impossible to enforce ... We shouldn't put restrictions in place to inhibit growth and innovation' (quoted in Freedman 2008: 126). This was only a mild version of comments made by James Murdoch, the CEO of BSkyB, who in the previous year had argued that a 'totally new approach which recognizes the new on-demand world we live in is badly needed ... there is a long way to go before consumers enjoy the sovereignty that is their right. We don't need more controls to achieve that. We need a bonfire of controls' (quoted in Freedman 2008: 127). In the end, the revised Directive (EC 2010) accepted many of these arguments and recommended a far more deregulatory approach to on-demand services than those still maintained on broadcast outlets.

We find similar arguments being proposed in relation to the vexed question of net neutrality, the regulatory response to the ability of certain providers to block, restrict or segregate content online. While there are some prominent advocates of government intervention to protect principles of non-discrimination and equality of access (including Tim Berners-Lee, the founder of the Web

[Berners-Lee 2010]), many commentators have insisted that formal government protection of neutrality is an affront to the very principles of openness, consumer sovereignty and decentralisation that characterise the internet's appeal. Larry Downes (2009: 128–37), for example, argues that net neutrality legislation will be both hard to police and counter-productive because the internet's architecture is already based on a concept of neutrality that is intrinsic to, not imposed on, its networks. Furthermore, laws that have been passed in relation to the internet are, for the most part, 'ignored, thanks to the Internet's ability to treat regulation as a network failure and reroute around the problem' (2009: 137). In the op-ed pages of the *New York Times*, a group of prominent neoliberal economists even went so far as to praise the *European* approach to net neutrality as a model example of negative policy: 'Perhaps the most noteworthy things about the European regulations is what they do not do. They do not prescribe business or pricing models for European telecommunications companies' (Mayo et al. 2010). Forcing 'heavy-handed rules' on such a dynamic system will, from this perspective, only squash innovation and distort competition.

Indeed, 'official' contributions to net neutrality debates tend to rely heavily on legal and economic arguments that lack a focus on broader theories of the public interest, citizenship or, in particular, democracy. By reducing it to a mere 'traffic management' issue (Ofcom 2010), policy makers have sought to limit what should be a discussion about how best we should organise and facilitate the circulation online of information, media and culture to a much narrower pre-occupation with ill-defined notions of transparency, competition and 'openness' (see, for example, Genachowski 2010). In the UK, communications minister Ed Vaizey has challenged the need for neutrality regulations on the basis that the country already has a competitive broadband market and that a lightly regulated internet is 'good for business, good for the economy and good for people' (quoted in Halliday 2010). When forced to clarify his comments, Vaizey declared that he was not ruling out intervention in the future but that he was indeed against 'heavy handed' regulation and was not prepared 'to put regulatory hurdles in the way – the last 20 years have told us not to do that' (quoted in Warman 2010).

In the US, however, the FCC did, by the narrowest of margins, pass neutrality rules, albeit ones that were watered down following extensive lobbying by telecoms companies like AT& T and Verizon (Schatz and Raice 2010). The rules, which exempt wireless devices (precisely the technologies that are most likely to connect users to the internet in the future) were then immediately condemned by pro-regulation voices as 'Net Neutrality-lite' (Nichols 2010), but also attacked by anti-regulation figures like senior Republican Fred Upton as 'nothing less than an "assault" on the internet' (quoted in Kirchgaessner 2010). The fact that the FCC was able, in the end, to introduce neutrality regulations, no matter how diluted or unsatisfactory to many campaigners, suggests that it is perhaps possible to overstate the influence of libertarian ideas. On the other hand, the determination of the Republicans, together with some major industry figures, to overturn the rules demonstrates the continuing presence of pro-market, anti-state ideologies. The announcement in January 2011 that Verizon was suing the FCC for overreaching its authority and for potentially endangering the stability of the US internet market is further evidence that libertarian ideas do continue to play a significant role in internet regulation debates.

Limitations of governance regimes

Libertarian or not, one issue on which many internet activists continue to agree is the desirability of self-regulation and the use of non-state institutions for internet governance. This argument is made not just by free-market enthusiasts with a natural hostility to state intervention but also by activists who are keen to extend the principles of content-sharing networks and non-proprietorial practices into the regulatory layer of the internet. The success of Wikipedia, the widespread use of open source software and the popularity of peer-to-peer sites all suggest, as we have already discussed, that there is a need to move away from traditional top-down forms of regulatory authority and towards more consensual governance spaces like the World Summit on the Information Society (WSIS) and more flexible practices of self-regulation and self-governance.

Critics, however, point to a significant problem: that such practices have not led to an internet free from viruses, spam, illegal content and security risks or, of course, to an online environment independent of either corporate control or state influence. Jonathan Zittrain, for example, argues that the internet's 'generative' nature, its openness and unpredictability, are precisely the qualities that allow worms, viruses and malware increasingly to suffuse its networks. Indeed, as the internet has become further institutionalised and commercialised, a business model for 'bad code' (Zittrain 2009: 45) has emerged in which the threat to launch a cyberattack has serious financial consequences. 'The economics', argues Zittrain (2009: 47), 'is implacable: viruses are now valuable properties, and that makes for a burgeoning industry in virus making where volume matters'. Furthermore, the US, with its established systems of self-regulation, is at, or near, the top of the rankings when it comes to instances of malicious activity (2009: 49).

Others are critical about the viability of specific regimes of self-regulation. According to Peng Hwa Ang (2008), attempts to protect online privacy or to develop workable and popular content labelling and filtering systems have been generally disappointing. This is partly because there are few effective enforcement mechanisms and partly because internet users constitute such a diverse and diffuse group. 'The easiest solution to heterogeneity is to set the lowest standard. But that undermines the confidence of users in the self-regulatory regime. All things considered, therefore', Ang concludes (2008: 311), 'the conditions for self-regulation of the Internet are absent'. In relation to the UK in particular, Richard Collins challenges the myth 'that network governance and self-regulation is both pervasive and dominant' (2009: 51). Instead, Collins identifies a system in which hierarchical and horizontal forms of governance coexist and in which self-regulation offers only an unstable support for the system as a whole. Given that most industry players view each other as rivals rather than collaborators, and given the power of the largest firms to shape the self-regulatory agenda, Collins argues that the UK's 'self-regulatory governance structures may not be well adapted to securing long-term public interest objectives' (2009: 57). Largely unaccountable, reactive and susceptible to or driven by industry interests, self-regulation has proved to be an inconsistent advocate for a robust, competitive and equitable system.

Olivier Sylvain presents a more sustained critique of self-regulation in which he relates the 'delegation of rulemaking to nongovernmental bodies' directly to the neoliberal belief that 'unimpeded market competition is generally the most efficient and objective adjudicator of contests between market actors' (2010: 233). Governance schemes are, according to Sylvain, all too often based on engineering principles like decentralisation, user empowerment and interoperability that, while powerful in a technical sense, are not necessarily adequate for developing a public-minded communications policy. When Lessig argues that 'open code' ought to preclude the need for government intervention or when Froomkin claims that a private self-regulatory organisation like the IETF is based on a high level of discourse ethics, Sylvain replies that this kind of technological approach to governance is 'untenable' (2010: 231), for two main reasons. First, because not everyone in the internet community is sympathetic to social production and collaborative methods, and second, because the power to select or enforce common standards is distributed extremely unequally (2010: 232).

This is borne out by analysis of the emergence of one of the most important regulatory bodies, ICANN. While ICANN, as we saw earlier, was created with particular emphasis on its self-governance and autonomy, Milton Mueller (1999) claims that this was merely a rhetorical device designed to obscure key issues concerning the US government's determination to maintain oversight over the domain-naming process. Industry self-regulation, he argues, 'was an appealing label for a process that could be more accurately described as the US government brokering a behind-the-scenes deal among what it perceived as the major players – both private and governmental' (1999: 504). Outsiders, however, were more positive, reading self-regulation as 'an open invitation for the internet community to set aside their differences and come together to forge a new consensus' (1999: 506). This led to a twin-track process: one open, democratic and discursive, the other closed and opaque and led by private organisations like the Internet Assigned Numbers Authority (IANA) and IBM (1999: 506). According to Mueller, this has produced a clear contradiction between principles of self-organisation and the unaccountable lobbying that took place, as a result of which the 'Commerce Dept basically devolved global state power to ICANN' (1999: 516). In conclusion, the setting up of ICANN was 'part of the process by which established economic players and arrangements assimilate internetworking' (Mueller 2002: 267) and attempt to take control of the 'root', the internet's address system. Far from reflecting new forms of consensual politics, it owes its allegiance to old corporatist, hierarchical structures and deferential forms of behaviour.

At the supranational level, there are far more sympathetic critiques (for example Raboy, Landry and Shtern 2010) of fora like WSIS and the Internet Governance Forum (IGF) in which civil society and social movements can claim to have forced issues concerning the digital divide, universal access and democratic governance onto the agenda. Yet, despite the reforms that activists can point to as a result of sustained civil society engagement, Mueller argues that, at its core, multistakeholderism is process, more than ends, driven: 'While it does address the problem of democracy and participation, it mostly evades the key axes of national sovereignty and hierarchical power' (2010: 264). Zittrain echoes this point, arguing that dialogues at gatherings like WSIS 'end either in bland consensus pronouncements or in final documents that are agreed upon only because the range of participants has been narrowed' (2009: 242). According to Castells (2009: 115), the value of WSIS and IGF is undermined, as 'they are not directed towards specific corporations or organizations but at the user community at large'. They are weak precisely because they are unable to combat the unequal agenda-setting power of the most influential players and therefore continue to submit to 'relentless pressure from two essential sources of domination that still loom over our existence: capital and the state' (2009: 116).

Indeed, pro-state commentators tend to illustrate the argument that the state has not at all withdrawn from the governance sphere simply by facilitating new self-governance arrangements at a domestic and international level. Goldsmith and Wu, for example, describe how the US government achieved its aim to develop an internet system fit for purpose through outsourcing many operations. 'The United States, while talking about things like "bottom up governance" and "the Internet community" never actually ceded control over either ICANN or the root' (2006: 169). According to James Lewis, a proponent of the state's role in regulating the internet in response to the challenge of international competition, multistakeholder governance structures afford much-needed legitimacy to state institutions. 'Countries are beginning to assert sovereign control over their national cyberspace. The next steps will be to deploy technologies to let them enforce control *and to create multilateral governance structures to legitimize these actions*' (2010: 63, emphasis added).

The idea that such structures have been created, in part, to lend democratic legitimacy to processes that have at their heart the re-establishment of state oversight over the internet should not imply that self-governance *cannot* make a contribution to more participatory forms of regulation. But until multistakeholder bodies combine an interest in procedural matters with a willingness to campaign independently at the national and supranational level for an *alternative* agenda to those of the most powerful states and companies, they will continue to be marginalised. Meanwhile, tensions between state and civil society groups are still very much present in discussions about the role of the internet governance community. For example, in December 2010, a proposal by the United Nation's

Commission on Science and Technology for Development to include only member states in a working group on improvements to the IGF was met with a furious response by civil society actors who had effectively been written out of the discussions. Whether their demand is heard for 'an open and inclusive process that ensures a mechanism for the full and active participation of governments, the private sector and civil society from both developing and developed countries' (Internet Society 2010) depends on the extent to which they are able fully to mobilise the publics on whose behalf they are campaigning. Either way, multistakeholder governance has not proved to be a magic solution to the problems posed by entrenched state and corporate power.

The privatisation of internet regulation?

The claim that the internet is either 'regulated' or 'unregulated' is an unhelpful binary, not simply because it is outdated (indeed, it was never an adequate way of talking about the evolution of the internet) but also because it misses out on the complex nature of governance systems that combine market liberalism, state supervision and a nod towards consensual decision making. We have therefore moved from a redundant polarisation between 'non-regulability' and 'regulability' to a set of more subtle distinctions between different forms of regulation: statutory/ voluntary, formal/informal, national/supranational, hierarchical/diffuse. In doing this, we are reminded, first, of the blurred boundaries between 'governmental' and 'nongovernmental' approaches and, second, of certain continuities of new forms of governance with traditional forms of communications regulation.

For example, Cass Sunstein, whose plea in *Republic.com* (Sunstein 2002) for tighter regulation of online spaces in order to balance out political partisanship caused outrage amongst libertarians, had, by 2007, totally changed his tune. In an interview with Salon.com, he insisted that fresh laws were unnecessary, as the internet was already heavily regulated through existing legal frameworks: 'The equivalent of trespass is forbidden. You can't libel people on the Internet, you can't commit fraud over the Internet. So that's good' (quoted in Van Heuvelen 2007). The British legal scholar Jacob Rowbottom identifies an ongoing hierarchy in online expression and argues that while small-scale 'associative' activity should not be regulated, 'a small number of speakers, often with substantial economic resources behind them, will consistently command a mass audience. Consequently, there will be certain types of online speaker that are appropriate targets for mass media regulations' (2006: 501). Richard Collins (2009) argues that much regulatory literature makes the mistake of treating the internet as a completely novel technological environment, immune to all previous pressures, 'bounded and different from all other electronic media' (2009: 53). Instead, he stresses the 'interdependence' of internet and legacy media and, reflecting on various layers of internet regulation, writes that the '"shadow" of hierarchy always lies over market and network governance systems and often shapes the behaviour of such agents in such systems of governance' (2009: 61).

Zittrain, Benkler and Lessig all describe in some detail how this 'shadow' of hierarchy has been implicated in moves to re-regulate the communications environment on behalf of corporate interests seeking to 'gain and assert exclusivity in core resources necessary for information production and exchange' (Benkler 2006: 384). Statutory instruments, from the 1996 Telecoms Act in the US to the 2010 Digital Economy Act in the UK, were designed to update regulations for the digital age but, above all, to normalise the enclosure of the internet. According to Benkler, these shifts in the regulatory climate 'are skewing the institutional ecology in favor of business models and production practices that are based on exclusive proprietary claims; they are lobbied for by firms that collect large rents if these laws are expanded, followed, and enforced' (2006: 470).

This was particularly evident in the run-up to the FCC vote on network neutrality in December 2010, where, according to the *Wall Street Journal*, telecoms companies Verizon and AT&T held 'at least' nine meetings with senior FCC staff (Schatz 2010) in order to shape the rules to their advantage. Media activist Amy Goodman reported later that AT&T 'practically wrote the FCC rules that [FCC chair] Genachowski pushed through' (Goodman 2010). On a similar note, European Community proposals to regulate cookies, whereby users would be required to 'opt in' before cookies are placed on an individual's computer, was described by a representative of the Interactive Advertising Bureau, the trade group for online advertisers, as 'not something we could live with' (quoted in Sonne and Miller 2010). After intense lobbying, the proposals were watered down so that there was no requirement for users to permit individual cookies, but simply to adopt a 'yes or no' attitude to cookies in general. In the end, few could agree on precisely what the rules involved, leading Nellie Kroes, the commissioner in charge, to suggest a 'user-friendly' solution: that the industry should adopt self-regulatory guidelines.

The internet, as Lessig (2006) reminds us, has facilitated a re-thinking of the source and scope of regulatory power. Alongside the impact of code-based regulation, governments are not only re-regulating on behalf of powerful corporate actors but actually delegating regulatory responsibility and initiative to private companies themselves. The neoliberal state is not evacuating the regulatory field so much as launching joint ventures in which it finds itself as the junior partner in what it describes as process of 'networked governance'. According to Mueller (2010: 7), this type of governance refers to a situation in which internet companies 'establish their own policies and negotiate among themselves what is blocked and what is passed, what is authenticated and what is not'. This is a familiar form of self-regulation where operational control is exercised by private players operating under general guidelines passed down by public authorities.

But it also suggests a new dynamic of regulatory power. If we think of regulation in terms of the ability to structure access to and shape content on the internet, then powerful new regulators appear: not simply Comcast, Verizon and AT&T but Facebook, Yahoo! and, of course, Google. Reflecting on the importance of online gatekeepers, Jeffrey Rosen argues that it is private actors like Google who 'arguably have more influence over the contours of online expression than anyone else on the planet' (Rosen 2008). The fact that a small legal team takes the final decision on what content is suitable to be circulated on Google's search engines or on YouTube suggests that a fairly rigid form of hierarchical governance is in place. Indeed, for Rosen, '[v]oluntary self-regulation means that, for the foreseeable future, [deputy general counsel of Google, Nicole] Wong and her colleagues will continue to exercise extraordinary power over global speech online' (Rosen 2008). Franklin argues that this kind of gate-keeping power makes it more and more difficult to distinguish between public and private forms of regulation. 'Google administers or controls increasingly large parts of this [online] space where a growing percentage of global internet users' activities happens. Corporate actors' increasing power and influence in every day cyber spaces most of us occupy is, arguably, government-like' (Franklin 2010: 77).

Regulation, therefore, has not simply been subcontracted to private companies but embedded in 'regulating' technologies. Jonathan Zittrain argues that the most immediate danger to creative expression online may be not overt government censorship but the ways in which 'non-generative' devices and spaces (like Sky Plus, Tivo and the iPhone) restrict the range of uses and connections and thus constrain our behaviour (2009: 106). The increasing popularity of 'walled gardens' like portals or apps for the iPhone which do not permit any modification signal further evidence of the enclosure of the online environment and its potential 'lockdown'. As Zittrain puts it: 'The prospect of tethered appliances and software as service permits major regulatory intrusions to be implemented as minor technical adjustments of code or requests to service providers' (2009: 125). Even small technical decisions – an upgrade here, a copy-protection scheme there – can have profound regulatory consequences.

There remain many who put their faith in the power of social media, collaborative platforms or, as Zittrain does, in the 'generosity of spirit [which] is a society's powerful first line of moderation' (2009: 246) somehow to beat this threat of a 'lockdown'. They are, however, perhaps underestimating the power of corporations – whether traditional or emerging, 'bureaucratic' or 'innovative', software- or hardware-related – either to neutralise the threat of commons-based media or to assimilate their distinctive features into for-profit models (usually both). As we have seen from the last chapter, while the internet has thrown up a fast-changing array of sites destined to be 'the next big thing' – from Compuserve and America Online to MySpace and Bebo, Google and Facebook – one thing that has remained constant is the structure of a 'winner takes all' market which systematises the need for huge concentrations of online and offline capital. A key consequence of this, and perhaps this is genuinely novel, is that the internet has facilitated an era, partly because of technological characteristics but also partly because of the global roll-out of neoliberalism, in which it is not simply code but, increasingly, *capital* that regulates.

Conclusion

The internet is not the first technological system to serve both public and private interests – the ability of broadcasting and the press to facilitate significant public conversations has also been fully exploited by the market. Yet the internet is particularly susceptible to competing pressures, as, while it was established by public bodies and continues to operate on open protocols, its backbone and most of its access points are privately owned and operated. One response to this dichotomy is to accept that tensions between public and private (or between proprietorial and non-proprietorial) will be played out following a predetermined technological logic: that all information-based innovations go from being 'somebody's hobby to somebody's industry; from jury-rigged contraption to slick production marvel; from a freely accessible channel to one strictly controlled by a single corporation or cartel – from open to closed system. It is a progression so common as to seem inevitable' (Wu 2010: 7–8). Wu describes this as the 'Cycle' in much the same way as Chris Anderson talks about a 'natural path of industrialisation: invention, propagation, adoption, control' (Anderson 2010: 126) or Deborah Spar cites four inevitable phases of technological development: innovation, commercialisation, 'creative anarchy' and finally the imposition of rules (Spar 2001: 11). Technologies start out messy but end up tamed.

There is a danger in this deterministic reading of technological evolution that regulation, far from being an activity that seeks *actively* to shape and respond to concrete developments on the internet on the basis of particular views and beliefs, becomes a *fait accompli* followed by a shrug of the shoulders. According to this perspective, we would 'treat code-based environmental disasters – like the loss of privacy, like the censorship of censorware filters, like the disappearance of an intellectual commons – as if they were produced by gods, not by Man' (Lessig 2006: 338). But there is little need for this kind of fatalism: the internet is not a spiritual or transcendent object but a built environment based on the visions and actions of a range of architects. Mueller is quite right to emphasise that the history of the internet has not been predetermined and that its future is something to be contested: 'Those who projected that the state will automatically wither away in this sphere were clearly wrong. Those who rationalize as inevitable a reversion to a bordered and controlled Internet dominated by states are also wrong. Nothing is inevitable. Whatever happens, we will make happen' (Mueller 2010: 254).

In order to preserve and build on the democratic possibilities of the internet, we need therefore to have a robust notion of regulation for the public good that aims to halt the increasing enclosure of online spaces. Not all regulation is about banning content, spying on users or enforcing proprietary property relations. It is interesting that when the internet's underlying principles of openness and decentralisation are severely threatened, many commentators, including those traditionally reluctant to involve government, turn to the state for support and action. Zittrain argues, for example, that traditional regulators may be required 'when mere generosity of spirit among people of goodwill cannot resolve conflict'

(2009: 246), while Tim Berners-Lee, the founder of the Web, insists that net neutrality is essential to preserve a dynamic, innovative and egalitarian internet when these principles are threatened by the 'walled gardens' and 'closed silos' of social networks, proprietary programmes and insulated apps (Berners-Lee 2010). This requires an understanding of and a commitment to forms of regulation that are *not* subservient to corporate pressure, government priorities or elite control but, indeed, regulatory actions that are required precisely to fend off the distortion of the public good by special interests. And what else, other than a democratically accountable and fully representative state, would be capable of providing this? This may not be the state we have and therefore not the regulation to which we are currently exposed, but it is certainly the one to which we should aspire.

References

Anderson, C. (2010) 'The Web Is Dead: Long Live the Internet', *Wired*, September.

Ang, P. H. (2008) 'International Regulation of Internet Content: Possibilities and Limits', in W. Drake and E. Wilson III (eds) *Governing Global Electronic Networks: International Perspectives on Policy and Power*, Cambridge, MA: MIT Press, 305–30.

Army Counterintelligence Center (2008) 'Wikileaks.org – An Online Reference to Foreign Intelligence Services, Insurgents, or Terrorist Groups?', 18 March. Online. Available HTTP: <http://mirror.wikileaks.info/leak/us-intel-wikileaks.pdf> (accessed 18 January 2011).

Barlow, J. P. (1996) *A Cyberspace Independence Declaration*, 9 February. Online. Available HTTP: <http://w2.eff.org/Censorship/Internet_censorship_bills/barlow_0296.declaration> (accessed 13 January 2011).

Bell, E. (2009) 'Digital Media Cannot Be Contained by the Analogue Rulebook', *Media Guardian*, 23 March.

Benkler, Y. (2006) *The Wealth of Networks: How Social Production Transforms Markets and Freedom*, New Haven: Yale University Press.

Berners-Lee, T. (2010) 'Long Live the Web: A Call for Continued Open Standards and Neutrality', *Scientific American*, 22 November. Online. Available HTTP: <http://www.scientific.american.com/article.cfm?id=long-live-the-web> (accessed 5 January 2011).

Castells, M. (2001) *The Internet Galaxy: Reflections on the Internet, Business and Society*, Oxford: Oxford University Press.

——(2009) *Communication Power*, Oxford: Oxford University Press.

Cerf, V. (2002) 'The Internet Is for Everyone', *Internet Society*, April. Online. Available HTTP: <http://www.ietf.org/rfc/rfc3271.txt> (accessed 11 April 2010).

Collins, R. (2009) *Three Myths of Internet Governance: Making Sense of Networks, Governance and Regulation*, London: Intellect.

Daly, M. (2003) 'Governance and Social Policy', *Journal of Social Policy* 32 (1): 113–28.

de Bossey, C. (2005) 'Report of the Working Group on Internet Governance', June, 05.41622. Online. Available HTTP: <www.wgig.org/docs/WGIGREPORT.pdf> (accessed 5 January 2011).

Doctorow, C. (2010) 'Digital Economy Act: This Means War', guardian.co.uk, 16 April. Online. Available HTTP: <http://www.guardian.co.uk/technology/2010/apr/16/digital-economy-act-cory-doctorow?intcmp=239> (accessed 18 January 2011).

Downes, L. (2009) *The Laws of Disruption: Harnessing the New Forces that Govern Life and Business in the Digital Age*, New York: Basic Books.

Dyson, E. (1998) *Release 2.1: A Design for Living in the Digital Age*, London: Penguin.

European Commission (EC) (2010) 'Audiovisual Media Services Directive (2010/13/EU)', *Official Journal of the European Union*, 15 April, Brussels: EC.

Falque-Pierrotin, I. and Baup, L. (2007) 'Forum des droit sur l'internet: An Example from France', in C. Moller and A. Amouroux (eds) *Governing the Internet: Freedom and Regulation in the OSCE Region*, Vienna: OSCE, 163–78.

Federal Communications Commission (FCC) (2005) *Internet Policy Statement*, FCC 05–151. Washington, DC: FCC.

Foucault, M. (1977) *Discipline and Punish*, London: Allen Lane.

Franklin, M. I. (2009) 'Who's Who in the "Internet Governance Wars": Hail the "Phantom Menace"?' *International Studies Review* 11: 221–26.

——(2010) 'Digital Dilemmas: Transnational Politics in the Twenty-First Century', *Brown Journal of World Affairs* 16 (2), Spring/Summer: 67–85.

Freedman, D. (2008) *The Politics of Media Policy*, Cambridge: Polity.

Friedman, T. (2000) *The Lexus and the Olive Tree*, London: Harper Collins.

Froomkin, A. M. (2003) 'Habermas@Discourse.Net: Towards a Critical Theory of Cyberspace', *Harvard Law Review* 116 (3), January: 749–873.

Genachowski, J. (2010) 'Remarks on Preserving Internet Freedom and Openness', Washington, DC, 1 December. Online. Available HTTP: <http://www.openinternet.gov/speech-remarks-on-preserving-internet-freedom-and-openness.html> (accessed 5 January 2011).

Gilmore, J. (1993) John Gilmore's home page. Online. Available HTTP: <http://www.toad.com/gnu/> (accessed 15 January 2011).

Goldsmith, J. and Wu, T. (2006) *Who Controls the Internet? Illusions of a Borderless World*, Oxford: Oxford University Press.

Goodman, A. (2010) 'President Obama's Christmas Gift to AT&T (and Comcast and Verizon)', *truthdig*, 21 December. Online. Available HTTP: <http://www.truthdig.com/report/item/president_obamas_christmas_gift_to_att_and_comcast_and_verizon_20101221/> (accessed 5 January 2011).

Halliday, J. (2010) 'ISPs Should Be Free to Abandon Net Neutrality, Says Ed Vaizey', guardian.co.uk, 17 November. Online. Available HTTP: <http://www.guardian.co.uk/technology/2010/nov/17/net-neutrality-ed-vaizey> (accessed 19 November 2010).

Hals, T. (2010) 'WikiLeaks Shows Reach and Limits of Internet Speech', Reuters, 9 December. Online. Available HTTP: <http://www.reuters.com/article/idUSTRE6B85I420101209> (accessed 21 January 2011).

IFEX (2010) 'News Media and Websites Censored and Blocked for Carrying Leaked Cables', 20 December. Online. Available HTTP: <http://www.ifex.org/international/2010/12/20/news_websites_censored/> (accessed 21 January 2011).

Internet Society (2010) Letter to Commission on Science and Technology for Development, n.d. Online. Available HTTP: <http://isoc.org/wp/newsletter/files/2010/12/IGF-Working-Group-Decision1.pdf> (accesssed 20 January 2011).

Johnson, D. R. and Post, D. G. (1996) 'Law and Borders: The Rise of Law in Cyberspace', *Stanford Law Review* 48 (5): 1367–1402.

Kelly, K. (1995) *Out of Control: The New Biology of Machines*, London: Fourth Estate.

Kirchgaessner, S. (2010) 'Internet Rules Stir Republicans', FT.com, 2 December. Online. Available HTTP: <www.ft.com/cms/s/0/2df10252-fe57–11df-abac-00144feab49a.html> (accessed 5 January 2011).

Lessig, L. (2006) *Code 2.0*, New York: Basic Books.

Lewis, J. (2010) 'Sovereignty and the Role of Government in Cyberspace', *Brown Journal of World Affairs* 16 (2), Spring/Summer: 55–65.

Livingstone, S. (2010) 'Interactive, Engaging but Unequal: Critical Conclusions from Internet Studies', in J. Curran (ed.) *Mass Media and Society*, London: Bloomsbury, 122–42.

McQuail, D. (2005) *Mass Communication Theory*, 5th edn, London: Sage.

Mayo, J. et al. (2010) 'How to Regulate the Internet Tap', *New York Times*, 21 April. Online. Available HTTP: <www.nytimes.com/2010/04/21/opinion/21mayo.html> (accessed 27 April 2010).

Mueller, M. (1999) 'ICANN and Internet Governance: Sorting through the Debris of "Self-regulation"', *Info: The Journal of Policy, Regulation and Strategy for Telecommunications, Information and Media* 1 (6), December: 497–520.

——(2002) *Ruling the Root: Internet Governance and the Taming of Cyberspace*, Cambridge, MA: MIT Press.

——(2010) *Networks and States: The Global Politics of Internet Governance*, Cambridge, MA: MIT Press.

Negroponte, N. (1996) *Being Digital*, London: Coronet.

Nichols, J. (2010) 'In a Year of Deep Disappointments, the Deepest: Obama Pledged to Protect Internet Freedom; but His FCC Put It at Risk', *The Nation*, 31 December. Online. Available HTTP: <http://www.thenation.com/blog/157255/year-deep-disappointments-deepest-obama-pledged-protect-internet-freedom-his-fcc-put-it-> (accessed 5 January 2011).

OECD (2010) 'The Role of Internet Intermediaries in Advancing Public Policy Objectives', 16 June. Online. Available HTTP: <www.oecd.org/sti/ict/intermediaries> (accessed 5 January 2011).

Ofcom (2010) *Traffic Management and 'Net Neutrality'*, discussion document, 24 June, London: Ofcom.

Ohmae, K. (1995) *The End of the Nation State*, London: Harper Collins.

Ó Siochrú, S., Girard, B. and Mahan, A. (2002) *Global Media Governance: A Beginner's Guide*, Lanham, MD: Rowman & Littlefield.

Palmer, M. (2009) 'Google Tries to Avoid the Regulatory Noose', FT.com, 21 May, Online. Available HTTP: <http://www.ft.com/cms/s/0/cd5cf33c-452b-11de-b6c8-00144feabdc0.html#axzz1BIIP4ZGT> (accessed 15 January 2011).

Raboy, M., Landry, N. and Shtern, J. (2010) *Digital Solidarities, Communication Policy and Multi-stakeholder Global Governance: The Legacy of the World Summit on the Information Society*, New York: Peter Lang.

Robbins, P. (2009) Comments to the Westminster eForum, 'Taming the Wild Web?' – Online Content Regulation, 11 February. London: Westminster eForum.

Rosen, J. (2008) 'Google's Gatekeepers', *New York Times*, 30 November. Online. Available HTTP: <http://www.nytimes.com/2008/11/30/magazine/30google-t.html> (accessed 2 December 2008).

Rowbottom, J. (2006) 'Media Freedom and Political Debate in the Digital Era', *Modern Law Review* 69 (4), July: 489–513.

Schatz, A. (2010) 'Lobbying War over Net Heats Up', WSJ.com, 10 December. Online. Available HTTP: <http://online.wsj.com/.../SB10001424052748704720804576009713669482024.html> (accessed 5 January 2011).

Schatz, A. and Raice, S. (2010) 'Internet Gets New Rules of the Road', *Wall Street Journal*, 22 December.

Sonne, P. and Miller, J. (2010) 'EU Chews on Web Cookies', WSJ.com, 22 November. Online. Available HTTP: <http://online.wsj.com/.../SB10001424052748704444430457 5628610624607130.html> (accessed 5 January 2011).

Spar, D. (2001) *Ruling the Waves: Cycles of Discovery, Chaos, and Wealth from the Compass to the Internet*, New York: Harcourt.

Sunstein, C. (2002) *Republic.com*, Princeton: Princeton University Press.

Sylvain, O. (2010) 'Internet Governance and Democratic Legitimacy', *Federal Communications Law Journal* 62 (2): 205–73.

Tambini, D., Leonardi, D. and Marsden, C. (2007) *Codifying Cyberspace: Communications Self-regulation in the Age of Internet Convergence*, New York: Routledge.

Van Heuvelen, B. (2007) 'The Internet is Making Us Stupid', salon.com, 7 November. Online. Available HTTP: <http://www.salon.com/news/feature/2007/11/07/sunstein> (accessed 5 January 2011).

Warman, M. (2010) 'Ed Vaizey: My overriding Priority Is an Open Internet', telegraph.co.uk, 20 November. Online. Available HTTP: <http://www.telegraph.co.uk/technology/internet/8147661/Ed-Vaizey-My-overriding-priority-is-an-open-internet.html> (accessed 5 January 2011).

Webster, F. (2006) *Theories of the Information Society*, 3rd edn, London: Routledge.

Williams, R. (1974) *Television: Technology and Cultural Form*, London: Fontana.

Wu, T. (2010) *The Master Switch: The Rise and Fall of Information Empires*, New York: Knopf.

Zittrain, J. (2009) *The Future of the Internet*, London: Penguin.

Part III

Internet and power

Chapter 5

The internet and social networking

Natalie Fenton

The growth in social networking sites and their usage has been phenomenal. In 2011 Facebook was second only to Google as the world's most popular website (http://www.hitwise.co.uk) and it gained this status in a remarkably short time. Nielsen research (2010) shows that 22 per cent of all time spent on the internet is now spent on social networking sites. Other research shows that the average global daily time spent on Facebook is 25 minutes, as compared to 5 minutes for a popular news site (www.alexa.com, September 2009). In 2010 Facebook had over 500 million users – one in 13 people on earth – with over 250 million people logging on every day (http://www.onlineschools.org/blog/facebook-obsession/, April 2011). Social networking is an activity that is more popular with the young: 48 per cent of 18- to 34-year-olds check Facebook when they wake up, with 28 per cent doing so before even getting out of bed (http://www.onlineschools.org/blog/facebook-obsession/, April 2011). The popularity of and time spent on these sites and others that encourage active production and are characterised by a high level of interactivity have brought about new rituals of communication and prompted media theorists to reconsider the traditional contexts of mass communication and the traditional (and previously often separate) concerns of production, text and reception. In this newly communicative context the audience is described as 'prod-users' (Bruns 2008) or 'pro-sumers' (Tapscott and Williams 2008: 124–50), to account for the creative and interactive nature of much online activity.

Digital media, and the internet in particular, are transforming our means of gathering information and communicating with each other and contributing to both these practices through creative production. In informational terms, use of the internet clearly has the *potential* to influence the capacity of 'ordinary' citizens and resource-poor social or political groups to gain information and expertise through vastly increasing the range of information that is freely available to any internet user, on virtually any subject imaginable (Bimber 2002). In communicational terms, sites like YouTube (the video-sharing website) or MySpace (the home page-creation website) have acquired billions of users in only a couple of years, largely by 'word of mouth' – or, at least, via millions of communications carried out through online social contacts. At the time of writing Facebook has more than 500 million people active on the site – connecting with others, sharing thoughts and discussing concerns, forming groups and joining forces with others in mutual interests and activities. Twitter – the site that allows people to connect to others and follow their stream of thought through linked communications no more than 140 characters long – currently (December 2011) has over 100 million active users, with over 250 million tweets being sent every day attempting to prompt a particular ordering of information and the prioritising of certain subject matters (Infographic 2010).

These social networking sites are also claimed to break down the barriers between traditionally public and private spheres of communication, putting power into the hands of the user and thereby giving the details of private concerns a public presence and enabling the public domain of the official political and institutional realm to be more easily monitored by the private citizen (Papacharissi 2009). Hence, social networking brings forth a means of communication that is for the public, by the public (e.g. Rheingold 2002; Gillmor 2004; Beckett 2008; Shirky 2008). These theorists proffer positive interpretations that refer to social networking sites or person-to-person media or mass self-communication (Castells 2009) as both supporting the maintenance of pre-existing social networks while also helping strangers to connect on the basis of shared interests, political views or activities. In this manner social networking sites are heralded as novel, pervasive and conferring agency.

On the other hand, there are those who propose a more critical assessment, viewing the form and nature of communication on display as no more than an incessant version of a 'daily me' (Sunstein 2007) that personalises and depoliticises public issues and simply re-emphasises old inequalities while feeding corporations the necessary data for online marketing, business promotion and the exploitation of private affairs – a specifically anti-democratic turn leading to civic privatism. This approach emphasises political economic concerns, reminding us that the internet does not transcend global capitalism but is deeply involved with it by virtue of the corporate interests it supports and the discourses of capitalism and neoliberalism in which the people who use it are drenched (see Chapter 4). In this manner social networking is claimed to further inscribe the neoliberal production of self in forms of mediation that are deeply commodified while also being conducive to sociality. In other words, in developed Western democracies, where social media exist within social and political contexts that foreground individualisation, embedded in technological developments that encourage pervasive communication and an ever-connected online presence, social networking sites are seen as extending neoliberal ideology rather than contesting it.

Situating a discussion in a sterile binary framework, with the optimists on one side and the pessimists on the other, is often how debates on new technologies begin (whether referring to the radio, television or the computer). But both approaches in isolation are reductive (either in relation to technology or in relation to largely political economic factors) and can never fully appreciate the form of communication they are commenting upon. As a result, each approach misunderstands the nature and impact of the media (in this case, of digital social media) on the social and political contours of contemporary life, and in doing so misunderstands the nature of the social and the political and the complexity of power therein. Part of this misunderstanding comes from a media centrism that resists a deep and critical contextualisation of social and political life. As Couldry (2003) has suggested, once the media (in any form) presents itself as the centre of society and we organise our lives and orient our daily rituals and practice towards it, we run the risk of falling prey to 'the myth of the mediated centre' (2003: 47). Media rituals not only stress the significance of media but also allude to the importance of being 'in the media' and of being able to communicate your message to others – whether this be for financial, political or social gain. The more powerful and influential you are, the better placed you are to get your message across. The internet and social networking push this argument one step further. The millions of people who use social networking sites inhabit a mediated world that offers the possibility of more control than mainstream media, is mobile, interactive and holds endless creative potential, but is nonetheless mythic. The claimed ubiquity of the internet and social media stresses the significance of always being tuned in and online. The seductive power of this mythic centre circulates around social life and serves to obscure the reproduction of the dominant values of neoliberal society.

Once this is appreciated it has ramifications for media theory – in particular in situating the destabilisation of the old producer/consumer divide in a broader and deeper context that can recognise and take account of communicational life without fetishising the media forms that may enable it. In resisting a fetishised media centrism we are also encouraged to rethink the relationship between structure and agency, between political economic approaches and their relationship to those that emphasise the constructive ability of individuals, the importance of subjectivities and the relevance of identity. It is in this critical contextual frame that we need to understand mediation and its relationship to our social and cultural practices. In the rest of this chapter I offer a critical consideration of the four main arguments that seek to place the internet and social networking at the centre of this mythology.

Social media are communication led rather than information driven

Social networking sites operate through organic networks. Each user sends an invitation to join a particular community, whether to an individual or to an entire group, who are then encouraged to pass it on to their own network of friends. In this manner the networks can expand extremely quickly (e.g. Haythornthwaite 2005). As Papacharissi (2010) notes, social media have been invested with the ability to facilitate the development of strong relations with family members and friends and weaker relations with a range of acquaintances (Ellison, Steinfield and Lampe 2007). There is no doubt that the act of digital self-communication has become part of many people's everyday rituals. The daily rhythms and activities of life are informed by, punctuated by and inhabited by social media. As we post our photographs on Flickr, discuss the latest film on Facebook, alert people to a nugget of information on Twitter, we have a sense that we are participating in something that is going on out there; that rather than being told what to do or what to think through the linear provision of information, we can join in the telling through a pulsating network of digital social communication.

This is neither straightforward interactivity nor simple participation in a network but participation in a communicative act for a complex range of purposes that may be personal or public, social, political or cultural; or any or all of these at once (Papacharissi 2010). Social networking sites such as Facebook are only one aspect of the multi-faceted phenomena of social media that allow a click and link process to a news site, to a YouTube video, to a blog, to Twitter, sending links directly from your internet-enabled phone, through your social network site, in a thoroughly converged mediated experience. It is a form of communicative experience based on a sense of participation that is claimed to offer a sense of ownership that incurs emotional involvement (Donath 2007) through a commonly shared understanding of protocol and conduct that frames the network and speaks to identities that are reflexive, mobile and performative. Communicative involvement is the primary motivation and its aim is to perform the self anywhere at anytime, on whatever mode the sender decrees. Clearly, communication is never just about the act of communicating, and communicational desires and informational requirements often overlap. But in social networking the need to be linked in, to feel at once connected and in control of your forms of interaction and means of self-expression and, ultimately, the creative promotion of self, is argued to gain in importance.

This resonates with many people's knowledge and practice of social media and brings to the fore the affective dimension of communication that is critical to our understanding of contemporary mediated experiences. A form of media that is communication led rather than content driven highlights the psychological and personal incentives of interaction and participation over and above the politics of media content for public consumption. Social media is a form of communication that is, above all, connective, and this has tended to dominate much of the early writing on it. Because it is social and is felt to begin with the individual user choosing to communicate with whomsoever they desire, it also confers a high degree of autonomy to the communicator. This increased sociality is said to bring new understandings, as we are increasingly subjected to a wider range of viewpoints and encouraged to deliberate freely within a variety of networks. The enhanced autonomy is said to bring improved levels of power and control to the user. We should, however, remember that people rarely have democratic enhancement at the top of their agendas and use the internet far more for entertainment purposes than for informational gain (Althaus and Tewksbury 2000; Shah, Kwak and Holbert 2001). Neither should acknowledgement of the communicational intensity of social media devalue the importance of the political and the economic context in which this increased sociality takes place.

Put another way, in emphasising communicational desires and motivations – the need to connect and relate to others (which we should acknowledge as a major facet of social networking and part of its vast success) – we should not fall into the trap of diminishing the importance of who is communicating what to whom. A consideration of *who* is communicating is a sobering exercise. Usage of social media is highly uneven amongst participants and much content is dominated by a small percentage of people. A recent survey by the Harvard Business school (Heil and Piskorski 2009) found that 10 per cent of Twitter users generate more than 90 per cent of the content and most people have only tweeted once. The top 10 per cent are dominated by celebrities or mainstream media corporations such as CNN. Other recent statistics (Infographic 2010) show that 97 per cent of twitterers have fewer than 100 followers, with the likes of Britney Spears attracting 4.7 million. Participation, it seems, is still the preserve of a few.

A consideration of *what* they are communicating shows that the means to self-expression have also been found to be carefully controlled impressions of the self, structured around class affiliation (Papacharissi 2002a; 2002b; 2009) and cultures of taste (Liu 2007). This research suggests that, far from broadening our communicational horizons and deliberative understandings, social media work to reinforce already existing social hierarchies and further strengthen close(d) communities. Furthermore, it has also been argued that social networking sites predetermine content in a manner that prioritises consumption over friendship and community building, as Marwick (2005) points out:

> First, the rigid profile structure encourages the user to present him or herself in a way that is partly constructed by the application, not the user. [...] Secondly, the way that profiles are structured is not neutral; rather, power is embedded throughout the applications in a variety of ways. Generally, the user is portrayed not as a citizen, but as a consumer [...] applications encourage people to define themselves through the entertainment products they consume: music, movies, books, and television shows. [...] Not only are users treated as consumers, they are encouraged to consume others in a concept of networking that privileges social capital over friendship or community building. 'Networking', in business terms, is a goal-oriented process in which one's social circle is constantly expanded in order to connect with as many people as possible, in order to gain business advantages. [...] Third, SNSs [social networking sites] inherently exclude certain segments of the world population. For instance, the majority of sites are American applications that attract primarily US users.
>
> (Marwick 2005: 9–11)

For Castells (2009), the internet is shaped by a conflict between the global multimedia business networks that try to commodify it and the 'creative audience' that tries to establish a degree of citizen control over it and to declare its right to communicative freedom without corporate control or interference. He describes how all the corporate giants are

> trying to figure out how to re-commodify Internet-based autonomous mass self-communication. They are experimenting with ad-supported sites, pay sites, free streaming video portals, and pay portals. [...] Web 2.0 technologies empowered consumers to produce and distribute their own content. The viral success of these technologies propelled media organizations to harness the production power of traditional consumers.
>
> (Castells 2009: 97)

The capacity for social media to bring into existence multiple and diverse voices with an apparent unprecedented autonomy in the modes of communication is frequently claimed to be a central facet of the productive creativity of the prod-user. But all of our online comings and goings leave digital footprints that can be tracked, analysed and commodified. In this manner, the dense matrix of information created through social media increases concentration and aids deep commodification (Fuchs 2009a).

In this vein, Castells (2009) subjects to economic critique the global multimedia giants – Apple, Bertelsmann, CBS, Disney, Google, Microsoft, NBC Universal, News Corporation, Time Warner, Yahoo! Amongst these global corporate giants he reveals 'increasing economic concentration, the usage of a diversity of platforms, the customization and segmentation of audiences, and economies of synergy' (Fuchs 2009a: 97). Creative capacity is, as he acknowledges, shaped, controlled and curtailed by the growing concentration and integration of corporate media and network operators around the world. Geveran (2009) also notes how social marketing is among the newest advertising trends now emerging on the internet. Using online social networks such as Facebook or MySpace, marketers can send personalised promotional messages featuring an ordinary customer to that customer's friends. Because they reveal a customer's browsing and buying patterns, and because they feature implied endorsements, the messages raise significant concerns about disclosure of personal matters, information quality and individuals' ability to control the commercial exploitation of their identity.

The concept of autonomy has a long history and is frequently connected to acts of resistance and the ability to rise above dominant ideologies and 'be yourself'. It is useful to note Castoriadis' (1991) distinction between individualistic autonomy, social autonomy (through equality of participation) and autonomy as political subjectivity (that liberates the imagination). In this critique of autonomy, Castoriadis confronts autonomy within the system of neoliberal capitalism (individualist), as opposed to autonomy that seeks to challenge the system (social) or transcend the system (through political subjectivity). Of course, while these theoretical distinctions are useful in enabling us to interrogate the term, in daily life, facilitated by converged media, we may well engage in all three forms of autonomy at once. So I may go on to my social networking site and comment on the latest celebrity gossip story, then click and link my way to a petition on ending child poverty while updating my blog that tells everyone what I've just done and how I think the world could be a better place. As both Papacharissi (2010) and Fuchs (2009a) signal, this chimes with Habermas' (1996) understanding of 'the co-originality of private autonomy and public autonomy' (1996: 104) – though they may be opposed, they are internally related and 'reciprocally presuppose each other' (Habermas 1996: 417). In other words, it acknowledges the deep context in which any form of autonomy is situated and seeks to understand its various manifestations in relation to it. Autonomy enacted through communication-led media may in fact amount to little more than an active endorsement of individualisation and an extension of a neoliberal approach that prioritises the self, and seeks to market the self and reproduce the self in myriad ways for the sole advantage of the self.

Castells' (2009) own empirical results seem to suggest that digital citizens are far from being autonomous from capital. As Fuchs (2009b: 95) points out, 'on the vast majority of platforms that they visit, their data and usage behaviour is stored and assessed in order to generate profit by targeted advertising. Indeed, the users who google data, upload or watch videos on YouTube, upload or browse personal images on Flickr, or accumulate friends with whom they exchange content or communicate online via social networking platforms like MySpace or Facebook, constitute an "audience commodity" (Smythe 1994) that is sold to advertisers. The difference between the audience commodity of traditional mass media and of the internet is that on the internet the users are also content producers'. The contemporary turn of phrase 'user-generated content' is a catch-all description of the endless creative activity, communication, community building and content production online. But this still does not escape the fact that this user activity is commodified in precisely the way we argued in Chapter 4. In fact we are excessively and ever more deeply commodified as so much more of our daily habits and rituals take an IT form. Again as Fuchs (2009b: 31) notes, during much of the time that users spend online, they produce 'profit for large corporations like Google, News Corporation (which owns MySpace), or Yahoo! (which owns Flickr). Advertisements on the internet are frequently personalized – this is made possible by the surveillance of, storing of, and assessing of user activities and user data with the help of computers and databases'. The audience-turned-producer does not, in this context, signify a democratisation of the media towards a truly participatory system. It certainly does not confer autonomy from capital but, rather, the profound and subcybernetic commodification of online human creativity.

Zittrain (2009) also worries about a shift in control of our technological environment away from individuals and towards consolidated private gate-keepers and commercial enterprises seeking to harness profit and retain brand, while all the time the wider environment is also controllable by state regulators. The private spaces in which we exert our creative autonomy are gradually being ensnared by commercial enterprises as spaces of commercial transaction (Fuchs, 2009b). Seen from this angle, the participation and autonomy that have been heralded as revolutionary could also amount to the automatic co-creation of consumer profiles (e.g. Hamelink 2000; Turrow 2001).

Social media allow or encourage deliberation and dissent through multiplicity and polycentrality

An emphasis on communication and the multiple ways in which this can now take place with a variety of people through social media is suggestive of the pluralisation of social relationships as discussed above; but social media are also claimed to aid democracy through an increase in the sheer number of spaces available for deliberation and dissent. This is an argument for information abundance freed from the shackles of a mass communication system that broadcast from one to many.

Within online discussion research, some scholars argue that internet communication expands our horizons and broadens our understandings by offering a multitude of sites for debate among persons of varied opinions and beliefs. Holt (2004) states that the ability of the internet to unite those of disparate backgrounds has great potential for fostering debate and discussion of issues in the civic arena. Furthermore, research has shown that online political discussion serves to expose participants to non-likeminded partners (Brundidge 2006). Yet, despite the potential of the internet to bring opposing camps together in a common space and provide exposure to different ideas, other evidence suggests that, looked at from a different vantage point, this may not necessarily be occurring. The structure of the internet has been found to offer conditions particularly conducive to selective exposure to media content (Bimber and Davis 2003). For example, on Friendster and MySpace particular cultural tastes and reference points are carefully displayed and managed to indicate a clear sense of relation to particular cultures and allegiance to certain groups (Liu 2007). Some evidence indicates that selective exposure also occurs in online political discussion arenas, which may lead to political polarisation. For example, scholars have noted that virtual communities are fairly homogeneous in terms of values and viewpoints (Dahlberg and Siapera 2007), and that participants in an online discussion often hold comparable political perspectives (Wilhelm 1999). For members of social networking sites, belonging to certain networks and not to others is also felt to communicate social status (Papacharissi 2009).

Multiplicity, or sheer abundance of information available to us, has also been argued to breed misinformation and lack of understanding (Patterson 2010) because the daily habits and rituals of news have changed. People are no longer required to sit in front of the television for a set period of time each day or to read the newspaper over breakfast. Instead we do news snacking. But there are so many other more tempting treats on offer that 'healthy' news snacking is rapidly replaced by the more immediately gratifying tasty tit-bits of entertainment. Even more worryingly, Patterson identifies a pattern whereby, in a high-choice media environment, the less-well informed are more inclined to opt for entertainment while the better-informed include the news junkies, leading to increasing inequality of knowledge between the more-informed and the less-informed. Patterson (2010: 20) also argues that speed 'increases sensation but decreases learning', noting that about 60 per cent of those who regularly read a daily newspaper spend at least half an hour doing so, compared to only 40 per cent of those who read an online daily newspaper.

This raises important issues for news and information in a world of social media where genre categories are also blurred and often difficult to tell apart. How do you distinguish between the facts – albeit contextualised and problematised – and the noise and increasing and ever-expanding volume of comment, opinion and propaganda? In Alexander Wolfe's column on InformationWeek, he addresses the issues and overwhelming impact of real-time live-citizen journalism:

> Indeed, the sheer volume of 'mumbai' tweets would seem to militate against the notion that there's anything of value easily accessible within. Since going through the first 100 pages of tweets only takes you back several hours, I did random searches on postings from Wed., Nov. 25; Thurs., Nov. 27, and Friday, Nov. 28, and couldn't come up with much hard information.

Another argument is the same in reverse – that there is so much audience content online that it enables journalists to see a broader world and connect with a wider range of news sources that will ultimately democratise the news product itself. But Örnebring (2008: 783) finds that even when audience content gained from sources such as social media is used as a means of generating news stories, it is usually in a very restricted range of areas: 'the overall impression is that users are mostly empowered to create popular culture-oriented content and personal/everyday life-oriented content rather than news/informational content'.

Further research in the UK by the Carnegie Trust (2010) found evidence of diminishing arenas for public deliberation, along with the marginalisation of dissent, especially in relation to those who lack power or confidence to voice their concerns or those who have non-mainstream views. This narrowing of the public sphere appears to be happening despite the expansion of mediated space and a multiplicity of media platforms and claims regarding interactivity, speed and the international reach of online communications.

Polycentrality, the notion that power is spread more widely in an environment where anyone can set up a website, can also be challenged on the grounds that social and political elites have greater cultural and economic capital at their disposal to harness the power of social media to their advantage. It is inevitable that as soon as a form of technology is seen to be a useful means of relaying information and connecting with people, particularly people who may otherwise not engage with their message, then political elites will try to find ways of exploiting it to their advantage. So political leaders post video blogs on YouTube, senior politicians apparently Twitter their way through their days while attempting to perform their political duties. On 30 December 2008 Twitter was used as a real-time news conference podium by the Consulate General of Israel in New York and featured on the news and commentary blog Israel Politik. David Saranga, Israel Consul of Media and Public Affairs in New York, answered questions regarding the situation in the Middle East in relation to Israel and Gaza and all parties involved. Questions were submitted to its Twitter account, @IsraelConsulate, and attempts were made to respond to the questions through the 140-character limit, with those requiring lengthy answers being posted on the Israel Politik blog. When asked why it chose to go on Twitter, the Israeli consulate said that it saw debate on Twitter and saw people who had unreliable information. It felt, in response, that Twitter would be a good way to put an official voice out there. This is now common practice.

Barack Obama's Twitter account brought up-to-the-minute information on the US President elect's life and activities before and after the election. Other presidential candidates soon jumped on the social media bandwagon, and continue to use blogs and Twitter, along with other microblog tools, to get their messages out to the public, creating the next generation of 'transparent' politicians. Similarly, as a mass medium that is often working directly alongside other converged media, the internet is also claimed to replicate the same types of control and function, with the same types of commercial concerns, as any other medium (Margolis, Resnick and Tu 1997; McChesney 1996), thereby reproducing homogeneity of content rather than challenging existing structures.

Research in this vein (e.g. Agre 2002; Hindman 2009) indicates that social media do not deliver the liberatory potential through multiplicity and polycentrality that they are said to possess. Rather, romanticised retrospectives of past and future civic engagement frequently impose language and expectations that misrepresent what actually happens in the mediations of the present. More pointedly, Andrejevic (2008: 612) argues that 'the trumpeting of the subversive power of interactivity contributes to the deployment of what might be described as "the mass society repressive hypothesis" which pays lip service to revolution even as it stimulates the productivity of consumer labor'.

Of course this should not undermine the ability of social media as a potential route to counter-expression in authoritarian regimes or developing democracies. The need to take control of one's own life in developed capitalist neoliberal democracies is quite different from the need to claim control in oppressive regimes where it is difficult to get information out and dangerous to express political subjectivity. In such countries, the use of social media has undoubtedly enabled otherwise repressed voices to be heard. In February 2005, the Nepalese government shut down all international internet connections after the king imposed martial law, though they were only down for a short time. During that time, many technologically creative people were able to get some information out via social media channels. The government shutdown of internet connections inside and outside Burma (Myanmar) in 2007 led to overwhelming support from outside of the country to get news and information to the world through social media tools, especially blogs, Twitter and Flickr, creating a form of underground network for internet communications and social media (see Chapter 6). Similarly, in Egypt in 2011, protesters used social media like Facebook and Twitter to garner momentum for attendance at demonstrations and spread news of the revolution to the rest of the world. Even when Egyptian authorities shut off internet access, speak2tweet enabled people to call through their messages, which were recorded and put out instantly on Twitter using the hashtag #Egypt (see Chapter 2).

Social media are predicated on self-communication to a mass audience

For Castells, a novel quality of communication in contemporary society is mass self-communication. This builds on the positive proclamations of multiplicity and polycentrality but centres more directly on the enhanced power of the individual:

> It is mass communication because it can potentially reach a global audience, as in the posting of a video on YouTube, a blog with RSS links to a number of web sources, or a message to a massive e-mail list. At the same time, it is self-communication because the production of the message is self-generated, the definition of the potential receiver(s) is self-directed, and the retrieval of specific messages or content from the World Wide Web and electronic networks is self-selected. The three forms of communication (interpersonal, mass communication, and mass self communication) coexist, interact, and complement each other rather than substituting for one another. What is historically novel, with considerable consequences for social organization and cultural change, is the articulation of all forms of communication into a composite, interactive, digital hypertext that includes, mixes, and recombines in their diversity the whole range of cultural expressions conveyed by human interaction.
>
> (Castells 2009: 55, see also p. 70)

The personalised content provided by social media, the ability to be publicly private and privately public (Papacharissi 2009), retains an emphasis on the self and on personhood rather than citizenship. In their private sphere (as defined by themselves) people connect with others on the basis of shared social, political and cultural agendas. Here, importantly, they experience mutuality, closeness and empathy (Coleman 2005) that may be lacking elsewhere in advanced capitalist societies. The spaces afforded by social media are mobile – they could be in train stations, cafés, the workplace or on the bus – but they allow for acts of association that bring with them notions of being in control, having autonomy and expressing the self. They frequently serve as alternatives to face-to-face interaction within or across networks, locally, nationally or globally, and have been linked to the generation of social capital (Hampton and Wellman 2001, 2003). An increase in emphasis of the values of self-expression certainly seems to point to the development of new social habits. And if we accept that the public and private spheres are ever overlapping and interlinked in an online world, then they are also likely to have political consequences too.

Castells sees mass self-communication as the 'interactive production of meaning' (2009: 132) through 'the creative audience' (2009: 127) whereby the self is realised through the creative process. He argues that in mass self-communication traditional forms of access control do not apply. Anyone can upload a video to the internet, write a blog, start a chat forum, or create an e-mail list – in other words they have creative autonomy (see Fuchs 2009a). Access in this case is the norm and blocking internet access is the exception (Castells 2009: 204). This may be true, but although in principle everyone can produce and diffuse information easily with the help of the internet, not all information is visible to the same degree and gets the same attention. Even accepting that social media engender a form of self-communication that is expressive and creative, self-communication to a mass audience is still the individual trying to be heard above the organisation, still the small organisation trying to shout louder than the large organisation. Social media cannot escape, and indeed are part of, the stratified online eyeball economy. And in this economy the traditional and the mainstream are still dominant. Mainstream news and information sites still attract the most traffic, just as certain celebrities and elites generate the largest networks.

In 2008, the year of the US presidential election, the popular success of the Obama campaign was said to be largely the result of the employment of social media. But research by the Pew Internet and American Life Project (2008) showed that a mere 10 per cent of US internet users posted political comments on social networking sites and 8 per cent posted comments on blogs. Furthermore, TV websites such as cnn.com, abcnews.com or msnbcnews.com provided the primary news source for 64 per cent of online users. The likes of news aggregator sites such as Google or Yahoo! (that draw much of their content from mainstream news organisations) were visited by 54 per cent of users, with 34 per cent using the websites of mainstream national newspapers. Digitally connected citizens still prefer the websites of major media organisations or television for information on public affairs over internet-based news organisations (Kohut 2008) or social media sites. And even when they do go to internet-based news organisations the same hierarchies apply. In our own research investigating a wide range of alternative news platforms such as Indymedia and openDemocracy as part of the broader research into new media and the news, we explored how much traffic non-mainstream, alternative sites received. Alexa traffic rankings (based on the percentage of traffic held by each website over the total amount of web traffic) put openDemocracy (an alternative news webzine) first in the league of alternative news sites at 36,694th most-visited site and Indymedia 2nd at 61,148th most-visited site.[1] BBC Online was ranked number 44, CNN Online number 52, the New York Times Online number 115 (data source: alexa.com, top 1, 000, 000, 000 sites, 2008). Even within the category of alternative news sites there was a concentration of traffic. Of the top 19 alternative news sites in Britain, the top 5 received more than double the traffic of the rest and more traffic than all the other websites put together. These sites are the ones that are better resourced and have managed to survive economically to build an audience over time. The curve of distribution for web audiences even amongst alternative media sites is very steep. Traffic is overwhelmingly directed to a few sites. The most visible websites are also the ones with the most incoming links and are more likely to have links to the mainstream media. Thus, the major platforms for political information remain the online versions of the established news sources and corporate mass media. 'Mass self-communication' via social media is clearly present and forms an important source of additional and often experiential insight, but this is framed by and subsumed under the influence of established powerful media actors.

Mass self-communication must also be understood through the social and political context of which it is a part. In advanced capitalist societies in the West, such as the US or the UK, where a politics of individualism is prevalent as part of a neoliberal approach, mass self-communication through social media is more likely to be largely self-referential and motivated by personal fulfilment (Kaye 2007; Papacharissi 2007) that is resonant of a materialistic and market-dominated culture (Scammell 2000). Indeed social media in these contexts lend themselves very neatly to what could be termed the neoliberal production of self wherein, as Margaret Thatcher once famously stated, 'there is no such thing as society, there are only individuals' – albeit a mass of individuals networked to each other. This self-expressive, thoroughly networked individual may be alone, but they are not lonely or isolated, at least not while they have their social media 'friends'. The network, the notion of unlimited, myriad connections to others, is based on the individual as a self-communicator but can also work to deny the deeper structures of inequality online. Similarly Miller (2008: 399) states that

> In the drift from blogging, to social networking, to microblogging we see a shift from dialogue and communication between actors in a network, where the point of the network was to facilitate an exchange of substantive content, to a situation where the maintenance of a network itself has become the primary focus. Here communication has been subordinated to the role of the simple maintenance of ever expanding networks and the notion of a connected presence ... The movement from blogging, to social networking,

to microblogging demonstrates the simultaneous movements away from communities, narratives, substantive communication, and towards networks, databases and phatic communion.

Phatic communications focus purely on social (networking) and not on informational or dialogic intents. As such, self-expression may well offer moments of individual control and a freeing of the creative imaginary, but it can also be fragmentary and disconnected from institutions of power. As Castells (2009) notes, we are indeed living through a paradigmatic shift in the articulation of all forms of communication that mixes and recombines forms of cultural expression while expanding the possibility for voices and their potential reach. But, the self that is given enhanced prominence in social media must not be reduced to the technological capacity of the form of communication under consideration; rather, it must be firmly understood in relation to the socio-structural context from which the means of expression is given voice and volume.

Social media offer a new form of social telling

If traditional news media have been claimed to function as a fourth estate holding the institutions of the state to account, Dutton (2007) argues that new media bring forth a new 'pro-social' dimension that exceeds the limitations of traditional media, leading to a 'Fifth Estate' that reaches beyond and moves across the boundaries of existing institutions, becoming an alternative source of news as well as a citizen-check on public life and private enterprise. In this manner they proffer a new form of social telling.

This has also been closely linked to the concept of monitorial democracy (Keane 2009), a variety of 'post representative politics' defined by the rapid growth of many different kinds of extra-parliamentary, power-scrutinising mechanisms that keep politicians, governments and political parties on their toes. Keane (2009: 15) describes monitory democracy as being indelibly linked to a digital age of multimedia-saturated societies: 'societies whose structures of power are continuously "bitten" by monitory institutions operating within a new galaxy of media defined by the ethos of communicative abundance'. Social media present a certain form of publicly private monitorial endeavour. Indeed, there are several examples of instances where a wave of twittering has caused an issue to go viral and forced a rethink by either mainstream news media, corporate business or political powers that be.

When the circumstances of the death of the gay pop star Stephen Gately, of the boy band Boyzone, were claimed by a UK *Daily Mail* tabloid newspaper columnist to be linked to his sexuality, it produced a storm of protest on Twitter, led by the celebrities Stephen Fry and Derren Brown. Fry wrote: 'I gather a repulsive nobody writing in a paper no-one with any decency would be seen dead with has written something loathsome and inhumane. Disgusted with Daily

Mail's Jan Moir? Complain where it matters. She breaches 1, 3, 5 and 12 of the code' (cited by Booth, *Guardian*, 17.10.09: p. 2). Complaints poured in to the Press Complaints Commission at the fastest rate in its history, causing its website to crash. Several mainstream newspapers reported the response and it was a point of discussion on the main BBC1 political discussion programme *Question Time*. Although it is unknown whether Jan Moir or the *Daily Mail* suffered as a consequence of this outpouring of anti-homophobic sentiment, the incident is indicative of the way in which a buzz can be created around a particular issue within a very short space of time and certain (undesirable) discourses can be subject to widespread criticism in a social media world.

In a similar demonstration of social media acting for democratic gain, an attempt to prevent the *Guardian* newspaper writing about a report on toxic waste being dumped off the Ivory Coast by the oil-trading company Trafigura, through the issuing of an injunction to keep it secret, was foiled by a combination of web users and Parliament. The *Guardian* had been embroiled in a five-week legal battle to reveal the details of the damning Minton Report, but an MP tabled a parliamentary question revealing the existence of the injunction. The lawyers operating for the oil firm, Carter-Ruck, immediately warned the newspaper that it would be in contempt of court if it published the information discussed in Parliament. The *Guardian* then ran a story on the fact that it had been prevented from publishing the proceedings of Parliament and within 12 hours bloggers had discovered the banned information (many through the WikiLeaks website – often used by whistleblowers to publish information banned by the courts in a particular country), millions of people knew of the report and Trafigura had become one of the most searched-for internet terms.

Both of these examples, notably, originated with the mainstream news media. But the novelty in this way of telling is the speed at which someone or something can be 'found out' through the search facilities of the internet as archive and library; the fact that anyone with access to a computer connected to the internet can contribute to the telling; and that the manner of being told can create an atmosphere around a particular issue or concern provoking mainstream publicity and political response. Twitter's greatest strength is its ability to provide a snapshot of what anyone is discussing, anywhere in the world, right at the time of asking. For example, in October 2009 Nick Griffin, leader of the British National Party (a far-right neo-fascist political party in the UK), made a controversial appearance on the BBC1 television discussion panel *Question Time*. At the time, a quick Google search for 'Nick Griffin' revealed some interesting results, including a profile on the BBC website and an editorial from the *Guardian* newspaper. But searching Twitter for the same term produced a detailed and compelling insight into the views of tens of thousands of people about the whole issue.

Twitter's ambition to be the pulse of the planet, allowing us to participate in a global conversation among the web community, is seductive, but this particular regime of attention is also still structured by the privileged few (Heil and Piskorski 2009). The Pew Internet and American Life Project (Smith 2010) found that the more educated you are, the more likely you are to be on Twitter. Similarly, Cellan-Jones (2009) noted how, at the G20 protests in London, Twitter was mainly used in broadcast mode to relay messages from the mainstream media. The popularity of Twitter can then also be argued to represent a concentration of power over communication, rather than the radical explosion of a two-way, peer-to-peer communication network, as has been claimed.

In October 2009 Twitter signed a deal with both Google and Microsoft to allow each company to include 'tweets' in its respective search engines as soon as they are posted, allowing real-time searching and increasing the competition between the two search engine rivals. Partnering with Twitter allows both sites to leverage data from the site's millions of active users, providing a ready-made package of real-time views and opinions at the click of a mouse. Both companies use their algorithms to try to identify the sorts of messages that users are likely to find most relevant, not just those that are posted most recently, as Twitter does with its own search service. And therein lies the rub. How do Google and Microsoft prioritise certain tweets over others? Do they have democratic intent as their ambition, or profit from advertising as their purpose?

So, do social media offer a new form of telling? Again, we have to come back to who is telling what to whom. Who is doing the telling is still dominated by a few, well-educated people who can occasionally set the news agenda but more often than not respond to the news agenda already set; rarely do they shift the framework of news. What are they telling? Are they telling tales or telling the truth? In an environment where speed is of the essence, fact checking is bound to be a casualty.

In this new form of social telling, where many voices contribute to the cacophony of online noise, digital presence is delineated both by market power and by social power. Paradoxically, it is often hard to speak in a whisper and not be overheard. The ability to trace and track information, and therefore the individuals that send it, also 'tells' the authorities and the institutions of policing and control precisely what is being said and by whom. Social media may provide a new way of telling, but in doing so they also aid surveillance and censorship – a case of us watching them watching us watching them (Khiabany 2010). As well as having an interest in and power to permanently control the online behaviour and personal data of users in order to accumulate capital with the help of targeted advertising (Fuchs 2009), corporate platform owners also hold the power to switch users off the networks or to switch off entire networks. This may be rare, but can be used to good effect. Furthermore, social media have been incorporated into police control and surveillance techniques for identifying deviants, criminals and terrorists. Rhoads and Chao (2009) discuss how the Iranian government is using social media to survey its citizens, to anticipate their plans, to identify dissidents and to counter them. They argue that when Iran keeps the internet open it does so to provide it with much richer information to spy on its citizens. Golumbia (2009) has also argued that Twitter is being used to control and monitor dissidence.

In the UK, Ofcom (2009) has published research showing that 54 per cent of 11- to 16-year-olds in the UK say young people need advice about how to keep their online personal information private. The updates of Facebook's more than 500 million users, meanwhile, could eventually provide an even richer trove of information than Twitter for the corporate giants of Google and Microsoft. Facebook users produce more than 45 million status updates each day. However, most of these are private, and hidden from search engines. But Facebook has begun a campaign to encourage users to make more of their information public, allowing access to data that can help to garner our attention for commercial gain.

As Benkler makes clear, the reversal of the economic concentrations of industrial media production is only partial; the forms of nonmarket 'sharing' Benkler celebrates, and the alternative information infrastructure they apparently enable, will, at best, exist *alongside* market-based media structures (2006: 121, 23). But that does not dim his vision of a completely new model of social storytelling; indeed he argues that 'we have an opportunity to change the way we create and exchange information, knowledge and culture' (2006: 473, cf. 162–65). But as David Harvey (2005: 3) notes, neoliberalism's endeavour to 'bring all human action into the domain of the market [requires] technologies of information creation and capacities to accumulate, store, transfer, analyse and use massive databases to guide decisions in the global marketplace – networked telecommunications and globalised neoliberalism make perfect partners'.

Thus we have to recognise that in all the radical potential of social media as social critique, as monitorial democracy, as a new way of telling, the relationship between capitalism and critique is complex. Boltanski and Chiapello (2005) suggest that critique both reinforces and transforms capitalism. Critique is always formed out of the dominant power structure and therefore always carries the socio-historic imprint of that birth. Similarly, critique must always struggle within the system that is dominant – in the case of the UK this means neoliberalism. The internet, as a technology, as a means of communication, does not transcend neoliberalism, it is part of it, although it holds the potential to expose its inadequacies. Seen in this context it is always more likely that social media will replicate and entrench social inequalities rather than liberate them. As Marwick says,

> [a]ssuming that social networks are discretely explanatory for human behaviour, then, ignores not only the influence of systemic power relations related to gender, sexuality, race, class etc. on behaviour, but also how the subject's own ability for empirical action is influenced by the larger interrelated context in which he or she is situated. Social networking applications remove these 'webs of power' while simultaneously exposing identity self-presentation and relational ties, with the result of removing value and signification from the network.
>
> (Marwick 2005: 12)

But there is a further anxiety that rests not simply on access to resources but rather on inclusion in social networks. An article in *Wired* (June 2009) about Facebook's plans to rule the world stated:

> For the last decade or so, the Web has been defined by Google's algorithms – rigorous and efficient equations that peruse practically every byte of online activity to build a dispassionate atlas of the online world. Facebook CEO Mark Zuckerberg envisions a more personalized, humanized Web, where our network of friends, colleagues, peers, and family is our primary source of information, just as it is offline. In Zuckerberg's vision, users will query this 'social graph' to find a doctor, the best camera, or someone to hire – rather than tapping the cold mathematics of a Google search.

In other words, our circle of friends, our social network facilitated through social media, will become our primary source of information. If we accept the argument that networks online, on the whole, intensify and expand exchanges of like-minded people, this is potentially of enormous concern. Zones of exclusion established on the basis of class, race and gender sustain inequalities. Why do we think the network of networks will somehow transcend previous inequalities, when the evidence on the ground is quite the opposite? Why do we still fall into the trap of thinking about the internet as an independent factor, when, as with other earlier research on media reception, it has been shown that its use and purpose are clearly motivated by social and political background and past and present civic activities that the individual brings with them (Jennings and Zeitner 2003), although the habits of media use may have changed?

The corollary of this is the possibility that our experience of the internet itself may in some way actually hide what's going on, that it may serve to induct us into a privileged stratum of global society and blind us to the need for radical change. This could be the outcome of self-representation through social media – the capacity to imagine ourselves only through the means of mediated self-expression and not as acting citizens – the 'politics of being' dissociated from 'being political' (see Chapter 6).

Conclusion

> [W]e should no longer be thinking of something called Information Society [...] but rather a Communicational Society [...], because it is in our communication with each other that ICTs intrude most directly into the core of social existence.
>
> (Silverstone and Osimo 2005)

The communicational society that Silverstone refers to promises a new transcendental space, a cooperative society (or form of participatory democracy), that is immanent in society as such (as far as socio-political conditions allow) and is potentially advanced by information and information technology. But this notion of a good and equal (and deliberative) society isn't reached automatically through communicational means because there is an inherent antagonism between cooperation and competition in capitalism (Andrejevic 2007), and hence also in the communicational society, that threatens the potentials for participatory democracy. The means of communication produces *potentials* that *may* undermine competition but at the same time also produce new forms of domination and competition. Digital media have brought about converged platforms and converged practice – consumers are producers and can directly create meaning; meaning making is no longer the preserve of the purely interpretative but combines with the act of making/producing, but they do so in specific social, economic and political contexts. In the case of Western developed democracies this is the context of neoliberal capitalism.

Castells (2009) may be right to stress that the internet offers *possibilities* for counter-power and the creation of autonomous spaces. But unfortunately, as Fuchs (2009a: 95) argues, spaces that are autonomous from capital and state power are not easy to come by. They certainly do not automatically exist in social media 'but are invariably subsumed under the corporate logic that dominates'. This does not mean that these spaces cannot exist in the future, but to understand how they might exist we have to have a critical analysis of what inhibits them.

The monitorial power that Castells (2009) sees as part of mass-self-communication – the ability to monitor, reveal and hold to account – is greatly increased in a vastly expanded and speeded-up digital age. But this takes place in a context where those in power 'have made it their priority to harness the potential of mass self communication in the service of their specific interests' (p. 414). But even as Castells acknowledges the enduring dominance of capital and state, he also sees the creativity unleashed online as having the potential to challenge corporate power, and dismantle government authority (p. 420). This is an argument that resides essentially on the basis of the politics of access to production – once you have it, then communicative freedom is yours; without due consideration of the terms on which that access is structured. Fuchs (2008, 2009a) argues that the typical Web 2.0 business strategy is not 'selling people access' but giving them access for free and selling the people (or rather data that is generated about those people) to third parties in order to generate profit. This relationship is clearly highly unequal. He cautions wisely that we would do well to remember that the actual power of corporations in Web 2.0 is far larger than the actual political counter-power that is exercised by the users.

The values of individualism and self-expression prevalent in late-modern neoliberal societies concord with a private sphere that functions as the basis for civic engagement. The mobility of this private sphere also allows everyday routines to be interwoven to render the individual permanently reachable in a manner that exerts phenomenal control over our lives (Castells, Fernandez-Ardevol, Linchuan Qiu and Sey 2006; Ling and Donner 2009). As Jodi Dean (2009) notes, the mythic dimension of the openness of new media that has brought about a hegemonic discourse based on the rhetoric of multiplicity and pluralism, autonomy, access and participation that apparently lead automatically to a more pluralistic society and enhanced democracy also happens to coincide with extreme corporatisation, financialisation and privatisation across the globe.

As Norval (2007: 102) reminds us, we must avoid 'assum[ing] the existence of a framework of politics in which in principle every voice could be heard, without giving attention to the very structuring of those frameworks and the ways in which the visibility of subjects is structured'. Creative autonomy is pretty difficult to express under conditions of material poverty, exploitation and oppression. Individual particularities and political desires alone, even if they are articulated together and facilitated by new communication technologies, will not reclaim and rebuild the institutions necessary to reveal and sustain a new political order.

Genuine democratisation requires the real and material participation of the oppressed and excluded; the real and material recognition of difference, along with the space for contestation and an understanding and response to its meaning. This is not an argument simply for inclusivity, multiplicity, participation or for the creative autonomy of everyone, as these claims alone can only ever take us to first base. They may well be suggestive of possible changes in the dynamics of action. But acknowledging this should not give way to a fetishisation of autonomy through notions of participation or interactivity.

Networks are not inherently liberatory; network openness does not lead us directly to democracy. The practices of new media *may* be liberating for the user but not necessarily democratising for society. We would be wise to remember that the wider social contexts in which networks are formed and exist have a political architecture that predates the internet. An emphasis on creative autonomy lends itself too neatly to individualistic politics that inhibit progressive social change. While social networking forces us to recognise the destabilisation of the producer and the consumer and the blurring of the social and political public spheres, to be fully understood it must be considered contextually. In certain contexts, expansions in networked communications media reinforce the hegemony of democratic rhetoric (Dean 2010) – fetishising speech, opinion and participation. It suggests to us that the numbers of friends you have on Facebook, the number of page-hits on your blog are markers of success. This networked communication may well expand the possibilities of contestation but may also increasingly embed mainstream media's priorities and interests ever more deeply into the ontology of the political. This helps further to establish the norms and values of commercial media while diverting attention from corporate and financial influence, access to structures of decision making and the narrowing of political struggle to reality entertainment.

The key question is: do social media do no more than serve ego-centred needs and reflect practices structured around the self? The civically motivated yet self-absorbed user of social media sees the endless possibility of online connectivity against the banality of the social order. The motivation is often fed by a desire to connect the self to society. As Bimber (2000) notes, while online technologies 'contribute

toward greater fragmentation and pluralism in the structure of civic engagement', their tendency to 'deinstitutionalise politics, fragment communication and
accelerate the pace of the public agenda and decision-making may undermine
the coherence of the public sphere' (2000: 323–33). Social media are not first
and foremost about social good or political engagement; their primary function
is expressive and, as such, they are best understood in terms of their potential for
articulating the (often contradictory) dynamics of political environments rather
than recasting or regenerating the structures that uphold them.

Note

1 This formed part of a large Leverhulme funded research project into new media and
the news (see Fenton 2010). Thanks to Paolo Gerbaudo for his analysis on this part of
the research.

References

Agre, P. E. (2002) 'Real-time Politics: The Internet and the Political Process', *Information
Society* 18 (5): 311–31.
Althaus, S. L. and Tewksbury, D. (2000) 'Patterns of Internet and Traditional Media Use
in a Networked Community', *Political Communication* 17: 21–45.
Andrejevic, M. (2004) 'The Web Cam Subculture and the Digital Enclosure', in
N. Couldry and A. McCarthy (eds) *Media Space: Place, Scale and Culture in a Media Age*,
Oxon: Routledge, 193–209.
——(2007) *iSpy: Surveillance and Power in the Interactive Era*, Kansas: University of Kansas
Press.
——(2008) 'Theory Review: Power, Knowledge, and Governance: Foucault's Relevance
to Journalism Studies', *Journalism Studies* 9 (4): 605–14.
Barber, B., Mattson, K. and Peterson, J. (1997) *The State of Electronically Enhanced Democracy:
A Survey of the Internet*. A report for the Markle Foundation. New Brunswick, NJ: Walt
Whitman Center for Culture and Politics of Democracy.
Baron, N. (2008) *Always on: Language in an Online and Mobile World*, Oxford: Oxford
University Press.
Beckett, C. (2008) *SuperMedia: Saving Journalism so It Can Save the World*, Oxford:
Wiley-Blackwell.
Bell, D. (2007) *Cyberculture Theorists. Manuel Castells and Donna Haraway*, New York: Routledge.
Benkler, Y. (2006) *The Wealth of Networks. How Social Production Transforms Markets and
Freedom*, New Haven, London: Yale University Press.
Best, S. J., Chmielewski, B. and Krueger, B. S. (2005) 'Selective Exposure to Online
Foreign News during the Conflict with Iraq', *Harvard International Journal of Press/Politics*,
10 (4): 52–70.
Bimber, B. (2000) 'The Study of Information Technology and Civic Engagement', *Political
Communication* 17 (4): 329–33.
——(2002) *Information and American Democracy: Technology in the Evolution of Political Power*,
Cambridge: Cambridge University Press.
Bimber, B. and Davis, R. (2003) *Campaigning Online: The Internet in U.S. Elections*, New York:
Oxford University Press.

Boltanski, L. and Chiapello, E. (2005) *The New Spirit of Capitalism*, trans. G. Elliott, London: Verso.

Brodzinsky, S. (2008) 'Facebook Used to Target Colombia's FARC with Global Rally', Christian *Science Monitor*, 4 February. Online. Available HTTP: <http://www.csmonitor. com/2008/0204/p04s02-woam.html> (accessed 22 November 2008).

Brundidge, J. (2006) 'The Contribution of the Internet to the Heterogeneity of Political Discussion Networks: Does the Medium Matter?' Paper presented at the annual meeting of the International Communication Association, Dresden International Congress Centre, Dresden, Germany, 16 June. Online. Available HTTP: <http://www.allacademic. com/meta/p_mla_apa_research_citation/0/9/2/6/5/p92653_index.html>.

Bruns, A. (2008) *Blogs, Wikipedia, Second Life and Beyond*, New York: Peter Lang.

Carnegie Trust UK (2010) *Enabling Dissent*, London: Carnegie Trust UK.

Castells, M. (1998) *The Information Age. Economy, Society and Culture*, Cambridge, MA: Blackwell.

——(2009) *Communication Power*, Oxford: Oxford University Press.

Castells, M., Fernandez-Ardevol, J., Linchuan Qiu, J. and Sey, A. (2006) *Mobile Communication and Society*, Cambridge, MA: MIT Press.

Castoriadis, C. (1991) *Philosophy, Politics and Autonomy: Essay in Political Philosophy*, New York: Oxford University Press.

Cellan-Jones, R. (2009) 'Do Anarchists Tweet?', BBC News website, 2 April. Online. Available HTTP: <http://www.bbc.co.uk/blogs/technology/2009/04/do_anarchists_ tweet.html> (accessed October 2011).

Coleman, S. (2005) 'The Lonely Citizen: Indirect Representation in an Age of Networks', *Political Communication* 22 (2): 180–90.

comScore (2007) 'Social Networking Goes Global'. Online. Available HTTP: <http:// www.comscore.com/press/release.asp?press=555> (accessed 7 July 2009).

Couldry, N. (2003) *Media Rituals: A Critical Approach*, London: Routledge.

Council of Foreign Relations (2008) 'FARC, ELN: Colombia's Left-Wing Guerrillas'. Online. Available HTTP: <http://www.cfr.org/publication/9272/> (accessed 23 May 2008).

Current.com (2008) 'Facebook Users Spawn Grassroots Protest of Colombia's FARC'. Online. Available HTTP: <http://current.com/items/88832752/facebook_users_ spawn_grassroots_protest_of_colombia_s_farc.htm> (23 November 2008).

Dahlberg, L. and Siapera, E. (eds) (2007) *Radical Democracy and the Internet: Interrogating Theory and Practice*, London: Palgrave Macmillan.

Davis, R. (1999) *The Web of Politics: The Internet's Impact on the American Political System*, Oxford: Oxford University Press.

Dean, J. (2009) *Democracy and other Neoliberal Fantasies: Communicative Capitalism and Left Politics*, Durham, NC: Duke University Press.

Donath, J. (2007) 'Signals in Social Supernets', *Journal of Computer-Mediated Communication* 13 (1): article 12. Online. Available HTTP: <http://jcmc.indiana.edu/vol13/issue1/ donath.html> (accessed August 2011).

Dutton, W. (2007) *Through the Network of Networks: The Fifth Estate*, Oxford: Oxford Internet Institute.

Ellison, N., Steinfield, C. and Lampe, C. (2007) 'The Benefits of Facebook "Friends": Social Capital and College Students' Use of Online Social Network Sites', *Journal of Computer-Mediated Communication* 12 (4): 43–68.

Facebook Group (2008) 'One Million Voices Against FARC' (English version). Online. Available HTTP: <http://www.facebook.com/group.php?gid=21343878704> (accessed 23 May 2008).

Facebook, Inc. (2008a) Create a Group. Online. Available HTTP: <http://www.face-book.com/groups/create.php> (accessed 27 April 2008).

——(2008b) Press Room. Online. Available HTTP: <http://www.facebook.com/press/info.php?statistics> (accessed 26 April 2008).

Facebook Statistics (2008). Online. Available HTTP: <http://www.facebook.com/press/info.php?statistics> (accessed 23 May 2008).

Fenton, N. (ed.) (2010) *New Media, Old News: Journalism and Democracy in the Digital Age*, London: Sage.

Fuchs, C. (2008) *Internet and Society. Social Theory in the Information Age*, New York: Routledge.

——(2009) 'Information and Communication Technologies and Society: A Contribution to the Critique of the Political Economy of the Internet', *European Journal of Communication* 24 (1): 69–87.

——(2009a) 'Some Reflections on Manuel Castells' Book "Communication Power"', *tripleC* 7 (1): 94–108.

——(2009b) *Social Networking Sites and the Surveillance Society. A Critical Case Study of the Usage of studiVZ, Facebook, and MySpace by Students in Salzburg in the Context of Electronic Surveillance*, ICT& S Center Research Report. Online. Available HTTP: <http://fuchs.uti.at/wp-content/uploads/studivz.pdf> (accessed October 2011).

Geveran, W. (2009) 'Disclosure, Endorsement, and Identity in Social Marketing', *University of Illinois Law Review*, 1105. Online. Available HTTP: <http://home.law.uiuc.edu/lrev/publications/2000s/2009/2009_4/McGeveran.pdf> (accessed August 2011).

Gillmor, D. (2004) *We the Media: Grassroots Journalism by the People, for the People*, Sebastopol, CA: O'Reilly Media.

Golumbia, D. (2009) *The Cultural Logic of Computation*, Harvard, MA: Harvard University Press.

Habermas, J. (1996) *Between Facts and Norms: Contributions to a Discourse Theory of Law and Democracy*, Cambridge: Polity Press.

Hamelink, C. (2000) *The Ethics of Cyberspace*, London: Sage.

Hampton, K. (2002) 'Place-based and IT Mediated "Community"', *Planning Theory and Practice* 3 (2): 228–31.

Hampton, K. and Wellman, B. (2001) 'Long Distance Community in the Network Society – Contact and Support Beyond Netville', *American Behavioral Scientist*, 45 (3): 476–95.

——(2003) 'Neighboring in Netville: How the Internet Supports Community and Social Capital in a Wired Suburb', *City and Community* 2 (4): 277–311.

Harvey, D. (2005) *A Brief History of Neoliberalism*, Oxford: Oxford University Press.

Haythornthwaite, C. (2005) 'Social Networks and Internet Connectivity Effects', *Information, Communication and Society* 8 (2): 125–47.

Heil, B. and Piskorski, M. (2009) 'New Twitter Research: Men Follow Men and Nobody Tweets'. Online. Available HTTP: <http://blogs.harvardbusiness.org/cs/2009/06/new_twitter_research_men_follo.html> (accessed October 2011).

Herman, E. S. and McChesney, R. W. (1997) *The Global Media. The New Missionaries of Global Capitalism*, London, Washington: Cassell.

Hill, K. A. and Hughes, J. E. (1998) *Cyberpolitics: Citizen Activism in the Age of the Internet*, Lanham, MD: Rowman and Littlefield.

Hindman, M. (2009) *The Myth of Digital Democracy*, Princeton: Princeton University Press.

Holguín, C. (2008) 'Colombia: Networks of Dissent and Power', *OpenDemocracy. Free thinking for the world*, 4 February. Online. Available HTTP: <http://www.opendemocracy.net/article/democracy_power/politics_protest/facebook_farc> (accessed 22 November 2008).

Holt, R. (2004) *Dialogue on the Internet: Language, Civic Identity, and Computer-mediated Communication*, Westport, CT: Praeger.

Holton, R. J. (1998) *Globalization and the Nation-state*, London: Macmillan Press.

Infographic (2010) 'Infographic: Twitter Statistics, Facts and Figures'. Online. Available HTTP: <http://www.digitalbuzzblog.com/infographic-twitter-statistics-facts-figures/> (accessed May 2010).

Internet World Stats (2007) http://www.internetworldstats.com/sa/co.htm (accessed 22 May 2008).

Kaye, B. K. (2007) 'Blog Use Motivations', in M. Tremayne (ed.) *Blogging, Citizenship and the Future of the Media*, New York: Routledge, 127–48.

Keane, J. (2009) *The Life and Death of Democracy*, London: Simon and Schuster.

Khiabany, G. (2010) 'Media Power, People Power and Politics of Media in Iran', paper presented to the IAMCR conference, Braga, Portugal.

Kohut, A. (2008, January) 'Social Networking and Online Videos Take off: Internet's Broader Role in Campaign 2008', The Pew Research Center for the People and the Press. Online. Available HTTP: <http://www.pewinternet.org/pdfs/Pew_MediaSources_jan08.pdf> (accessed March 2008).

Jennings, M. K. and Zeitner, V. (2003) 'Internet Use and Civic Engagement: A Longitudinal Analysis', *Public Opinion Quarterly* 67: 311–34.

Ling, R. and Donner, J. (2009) *Mobile Communication*, Cambridge: Polity.

Liu, H. (2007) 'Social Networking Profiles as Taste Perfomances', *Journal of Computer-Mediated Communication* 13 (1): article 13. Online. Available HTTP: <http://jcmc/indiana.edu/vol13/issue1/liu.html> (accessed October 2010).

McChesney, R. (1996) 'The Internet and US Communication Policy Making in Historical and Critical Perspective', *Journal of Computer-Mediated Communication* 1 (4). Online. Available HTTP: <http://jcmc.indiana.edu/vol1/issue4/mcchesney.html> (accessed October 2010).

Margolis, M., Resnick, D. and Tu, C. (1997) 'Campaigning on the Internet: Parties and Candidates on the World Wide Web in the 1996 Primary Season', *Harvard International Journal of Press and Politics* 2: 59–78.

Marwick, A. E. (2005) *Selling Your Self: Online Identity in the Age of a Commodified Internet*, Washington: University of Washington Press.

Miller, V. (2008) 'New Media, Networking, and Phatic Culture', *Convergence* 14 (4): 387–400.

Nielsen (2010) 'Social Networks/Blogs Accounts for One in Every Four and a Half Minutes Online'. Online. Available HTTP: <http://blog.nielsen.com/nielsenwire/online_mobile/social-media-accounts-for-22-percent-of-time-online/> (accessed October 2011).

Norris, P. (2004) 'The Digital Divide', in F. Webster (ed.) *The Information Society Reader*, New York: Routledge, 273–86.

Norval, A. (2007) *Aversive Democracy*, Cambridge: Cambridge University Press.

Ofcom (2009) 'Children's and Young People's Access to Online Content on Mobile Devices, Games Consoles and Portable Media Players'. Online. Available HTTP: <http://www.ofcom.org.uk/advice/media_literacy/medlitpub/medlitpubrss/online_access.pdf?dm_i=4KS,1QAM,9UK2L,64F1,1> (accessed January 2010).

Örnebring, H. (2008) 'The Consumer as Producer of What? User-generated Tabloid Content in The Sun (UK) and Aftonbladet (Sweden)', *Journalism Studies*, 9 (5): 771–85.

Papacharissi, Z. (2002a) 'The Self Online: The Utility of Personal Home Pages', *Journal of Broadcasting and Electronic Media* 44: 175–96.

——(2002b) 'The Presentation of Self in Virtual Life: Characteristics of Personal Home Pages', *Journalism and Mass Communication Quarterly* 79 (3): 643–60.

——(2007) 'The Blogger Revolution? Audiences as Media Producers', in M. Tremayne (ed.) *Blogging, Citizenship and the Future of the Media*, New York: Routledge, 21–38.

——(2009) 'The Virtual Geographies of Social Networks: A Comparative Analysis of Facebook, LinkedIn and ASmallWorld', *New Media and Society* 11 (1–2): 199–220.

——(2010) *A Private Sphere: Democracy in a Digital Age*, Cambridge: Polity.

Patterson, T. (2010) 'Media Abundance and Democracy', *Media, Journalismo e Democracia* 17 (9): 13–31.

Pew Internet and American Life Project (2008) *The Internet's Role in Campaign 2008*. Online. Available HTTP: <http://www.pewinternet.org/Reports/2009/6-The-Internets-Role-in-Campaign-2008.aspx> (accessed 5 October 2011).

Porta, D. D. and Tarrow, S. (2005) 'Transnational Process and Social Activism: An Introduction', in D. D. Porta and S. Tarrow (eds) *Transnational Protest and Global Activism*, Lanham, MD: Rowman and Littlefield, 1–19.

Poster, M. (2006) *Information Please. Culture and Politics in the Age of Digital Machines*, Durham, London: Duke University Press.

Puopolo, S. (2000) 'The Web and U.S. Senatorial Campaigns 2000', *American Behavioral Scientist* 44: 2030–47.

Quantcast (2008) Facebook.com. Online. Available HTTP: <http://www.quantcast.com/facebook.com> (accessed 30 June 2008).

Rainie, L. and Madden, M. (2005) 'Podcasting', Pew Internet and Life Project, Washington, DC. Online. Available HTTP: <http://www.pewinternet.org/pdfs/PIP_podcasting2005.pdf> (accessed 3 October 2007).

Rheingold, H. (2002) *Smart Mobs. The Next Social Revolution*, Cambridge, MA: Perseus Books Group.

——(2008) 'From Facebook to the Streets of Colombia', in *SmartMobs. The Next Social Revolution. Mobile Communication, Pervasive Computing, Wireless Networks, Collective Action*. Online. Available HTTP: <http://www.smartmobs.com/2008/02/04/fromfacebook-to-the-streets-of-colombia/> (accessed 22 May 2008).

Rhoads, C. and Chao, L. (2009) 'Iran's Web Spying Aided by Western Technology', *Wall Street Journal*, 22 June. Online. Available HTTP: <http://online.wsj.com/article/SB124562668777335653.html> (accessed October 2009).

Sassen, S. (2007) 'Electronic Networks, Power, and Democracy', in R. Mansell, C. Avgerou, D. Quah and R. Silverstone, R. (eds) *The Oxford Handbook of New Media*, Oxford: Oxford University Press, 339–61.

Scammell, M. (2000) 'The Internet and Citizen Engagement: The Age of the Citizen Consumer', *Political Communication* 17 (4): 351–55.

Sennett, R. (1974) *The Fall of Public Man*, New York: Random House.

Shah, D. V., Kwak, N. and Holbert, R. L. (2001) 'Connecting and Disconnecting with Civic Life: Patterns of Internet Use and the Production of Social Capital', *Political Communication* 18: 141–62.

Shirky, C. (2008) *Here Comes Everybody: The Power of Organizations without Organization*, London: Allen Lane.

Silverstone, R. and Osimo, D. (2005) 'Interview with Prof. Roger Silverstone', *Communication & Strategies* 59: 101.

Smith, A. (2010) 'Who Tweets?', Pew Research Center Publications. Online. Available HTTP: <http://pewresearch.org/pubs/1821/twitter-users-profile-exclusive-examination> (accessed October 2011).

Smith, A. and Raine, L. (2008) 'The Internet and the 2008 Election'. Pew Internet and Life Project. Washington, DC. Online. Available HTTP: <http://www.pewinternet.org/pdfs/PIP_2008_election.pdf> (accessed 8 July 2008).

Smythe, D. W. (1994) 'Communications: Blindspot of Western Marxism', in T. Guback (ed.) *Counterclockwise: Perspectives on Communication*, Boulder, CO: Westview Press, 263–91.

Streck, J. M. (1998) 'Pulling the Plug on Electronic Town Meetings: Participatory Democracy and the Reality of the Usenet', in C. Toulouse and T. W. Luke (eds) *The Politics of Cyberspace: a New Political Science Reader*, New York: Routledge, 8–48.

Sunstein, C. (2007) *Republic.Com 2.0*, Princeton: Princeton University Press.

Tapscott, D. and Williams, A. (2008) *Wikinomics: How Mass Collaboration Changes Everything*, London: Atlantic Books.

Turrow, J. (2001) 'Family Boundaries, Commercialism and the Internet: a Framework for Research', *Journal of Applied Developmental Psychology* 22 (1): 73–86.

Wilhelm, A. G. (1999) 'Virtual Sounding Boards: How Deliberative Is Online Political Discussion?', in B. N. Hague and B. D. Loader (eds) *Digital Democracy*, London: Routledge, 54–78.

Williams, C. B. and Gulati, G. J. (2007) 'Social Networks in Political Campaigns: Facebook and the 2006 Midterm Elections', paper presented at the Annual Meeting of the American Political Science Association, Chicago. Online. Available HTTP: <http://www.bentley.edu/news-events/pdf/Facebook_APSA_2007_final.pdf> (accessed 27 March 2008).

Zittrain, J. (2009) *The Future of the Internet*, London: Penguin.

Chapter 6

The internet and radical politics

Natalie Fenton

Introduction

The capacity of the internet to build and mobilise political networks of resistance to counter dominant power structures, both nationally and internationally, has been well documented (e.g. Diani 2001; Downey and Fenton 2003; Fenton and Downey 2008; Hill and Hughes 1998; Keck and Sikkink 1998; Salter 2003). This is a literature that goes beyond the habitual day-to-day communicative realm of the internet that focuses on the individual (albeit the individual in a connected world), and speaks to the radical collective possibilities of online political mobilisation. Many of these forms of radical oppositional politics emerge out of complex social and political histories wherein politics itself has shifted from a traditional focus on institutions processed via formal, organised systems to a concern with more disparate social movement alignments (Hardt and Negri 2004; Loader 2007) that operate via informal networks and resonate with a politics more loosely connected to issues relating to lifestyle than social class. This shift has challenged traditional forms of political representation while responding to the changed social, political and technological conditions and circumstances under which political citizenship is enacted.

This chapter considers the claims made for the internet and the revival of radical oppositional politics, in both domestic and international contexts, under the organising themes of multiplicity, interactivity and autonomy that sum up many of the assertions made in relation to the radical potential of the internet. In doing so, it tackles a literature that points to an emergent sense of the political that resides in multiple belongings (people with overlapping memberships linked through a myriad of networks) and flexible identities (characterised by inclusiveness and a positive emphasis on diversity and cross-fertilisation) that is, as yet, barely appreciated.

These claims are then considered in relation to the counter-arguments by those who interpret multiplicity not as political pluralism but as political dissipation and fragmentation (Habermas 1998) and interactivity as illusive rather than deliberative (Sunstein 2001). In other words, rather than the internet signalling a newly vital oppositional political culture, we are witnessing an era of easy-come, easy-go politics where you are only ever one click away from a petition; a technological form that encourages issue drift whereby individuals shift focus from one issue to another or one website to another with little commitment or even thought; where collective political identity has a memory that is short lived and easily deleted.

Both assessments are incomplete. The former, more excitable and often exciting approach focuses on passions stirred and protests realised, yet fails to take account of the prevailing conditions and particular contexts of power and control. The latter, more sober and frequently cynical approach fails to take account of the felt experience of real and potential political solidarity and the desire for a democracy that is yet to come.

Whichever way you look at it, the internet is at the heart of radical politics in the digital age: it has galvanised local campaigning and facilitated transnational political movements. These activities combine collective action and individual subjectivities, mixing personal expressions of political allegiance with public debate in an online context that has enabled the spaces of action and debate to expand from local/national configurations and terrestrial media to 'global' counter-summits and the internet such as the European and World Social Forums.[1] One of the striking differences between a transnational radical politics and the counter-politics of the nation-state is the former's lack of a common political identity and a rejection of broad, unifying meta-narratives of organisation such as socialism or communism. Rather, these forms of radical politics are characterised by their multiplicity and inclusivity as a network of networks, a politics of non-representation, where no one person speaks for another and differences are openly embraced.

The use of the internet for such radical oppositional purposes is described as a mediated activity that seeks to raise peoples' awareness, give a voice to those who do not have one, offer social empowerment, allow disparate people and causes to organise themselves and form alliances, and ultimately be used as a tool for social change. It is the ability to form networks and build alliances at the click of a mouse that is felt to be conducive to the building of oppositional political movements that can spread across national borders and merge a variety of topics under broadly common themes, though the themes may be subject to frequent change.

Sometimes such radical politics takes the form of new social movements that are themselves often hybrid, contradictory and contingent and include a huge variety of voices and experiences. At other times, the oppositional politics on display is better described as an alliance of groups, organisations and individuals with a political affinity that coalesces at a particular moment in time. The differences within and between individual approaches to a radical politics and the collective response to a common cause or concern often raise many political dilemmas for activists. They are, however, intrinsic to understanding the vibrancy of a form of politics that prefers to operate with a variety of positions and perspectives and often from a highly personalised approach, as opposed to a traditional class politics of old that may rely on established political doctrines.

The internet has another characteristic that is well suited to radical politics – it is a medium that is more readily associated with young people (e.g. Ester and Vinken 2003; Livingstone and Bovill, 2002; Loader 2007); and young people, in particular, are increasingly associated with disengagement from mainstream politics (e.g. Park 2004; Wilkinson and Mulgan 1995) and engagement with the internet (Livingstone et al. 2005; Ofcom 2010). The extensive literature that discusses young people and politics falls largely into two camps: one that talks of a disaffected youth and the other of citizen displacement (Loader 2007).

In the former, studies speak of the decline in the number of young people voting in conventional national party-political elections as indicative of extensive alienation of young people from society's central institutions, and warn of the long-term dangers this may have (Wilkinson and Mulgan 1995). In the latter, an engagement with traditional politics based on a sovereign nation-state is displaced: 'Young people are not necessarily any less interested in politics than previous generations, but ... traditional political activity no longer appears appropriate to address the concerns associated with contemporary youth cultures' (Loader 2007: 1). Rather, civil society or certain parts of it become foregrounded as alternative arenas of public trust, information and representation. It is argued that politically motivated young people tend to look to non-mainstream political arenas, often populated by non-governmental organisations and new social movements – alternative forms of political activism that work at the margins of the dominant public sphere (Bennett 2005; Hill and Hughes 1998; Kahn and Kellner 2004, 2007). It is further claimed that these forms of political engagement better fit the experience of social fragmentation and individualisation felt by citizens (Loader 2007), as well as being directly compatible with the structure and nature of communications via the internet – a medium that young people are commonly well acquainted with.

The combined elements of technology, youth and counter-traditional politics – each conducive to the others – mark out the internet as particularly suited to contemporary (transnational) political activism. The dual characteristics of the internet – of multiplicity and interactivity – are frequently assigned with radical liberatory potential. These acclaimed characteristics also speak to the nature of politics online, which is frequently associated with protest rather than a long-term fixed political project (Fenton 2006) – a bid for involvement and voice, along with a refusal to determine or even presume a singular policy or direct political outcome or end-point that may signal exclusion and/or hierarchy within any grouping or alliance. To some extent this is nothing new. Radical politics has always been at the forefront of mobilising protest and demonstration. A willingness and desire to participate in such political activism is one of the defining features of 'being radical'. What is unprecedented is that this is now happening on a transnational basis and at high speed, resulting in ever more complex networks of intensely expressive and often highly personalised forms of oppositional activism. The nature of these new struggles resides in the political embodiment of the diversity of social relations they embrace – an explicit contention to resist the perceived dogma of political narratives within traditional leftist politics believed by some activists to be the harbinger of outmoded understandings and values.

The internet and radical politics: multiplicity

More than a decade ago, Klein (2000) argued that the internet facilitates international communication among non-governmental organisations (NGOs) and allows protesters to respond on an international level to local events while requiring minimal resources and bureaucracy. This occurs through the sharing of experience and tactics on a transnational basis to inform and increase the capacity of local campaigns. According to Klein, the internet is more than an organising tool. It is also an organising model for a new form of political protest that is international, decentralised, with diverse interests but common targets; although these targets may be perpetually contested.

Salter (2003) also claimed that the internet is a novel technological asset for democratic communications precisely because of its decentred, textual capacities where content is most often provided by users. On this basis it accords with a contemporary radical politics that operates within more fluid and informal networks of action than the class and party politics of old; that lacks membership forms, statutes and other formal means of organising; that may have phases of visibility and phases of relative invisibility.

Both Klein and Salter were describing an emergent form of contentious politics that has partly developed from new social movements. This is a form of politics that cannot be identified by a party name or definitive ideology and is often liable to rapid change in form, approach and mission. These forms of oppositional politics may be based in, but spread quickly beyond, specific localities; they are usually non-hierarchical, with open protocols, open communication and self-generating information and identities that function via networks of activism and activists. Such networks are often staunchly anti-bureaucratic and anti-centralist, suspicious of large organised, formal and institutional politics. Furthermore, the ability of new communication technologies to operate globally and so respond to global economic agendas from a variety of contingent social and political contexts signals a potentially limitless myriad of online voices that have the possibility of coalescing at key protest events but emanate from contexts that may be starkly divergent.

Despite the variability and fluidity at the heart of these forms of radical politics that embrace difference, they are still founded on a level of commonality, even if this does not bear the class/labour configuration of a solidarity of old. Participants in these networks are drawn together by common elements in their value systems and political understandings – though this can be capricious and liable to frequent change (della Porta and Diani 1999; Keck and Sikkink 1998). This is a politics that makes a virtue out of a solidarity built on the value of difference that goes beyond a simple respect for otherness and involves an inclusive politics of voice. Marchart (2007) has called this a type of 'post-foundational politics', while others have claimed that the space of new media enables a broader range of voices and types of material to be communicated to a wider audience without the constraints of needing to comply with or follow a particular political creed or direction other than the expression of an affinity with a particular cause (Dean et al. 2006; Terranova 2004; Tormey 2005, 2006).

Several writers in this field refer to the anti-globalisation movement as one of the first transnational displays of this type of politics, although there had been many national precursors, such as the DIY movement in the UK (McKay 1998). 'The Battle of Seattle' did, however, bring the anti-globalisation (also referred to as the alter-globalisation or social justice) movement to the public's attention around the world. On 30 November 1999 an alliance of Labour and environmental activists congregated in Seattle in an attempt to make it impossible for delegates to the World Trade Organization (WTO) conference to meet. They were joined by consumer advocates, anti-capitalists and a variety of other grass-roots movements. Simultaneously, it is claimed that nearly 1,200 non-governmental organisations (NGOs) in 87 countries called for the wholesale reform of the WTO, many staging their own protests in their own countries (Guardian Online, 25.11.99, p. 4). Groups integrated the internet into their strategies. The International Civil Society website provided hourly updates about the major demonstrations in Seattle to a network of almost 700 NGOs in some 80 countries (Norris 2002). The Independent Media Center (www.indymedia.org) was established by various independent and alternative media organisations and activists for the purpose of providing grassroots coverage of the WTO protests in Seattle. The Center acted as a clearinghouse of information for journalists and provided up-to-the-minute reports, photos, audio and video footage through its website. The Center also produced its own newspaper, distributed throughout Seattle and to other cities via the internet, as well as hundreds of audio segments, transmitted through the web and internet radio station based in Seattle. During the Seattle demonstration the site, which used an open publishing system, logged more than 2 million hits and was featured on America Online, Yahoo!, CNN and BBC Online, among others.

The demonstration was heralded as a success for transnational internet activism. Consequently, hundreds of media activists set up independent media centres (IMCs) in London, Canada, Mexico City, Prague, Belgium, France and Italy over the following year. IMCs have since been established on every continent. They are part of a growing alternative online news presence that provides an interactive platform for politically progressive reports from 'the struggles for a world based on peace, freedom, co-operation, justice and solidarity; and against environmental degradation, neoliberal exploitation, war, racism and patriarchy. The reports cover a wide range of issues and social movements – from neighbourhood campaigns to grassroots mobilizations, from critical analysis to direct action' (http://london.indymedia.org/pages/mission-statement, February 2011).

Other online groups are less news oriented and exist explicitly for the facilitation of political action. *DigiActive* is an all-volunteer organisation dedicated to helping grassroots activists around the world use the internet and mobile phones to increase their impact. Their goal is a world of activists made more powerful and more effective through the use of digital technology. *DigiActive* was created because of a fundamental belief by the founders that digital tools are a great way to express the untapped people power that exists:

> Tools like the Internet and mobile phones let us communicate with other people who share our concerns, to disseminate a message of change, to organize and inform ourselves, to lobby the government, to take part in activism. Together, we call these activities digital activism: the methods by which citizens use digital tools to effect social and political change. We founded DigiActive because we want to spread digital activism around the world.
>
> (http://www.digiactive.org/about/)

Many similar groups – Cyberdissidents, Tactical Technology Collective, the Association for Progressive Communication, Counterfire, Netstrike, Electro-hippies, Electronic Disturbance Theatre, to name but a few, exist for similar purposes. Such groups operating online are claimed to offer infinite expansion of networks of communication, thereby spreading greater awareness (Hampton and Wellman 2003; Wellman et al. 2001), facilitating international communication among activists on multiple platforms with a vast range of issues and diversity of political perspectives. Of course, other groups also come into focus around particular campaigns and then fade away. Established NGOs, trade unions and other oppositional political platforms also mobilise and organise online, all hoping to garner individual support and swell a particular counter-politics to such an extent that it can't be ignored. This inclusivity is further enhanced by the accessibility of online communications, allowing protesters to respond on an international level to local events with minimal resources.

Multiplicity or more of the same?

Dig a little deeper, however, and the limitless multiplicity on offer is clearly challenged. Research on the digital divide (see Chapter 1) notes that internet users are younger, more highly educated and richer than non-users, more likely to be men than women and more likely to live in cities (Norris 2001; Warschauer 2003). These concerns do not just refer to access to the internet and the huge gaps prevalent between the global North and South; they also refer to online activity within developed nations and to traditional divides between the well-educated middle class who dominate public discourse and those on the peripheries or excluded altogether (Hindman 2008). Multiplicity, it would seem, is reserved for the privileged. In a survey on digital activism by DigiActive

(2009), digital activists, particularly in developing countries, were much more likely than the population at large to pay a monthly subscription fee to have internet access at home, to be able to afford a high-speed connection and to work in a white-collar job where internet access is also available. In short, digital activists are likely to be prosperous. They also found that intensity of use, rather than simple access, is a critical determinant of digital activism. Such high use is only possible for people with the ability to pay for it or in white-collar jobs where internet access is commonplace. Similarly, respondents with more features on their mobile phone – such as internet, video and GPS – are more likely to use their phones for political activism. This is another indicator of the importance of financial resources for the politically engaged, both quantitatively, in terms of greater technology access, and qualitatively, in terms of better (mobile) hardware. The conclusion is simple. The internet may be democratising, but more often than not its effects are felt most strongly in the global middle class.

This is not to diminish the use to which the communicative reach of the internet can be put for oppositional political mobilisation. We have witnessed many so-called 'Twitter revolutions', whether in Iran, Moldova, Tunisia or Egypt. Each of these is, of course, a social uprising facilitated by (but not embodied by) technology. But the technological endorsements continue unabated. Miladi (2011: 4), talking about the revolution in Tunisia in 2011, claims that:

> The mushrooming of social networks on Facebook and Twitter was by far the most instrumental factor in the escalation [of the protests]. Tens of thousands joined Facebook groups and got to know about the news developments and mobilised for further action. ... Bloggers have proven that they can challenge not only the state media and other independent (self-censored) newspapers and radio stations, but also the government discourse on what is really happening.

But, as noted in Chapter 5, the internet is also a prime site for surveillance and monitoring. During the uprising in Tunisia, a number of Facebook users inside the country discovered that their accounts were being phished by the government. According to reports (Elkin 2011), the Tunisian Internet Agency was modifying web pages by injecting them with JavaScript to steal user names and passwords on sites like Google, Yahoo! and Facebook. People logging onto the sites unknowingly had their sensitive login information stolen. The government then quickly moved to delete Facebook accounts and groups.

Alongside state censorship and criminalisation of internet activists (Morozov 2011), we should also remember to shine a bright light into the dark recesses of online facilitators of social movements and interrogate their practices. The Alliance of Youth Movements (AYM), established in 2008 as a not-for-profit organisation dedicated to helping grassroots activists to build their capacity and effect social change, held an inaugural summit in 2008 in New York City 'to identify, convene and engage 21st century movements online for the first time in history' (http://www.movements.org/blog/entry/welcome/). In 2011 AYM launched its website and began referring to itself as Movements.org. One of the founders of Movements.org is Jared Cohen, director of Google Ideas and an Adjunct Fellow at the Council on Foreign Relations, where he focuses on terrorism and counter-radicalisation, the impact of connection technologies and '21st century statecraft'.

Twenty-first-century statecraft is part of the US's new strategic approach to international diplomacy. It is heralded as a way of responding to the digital age, and to digital activism in particular. It claims to extend the reach of US diplomacy beyond government-to-government communications to civil society, adapting state intervention by reshaping development and diplomatic agendas through the use of the internet. 'This is 21st Century Statecraft – complementing traditional foreign policy tools with newly innovated and adapted instruments of statecraft that fully leverage the networks, technologies, and demographics of our interconnected world' (Ross 2011). Previously, Cohen served for four years as a member of the State Department's Policy Planning Staff under both secretaries of state Condoleezza Rice and Hillary Clinton. In this capacity, he advised on the Middle East, South Asia, counter-terrorism, counter-radicalisation and, of course, the development of the '21st century statecraft' agenda.

Another co-founder of Movements.org, Jason Liebman, co-founded Howcast Media. Howcast streams tens of millions of videos every month across its multi-platform distribution network. Howcast also works directly with brands, agencies and organisations such as GE, Proctor & Gamble, Kodak, 1-800-Flowers.com, Staples, US Department of State, US Department of Defense, American Red Cross and Ford Motor Company to create custom branded entertainment, innovative social media and targeted rich-media campaigns. Before Howcast, Liebman worked for four years at Google, where he played an integral role in growing strategic content licensing and monetisation relationships for YouTube, Google Video and AdSense. Prior to Google, he was at Applied Semantics before it was acquired by Google in 2003 – one of Google's largest acquisitions in its history. At Applied Semantics, he held several positions, including Executive Vice President of Sales and Business Development. In this role he was responsible for overseeing new monetisation products, including AdSense, and introducing them to web publishers. He began his career at Credit Suisse as an investment banker.

Of course, it does not necessarily follow that a corporate past, direct links to the US government and explicit connections to Google lead to dubious practice and state-engineered activism. And the activists attending Movements.org summits are doubtless genuine and intent on playing out a progressive social and political agenda. But the men behind the summit, the sponsors who are funding it (Pepsi, Google, MTV, CBS News, Edelman, Howcast, Meetup, Mobile Accord, YouTube, Facebook, MSN, National Geographic, Omnicom Group, Access 360, Gen next), the twenty-first-century statecraft agenda that is prodding it, are an immensely powerful state–corporate combine working to promote activism in 'problem spots' around the world that the US State Department would like to see 'chan-ged'. Cartalucci (2011: 2) claims that 'wherever protestors and movements are working to undermine governments non-conducive to corporate America's agenda, you will find Movements.org supporting their efforts'. Whichever way we look at it, the connections between Google, Facebook, Twitter, the US State Department and Movements.org certainly raise suspicions, and a straightforward celebration of the radical counter-political possibilities of new technology starts to appear exceedingly naive.

A simple retort to those who peddle a revolutionary homily to the likes of Twitter, but one that is often little heeded, is that the relationship between oppositional political activism and the internet cannot be adequately understood without a conceptual appreciation of power – who has it, in what circumstances and how is it manifest? This is the starting-point for understanding all social change and political upheaval, even within social movements themselves. But this is not simply an argument for political economic interrogation, as critical as this is. It is also a plea for a consideration of the social dimensions of political life and citizenship – what brings people together and why they seek solidarity. The political cannot be understood outside of relations of power or without the social. Only when we have a sense of what may constitute the political – economically, socially and technologically – alongside a better understanding of the nature of power therein and can interpret these contingent factors through a particular socio-geographic lens, then, and only then, can we begin to address the part played by the internet and its role in the complexity of modern-day living.

The examples below illustrate this point.

Student protests, UK, autumn 2010/winter 2011

Consider the mass student protests across the UK in autumn 2010/winter 2011. In response to the UK Coalition government's announcement of its intention to triple university fees to up to £9,000 a year, while also totally removing the teaching subsidy from arts, humanities and social science subjects and reducing by 40 per cent the subsidy to science, technology and engineering subjects, there were a series of mass demonstrations, flash protests and occupations of university buildings. The first large demonstration, on 10 November 2010, amassed in the region of 50,000 protestors, most of whom were young and many protesting for the first time, but also included lecturers, parents and others, worried that the right to higher education would cease to be open to a large segment of the British population unable to shoulder the huge debts they would accumulate whilst doing a degree in a privatised system (Solomon 2011). As in many acts of counter-government publicity, the internet was used to provide alternative mes-sages to government spin, to disseminate information on the likely consequences of the proposals, to organise protest events, mobilise demonstrators and spread cultural dissidence. In doing so it enabled many people to feel part of the action and express their anger. Amongst those who cared and got involved, the internet helped to create an atmosphere of political solidarity, hope, empowerment and possibility. For those students still at school, below voting age and who stood to lose the most from the proposals, social media unlocked a treasure trove of connections and means of oppositional expression that became key to organising their engagement and bringing them out onto the streets. Facebook groups supporting the action and enabling, in particular, student occupations of university buildings, facilitated deliberation and a form of voice and connection that had been much more difficult to establish prior to the internet.

Protestors spoke of being able to bypass institutions that had failed to represent them and take control of their own destiny through online organising (Casserly 2011). Live Twitter feeds were placed on mainstream news websites, inviting comments from people on the ground and in the action, often challenging the nature of representation from one of 'rioters', 'thugs' and 'criminals' while highlighting police brutality and the provocation of protestor containment via 'kettling'.[2] YouTube footage showed police charging horses into a crowd of protestors – a fact they had previously denied (Solomon 2011). But whereas the internet helped to facilitate the organisation of protest and protestors and spoke to the affective passions of the moment, the felt injustice of the policy proposals, it did not in itself create the political dissent. This was a result of many factors, not least a government that came to power through a coalition of the Conservative Party with the Liberal Democrat Party, which had campaigned vociferously on the removal of fees for university students. It was also key that almost all of the 'austerity measures' introduced by the government only four months after coming to power in its first emergency Comprehensive Spending Review to reduce the budget deficit had never been mentioned in the two parties' pre-election manifestos and campaigns (Deacon et al. 2011). Quite simply, representative democracy was felt to have failed. As one protestor said:

> It's increasingly obvious that the 'democratic channels' we've been encouraged to go through all our lives in order to effect change are completely useless, obsolete. They're nothing more than an illusion. It's what creates this cycle of protest, then go back to bed, then protest, then go back to bed again. You've made use of the right to protest, but they don't give a shit … they know the law is your limit … Protest isn't enough anymore.
>
> (Cited in Killick 2011)

The apparent brazen political disregard for democratic process was heaped on top of a deep mistrust of political parties and politicians that had developed over the previous two decades (Guardian Euro Poll 2011) and was most recently manifest in a raft of political scandals that emphasised the self-interest of politicians over the professed public interest of elected office. Without an understanding of this political history, the protests and the use of the internet to mobilise dissent and demonstrative action make little sense.

The contemporary context of political activism and (lack of) political engagement in mainstream traditional politics in the UK is indicative of several interrelated factors. The professionalisation of politics yields a public that is less trusting and more sceptical of traditional representative politics, and constantly deprived of voice and emotion through the processes of aggregate public opinion polling. New media technologies offer the potential for a form of democratic practice that has features of both participatory and direct democracy that are difficult to integrate within a globalised neoliberal society that turns to a system of representative democracy as a way of managing its mass and reach. When electoral democracy is deemed to have failed, a technology that infers individual control and is seen to side-step and frequently outwit the state is willingly embraced. It *feels* democratic because it feels dynamic and organic, a process that is led by the participants who, in turn, feel linked in and part of something bigger, raising the possibilities of a counter-political movement.

But the seductiveness of the counter-political possibilities online also tells a cautionary tale. During these student protests the internet made counter-political strategising more fragmented and exposed the difficulties in representative politics from within the more traditional forms of counter-politics such as the National Union of Students (NUS) and the Universities and Colleges Union (UCU) (Grant 2011; Killick 2011). In an environment where everyone has a voice on multiple platforms but no institution can contain, frame or coordinate those voices, then fragmentation and political dissolution can occur – a thoroughly contemporary anxiety of trade unions in a digital age (Ward and Lusoli 2003).

In January 2011, at another demonstration against student fees and cuts to higher education in Manchester, the then president of the NUS, Aaron Porter, was lambasted by protestors for not properly representing their views. Porter had sought to distance the NUS from outbreaks of violent protest and stood accused of accepting the 'establishment' line (Salter 2011). The multiple viewpoints that the internet invokes can be problematic from an old-fashioned standpoint of political organising. Loss of control of the message and, indeed, the demonstration or protest itself as people follow online networks and Twitter feeds, as splinter groups develop and grow apace and new ones form, sometimes out of conflict with established organisers (such as trade unions) or often out of communities with more precise subject identities (e.g. Artists Against the Cuts), create genuine difficulties for those in hierarchical political organisations seeking to direct carefully orchestrated and coordinated campaigns. As James Haywood, the Campaigns Officer for Goldsmiths (a college of the University of London) Student Union notes:

> [the demonstration at] Millbank didn't just inspire more people to protest; it decisively changed the whole attitude to protest in the UK. What is noticeable now is how, especially among the younger students, demonstrations are being reclaimed: people march where they want to march, they break away from police kettles, they look for buildings to occupy. No-one

waits for the unions or the organizers to give them orders. This is a new thing.

(Haywood 2011: 69)

The politics in practice in movements such as the above is highly porous and more organic than the politics of old. And while the example of the student protests in the UK operated both horizontally and vertically (Tormey 2006), the dynamic within the centralised organising forces of a hierarchical leadership-based system (from within a trade/student union movement) is clearly directly challenged by the leveller of networks of resistance. This form of networked politics links marginalised groups and builds counter-discourses, but endlessly resists the construction of a one-size-fits-all politics by insisting on the preservation of a multiplicity of political identities, viewpoints and approaches to political action.

It is easy to dismiss such (dis)organised political action and activists as anarchic, and indeed much of the mainstream news reporting did just that. But in seeking to understand this multiplicity and horizontality of new social movements (NSMs) that contrast starkly with a traditional politics based on class, we must also be prepared to take stock of representative politics – how *can* one individual represent a multiplicity of different views equally? Once we ask this question we are also faced with an interrogation of the assumptions built into the notion of liberal democracy itself. If liberal democracy is deemed to be failing in crucial ways based on the inability of a few elected representatives to account for the views of the many, then it should come as no surprise that oppositional politics that seeks to challenge such assumptions is emerging.

But of course, democracy means different things to different people in different places. The question this then raises is: are the notions of multiplicity and interactivity that seem to characterise much political activity online in terms of NSMs relevant in all contexts, or are we falling prey once more to a thoroughly westernised interpretation of theory and politics?

'The Green Revolution': Iran, 2009

Let us consider another example. In June 2009 the Iranian presidential election prompted widespread unrest as the sitting President Mahmoud Ahmadinejad won a further term of office, with official figures putting his win at 62.6 per cent of the vote on an 85 per cent turnout. Supporters of pro-reform candidate Mir Hossein Mousavi cried foul and clashed with riot police in Tehran, despite a ban on public protests. The protests in Iran sparked the organisation of global protest against the national elections, with protesters using the social-networking tool Twitter to communicate with the outside world when journalists' access was restricted. Iran's tenth presidential elections took place in a particular context where the government has a Supreme Leader, Ayatollah Ali Khamenei, more

powerful than the elected president, and two-thirds of the population are relatively young, being born after the revolution of 1979, and are more inclined
towards social media.

Iran also went from fewer than one million internet users in 2005 to around
23 million in 2008; in 2009 it was estimated that approximately 35 per cent of
the population of Iran were online; and the use of text messaging climbed from
30 per cent of the adult population in 2006 to 49 per cent in 2009. Despite the
use of satellite television and ownership of satellite dishes being banned since
1994, it was estimated that 25 per cent of the population of 70 million had
access to satellite television in 2009. In January 2009 the BBC launched its own
Persian-language television station, joining the existing Persian-language services,
BBC Persian radio and BBC's Persian-language website – also blocked by the
Iranian authorities (Ilves, 2009). The BBC received thousands of e-mails, photos
and videos of what was happening on the ground in Iran that were used not
only on BBC Persian TV but also on BBC channels in the UK, BBC World
News TV, BBC World Service radio and BBC Online (Ghoddosi 2009).

Before the election there were very few foreign correspondents from international news organisations in Tehran, and during the protests against the election
results foreign journalists were expelled from the country (Choudhari 2009).
Broadcasts in Iran by international news organisations, including those from the
BBC, were jammed and their websites blocked. After the protests domestic
media also came under fire. Several opposition newspapers were closed and
Reporters Without Borders stated that more than 39 journalists had been arrested
(http://en.rsf.org/iran-press-freedom-violations-recounted-31-12-2009,33433).

During the election the government, in an effort to crack down on the information leaving Iran, slowed internet connection and blocked social network and
video-sharing sites such as Facebook and YouTube, but Twitter continued on
account of its compatibility with SMS text messaging. Furthermore, as mobile
phone reception was turned off in some areas, Twitter feeds could still be
updated by 'relay' websites. After a large surge in SMS traffic in the run-up to
the election, multiple sources inside Iran reported that the country's SMS networks also went down just hours before the polls opened. Reporters Without
Borders reported that the SMS shut-down was part of an attempt to prevent
opposition supporters from collecting election results. By the time of the election,
all mobile phone services had been shut off in Tehran.

The Iran–Twitter fascination became a media phenomenon when the US
State Department announced that it had asked Twitter to postpone some
scheduled maintenance because, as Secretary Clinton said, 'keeping that line of
communications open and enabling people to share information, particularly at
a time when there was not many other sources of information, is an important
expression of the right to speak out and to be able to organize' (Tapper 2009).[3]
Jeff Jarvis called it 'the API revolution' (http://www.buzzmachine.com/2009/
06/17/the-api-revolution/), referring to the ability, via software called an API, of
third parties to 'use' other applications – for mobile phone providers, for example,

to route messages onto Twitter. Clay Shirky called it 'the big one' (http://blog.
ted.com/2009/06/qa_with_clay_sh.php):

> the first revolution that has been catapulted onto a global stage and trans-
> formed by social media. People throughout the world are not only listening
> but responding. They're engaging with individual participants, they're pas-
> sing on their messages to their friends, and they're even providing detailed
> instructions to enable web proxies allowing Internet access that the authorities
> can't immediately censor.

But it is hard to establish how much twittering was actually going on inside Iran.
The tweets circulated by expatriates in the United States tended to be in English,
as the Twitter interface did not support the use of Persian, although it is one of
the most blogged-in languages. And though many people seemed to be sending
tweets out of Iran, their use inside Iran was questioned. Mehdi Yahyanejad,
manager of a Persian-language news site based in Los Angeles, commented that
'Twitter's impact inside Iran is zero. Here, there is lots of buzz, but once you
look … you see most of it is Americans tweeting among themselves' (cited in
Musgrove 2009).

This raises three crucial issues: firstly, that a huge amount of noise and (false)
information generated by networks can make it difficult to separate the authentic
from the deliberately placed. Secondly, social media sites are not concerned first
and foremost with balance – in the above example most postings were in favour
of the opposition candidate, Mir Hossein Mousavi, who tended to attract the
support of younger, more computer-literate Iranians, as well as activists in the
West. And thirdly, social media tend to amplify inaccuracies, as speed generates
its own momentum and networks endlessly repeat errors. In this instance social
media claimed repeatedly that three million people protested in Tehran. Independent assessments put this at a few hundred thousand. Claiming another
'Twitter Revolution' clearly belies much deeper and more consequential concerns:

> Simple-minded Web 2.0 gurus latched on to the summer of discontent in
> Iran as the 'Twitter revolution'. But such technological determinism belies
> the long-existing political, cultural and sexual frustration, the sheer libidinal
> energy of a youthful population finding no outlets for its creativity and
> desires. It offers thin explanation that does not recognise Iran's repeated loss
> of political structure and practice and the need in each generation to build
> them anew, nor the manner in which politics becomes transmuted into
> forms of communication. Nor does it acknowledge both the extent of digital
> development in Iran and its control.
>
> (Sreberny 2009)

But perhaps more importantly, Sreberny and Khiabany (2010: xi), discussing the
explosion of blogging in Iran, point to the 'universalist assumptions' in much of

the literature on the internet and society that fail to offer a critical contextual analysis of particular situations, illustrating emphatically that we cannot understand what happened in Iran in 2009 without understanding 'the legacy of a revolutionary political culture, the perception and experience of repression by citizens, culturally preferred modes of expressivity as well as the meaning and experience of the Iranian diaspora and a deep-rooted Iranian cosmopolitanism' (2010: xi). Thus they argue for a multidimensional contextualisation that can take account of the deep and broad socio-political and cultural environment of the Islamic Republic.

In insisting on the need for context, Sreberny and Khiabany do precisely what Castells (2009) misses through his erudite but ultimately over-generalised assessment of 'communication power'. Castells (2009: 300) argues that social movements that engage in oppositional politics – 'the process aiming at political change (institutional change) in discontinuity with the logic embedded in political institutions' – now have the chance to enter the public space from multiple sources and bring about change. Through four case studies – the environmental movement, the movement for democratic globalisation, the spontaneous movement that emerged in Spain after the al- Qaeda attacks in March 2004, and the Obama presidential campaign – he shows how social movements try to reprogram communication networks and reconfigure the symbolic environment, thereby establishing a means of media counter-power. Examples he gives from these case studies include the networking of scientists, activists, opinion leaders and celebrities; the use of entertainment and popular culture for political causes; mobilisation and networking with the help of social networking sites (MySpace, Facebook etc.); celebrity advocacy; event management; alternative online media; video-sharing platforms (YouTube etc.); actionism; street theatre; hacking; electronic civil disobedience; flash mob activism supported by mobile phones; online fund raising; Obama's emotional political style that promised hope and change in order to stimulate enthusiasm and grassroots activism; online petitions; political blogging; or delocalised mobilisation and micro-targeting tactics supported by the internet.

In this argument the multiple prospects for intervention and manipulation coming from a myriad of social nodes combine to create a new symbolic counter-force that can shift dominant forms of representation. The counter-political response swells to such a size online that it simply cannot be ignored offline and is, in turn, taken up by the mass media. By using both horizontal communication networks and mainstream media to convey their images and messages, they increase their chances of enacting social and political change – 'even if they start from a subordinate position in institutional power, financial resources, or symbolic legitimacy' (Castells 2009: 302). But leaving change to chance alone predicated on the means of communication seems like a risky business that refuses a deep and broad interrogation of the conditions required for people power to overtake corporate and state power and for democracy to flourish, and leads to an over-emphasis on technology, to the detriment of social, political and economic context.

As noted in Chapter 5, networks are not inherently political, and identification and communication of injustice and inequality is only one part of political action. Publicising the failures of political states, whether they are authoritarian or neoliberal, and organising protest against them may increase the prospects of change through the mediation of solidarity, but transformation of political and economic systems cannot be tackled through communicational means alone.

Interactivity, participation and autonomy

Civic and political participation are frequently understood as prerequisites for citizen-based democracies to flourish. Facilitation of participation is a crucial factor in transnational internet activism. The interactive and participative capability of the internet to speed up and increase the circulation of struggle has been argued as key to the success of some campaigns, such as the anti-globalisation movement (Cleaver 1999), as well as the spread of pro-democracy protest in the Middle East in 2011 (Ghannam 2011; Miladi 2011). The nature of participation promoted by many contemporary forms of radical political mobilisation online is predicated upon a particular notion of individual autonomy connected directly to the celebration of multiplicity and difference: the ability to act and speak for oneself while also being part of a collective movement over which no one individual, or central hierarchy, has control.

The principle that no one speaks for the collective, that each takes control of their own political activism, is also at the heart of the networked politics of new social movements. One of the first social movements to explicitly embrace and endorse such an approach was the Zapatista Army of National Liberation (EZLN) in its political rebellion against neoliberal capitalism and, in particular, against the North American Free Trade Agreement (NAFTA), in pursuit of the liberation of Chiapas. From the outset, the Zapatista struggle, led by Subcomandante Marcos, differentiated itself from previous political movements through a disinterest in state power and hierarchical structures and a clear focus on autonomy and direct democracy (Graeber 2002; Klein 2002). Direct democracy in this context emphasises consensus over majority rule and refers to the open invitation to everyone to take part in politics. Concurrently, they also placed importance on interconnectedness and networking, using the internet to create a collective political identity that spread across the globe (Atton 2007; Castells 1997; Kowal 2002; Ribeiro 1998). Subcomandante Marcos deliberately resisted the status of leader and refused any name that would identify him as an individual. The conflict in Chiapas gave rise to the People's Global Action network (PGA), which led to the 1999 Seattle demonstrations and the creation of the movement for global justice (Day 2005; Graeber 2002; Holloway 2002), with the internet cemented as part of the repertoire of political action (Traugott 1995). The internet was also seen as evidence that radical politics can arise horizontally and take the form of networks, rather than hierarchical hegemonies as in a traditional trade union politics of labour.

The conceptualisation and enactment of autonomy in the networked sociality of contemporary radical politics has since been forged through a connection to anarchism and autonomous Marxism. These approaches imagine the network as an ever-open space of politics. From this perspective, the network is not simply the expression of networked individuals, but the manifestation of self-constituted, unhierarchical and affinity-based relationships which extend beyond state borders and have the combined notions of 'autonomy' (everyone's right to express their own political identity) and 'solidarity' (to overcome power/neoliberalism) at their core (Graeber 2002: 68).

This is partially explained through an appreciation of participation in contemporary radical politics being linked to disengagement with traditional party politics. In her extensive interviews with and questionnaires to activists della Porta (2005) discovers a relationship between mistrust for parties and representative institutions with very high trust and participation in social movements. The distinction between institutional politics and social movements rests upon the former acting as bureaucracies founded upon delegation of representation and the latter being founded on participation and direct engagement. This encourages us to move away from the notion of liberal deliberative democracy's being realisable only through the traditional political structures of the nation-state. Rather, it encourages us to think in terms of a decentred democracy that rejects the modernist version of a political project with a single coherent aim of social reform, allowing a more fluid and negotiable order to emerge, 'with plural authority structures along a number of different dimensions rather than a single location for public authority and power' (Bohman 2004: 148). Similarly, for Benkler (2006) the internet has the potential to change the practice of democracy radically because of its participatory and interactive attributes. It allows all citizens to alter their relationship to the public sphere, to become creators and primary subjects, to become engaged in social production. In this sense the internet is ascribed the powers of democratisation.

But participation rooted in autonomy is hotly contested on grounds of political efficacy, with the network society seen as producing localised, disaggregated, fragmented, diversified and divided political identities. Earlier work by Castells (1996) saw the fragmented nature of new media as limiting the capacity of new political movements to create coherent strategies due to the increasing individualisation of activists. Similarly, in an approach based on *dis*organisation, problems of quantity and chaos of information challenge the way analysis and action are integrated in decision-making processes – how issues are debated and decisions are reached can be at best unclear and at worst unfathomable. If, like Castells et al. (2006), we view this all-inclusive approach as leading to the fragmentation and dissolution of solidarity, this leads us ultimately to the conclusion that this is a form of politics that lacks direction and political agency. It is unclear why Castells changed his mind by 2009, but it is likely related to the increase in volume and intensity of such activity.

But even if we accept that through political conflict associational networks can emerge, civil society can be established and social change can occur, the problem remains: how can fragmented and multiple oppositional groupings function together for political ends? The key to understanding this approach to a 'post-foundational' (Marchart 2007) radical politics is to keep in mind that any end-point has multiple possibilities and there are many different routes to get to each. The reduction of political action to the construction of a single end-point that infers a rational, exclusionary approach whereby all other potential end-points are dismissed as ill-conceived or wrong is considered by many to be unacceptable; after all, why would someone participate in a politics that is established on someone else's terms and tries to flatten disagreement and stifle dissent: the markers of a failed and stale representative politics?

Participation on someone else's terms is understood as the misguided delivery of a homogenous ideal that attempts to remove uncertainty and unknowability and reduces politics to the 'administration of things' (Bhabha 1994). It is seen as removing creativity and autonomy from political action. Contemporary political activists talk of creating autonomous spaces of imagination and creativity that are contingent, open and unpredictable – an attempt to escape ideological politics and move to a dialogical politics where we continually acknowledge difference and learn from others. The political premise is one of anti-reductionism that refuses a monological process or vision. Such forms of resistance are united by a shared perception of an injustice rather than a common, determinate vision of a 'better world' that may follow.

But even if it is accepted that fragmented and multiple oppositional groupings can create their own political interventions via the internet, we still have to broach the next stage: how can a politics of solidarity (based often on a consensus of what people don't want) forged through difference (based often on what people do want) be realised and sustained? Can a commitment to the value of difference and an appreciation of everyone's right to dissent sustain a coherent and effective radical politics?

In their research of social movements Tarrow and della Porta (2005: 237) refer to the interconnections between online and offline participation as 'rooted cosmopolitans' (people and groups rooted in specific national contexts but involved in transnational networks of contacts and conflicts); 'multiple belongings' (activists with overlapping memberships linked with polycentric networks); and 'flexible identities' (characterised by inclusiveness and a positive emphasis on diversity and cross-fertilisation) (della Porta and Diani 1999; Keck and Sikkink 1998). Tormey (2005) notes that the politics at play here favours a praxis of micro-power and a micro-politics of and in everyday life directed against the master-signifier of ideological thought and 'by extension the coalescence of revolutionary struggle around some agreed place that it was the task of the "movement" to build or construct' (Tormey 2005: 403).

We can also see this perspective echoed in Deleuze and Guattari's *A Thousand Plateaus* (1988: 469–73), which argues against 'majoritarianism', the notion that there must be some scheme, project, goal or telos around which 'we' can be united, preferring a minoritarian stance that rejects the ultimately essentialist and pointless search for a universal blueprint. In order to resist incorporation into the dominant ideal there is, according to Deleuze and Guattari, a necessity to generate spaces in which micro-politics can become established and thrive. Such spaces of affinity and creativity, they argue, have the potential to develop activist networks of micro-politics that can converge, multiply and develop without an ideology or a strategy – spaces that are predicated on participation, learning, solidarity and proliferation. This has been referred to as 'swarming', whereby networks of affinity and association integrate and form multiple resistances and actions (Carty and Onyett 2006).

The work of Hardt and Negri (2000, 2004) attempts to broach a politics of the Multitude and has become a source of validation and direction for many people involved in online mobilisation and transnational political protest. Hardt and Negri (2004) call on us to reclaim the concept of democracy in its radical, utopian sense: the absolute democracy of 'the rule of everyone by everyone' (2004: 307). The multitude, they argue, is the first and only social subject capable of realising such a project. They propose a description of the Multitude as 'an open network of singularities that links together on the basis of the common they share and the common they produce' – a union which does not, however, in any way subordinate or erase the radical differences among those singularities. Brought together in multinodal forms of resistance, different groups combine and recombine in fluid networks expressive of 'life in common' (2004: 202). In other words, they form a multitude. Because of both its plurality and the sharing of life in common controlled by capital it is claimed that the Multitude contains the composition of true democracy.

The Multitude's ability to communicate, form alliances and forge solidarity – often through the very capitalist networks that oppress it – allows it to produce a common body of knowledge and ideas that can serve as a platform for democratic resistance, a union that does not in any way subordinate or erase the radical differences among those disparate groupings. As Oswell (2006: 97) states:

> if the people are defined by their identity, relation to sovereignty and represented homogeneity, the multitude in contrast is defined through its absolute heterogeneity and through its being a congregation of singularities.

Hardt and Negri (2004) point to anti-globalisation and anti-war protests as exercises in democracy motivated by people's desire to have a say over decisions that impact upon the world in which they live – operating at a transnational level. However, their call for a 'new science of democracy' (2004: 348) is difficult to pin down. Exactly how the Multitude can stand up and be counted is never set out. Both Laclau (2004) and Habermas (1998) are sceptical of the claims made for a minoritarian politics and the Multitude's ability to deliver a socially meaningful radical politics. Laclau (2004) has called this the antithesis of politics – an agency that does not articulate, represent or strategise. This is utopia without architecture and universality without meaning. A movement of antagonistic constitution does not offer direction on how such a community of diversity is organised, it merely enacts the right of resistance.

Habermas registers his ambivalence towards new information and communication technologies as a potential source of equal and inclusive communication, arguing that, far from ensuring political mobilisation and participation, the internet may contribute to the fragmentation of civil society:

> Whereas the growth of systems and networks multiplies possible contacts and exchanges of information, it does not lead per se to the expansion of an intersubjectively shared world and to the discursive interweaving of conceptions of relevance, themes, and contradictions from which political public spheres arise. The consciousness of planning, communicating and acting subjects seems to have simultaneously expanded and fragmented. The publics produced by the Internet remain closed off from one another like global villages. For the present it remains unclear whether an expanding public consciousness, though centered in the lifeworld, nevertheless has the ability to span systematically differentiated contexts, or whether the systemic processes, having become independent, have long since severed their ties with all contexts produced by political communication.
>
> (Habermas 1998: 120–21)

Greater pluralism is regarded by Habermas as a risk for deliberative democracy rather than its saviour. This concern is echoed by Sunstein, who argues that the internet has spawned large numbers of radical websites and discussion groups, allowing the public to bypass more moderate and balanced expressions of opinion in the mass media (which are also, he argues, subject to fragmentation for essentially technological reasons). Moreover, these sites tend to link only to sites that have similar views (Sunstein 2001: 59). Such findings are supported by other empirical work, such as Hill and Hughes (1998). Sunstein argues that, as a consequence, we are witnessing a group polarisation (2001: 65) that is likely to become more extreme with time. As such, Sunstein contends that two preconditions for a well-functioning, deliberative democracy are threatened by the growth of the internet and the advent of multi-channel broadcasting. First, people should be exposed to materials that they have not chosen in advance. This results in a reconsideration of the issues, and often recognition of the partial validity of opposing points of view. Second, people should have a range of common experiences, in order that they may come to an understanding with respect to particular issues (Downey and Fenton 2003).

But, as Mouffe (2005) contends, enacting the right of resistance, revealing political struggle and conflict in a diversity of forms is still crucial to the actual practice of democracy that can lead to multiple forms of unity and common action, such as we have seen in the uprisings in the Middle East in 2011. Where there is political conflict, the means of circulating information will always be a primary aim, and with the help of the internet such 'revolutionary' information can spread quickly and the flickers of possibility for change more readily turn into flames. The quick-form instant relay of protest and political struggles online is often far from rational and encourages affective responses in the passionate and frequently explicit renditions of struggle and resistance up close. Often these are in stark contrast to the oppressive politics on offer in authoritarian regimes or the increasingly bland and highly popularised yet deeply unappealing politics of neoliberal democracies.

Conclusion

The growing 'civic disengagement' of young people from state politics – the kind of politics that has been developed through modern history to fit and serve the political integration into 'nation-states' – along with the development of new communication technologies, has shifted political interests and hopes to new terrains that are borderless and global: a kind of politics well suited to the internet. But networks are not democratic institutions; they do not apportion membership or citizenship; they do not conform to legislative models of governance or a representative model of election. And it is partly these characteristics that make them attractive to young people: they are both different from conventional state-bound politics and they embrace difference. If there is a new politics emerging in new media it is a politics of non-representation; a politics of affect and antagonism. It includes a multiplicity of experiences that are contradictory and contingent.

Dahlgren (2009) notes that civic cultures are shaped by an array of factors: from family and schools, to group settings, relations of power (including social class, gender and ethnicity), economics, the legal system and organisational issues. He also notes that the resources that people can draw upon are more abundant amongst the more privileged and discusses how the media directly and routinely impact upon the character of civic cultures via their form, content, logics and modes of use. In terms of the internet, he notes that its significance is found not simply at the level of social institutions but also in a lived experience that is messy and contradictory.

Contemporary radical politics online are, on the one hand, magnifying the 'shift to a more fluid, issue-based group politics with less institutional coherence' (Bimber 1998: 135) where political engagement is integrated into everyday routines but rarely directed at policy change or resources. On the other hand, these often atomised expressions of social activism that move in and out of focus reflect a move to newer forms of civic engagement and open up the public sphere to disagreement over consensus. They are suggestive of a dramatic enlargement of how we think of politics and a radical development in our understanding of the mechanisms of social change. These forms of radical politics are open ended; there are no meta-narratives that shape the beginning, middle and end of a particular ideological approach. As such, they are ever incomplete, tacit and experiential, with an emphasis on horizontal sharing and exchanging of knowledge; a highly self-conscious and self-reflexive form of action and struggle that functions in an endless dynamic of experimentation and search for synthesis. But by choosing to emphasise multiplicity and creative autonomy we run the risk of providing an illusion of direct control through self-expression (see Chapter 5) and run the danger of ending up being comforted to the point of inaction, with no significant means of tempering communicative overload and no clear direction of travel. Furthermore, by reducing politics to either a liberal tolerance of difference or an anarchic, autonomous and ultimately individualistic politics we may prevent substantive questions from being asked and substantive change from happening.

Clearly, it is not quite as straightforward as it may seem. It feels a bit like making a soufflé. No matter how many times you do it, you never quite know whether it will rise or sink. But actually, if you take the time to research it properly you will find that there are certain conditions one can impose that make success more likely than failure – take eggs that are fresh but not too fresh, whisk the egg whites to the right consistency and make sure the oven is just hot enough. The conditions for political transformation facilitated by the internet, and indeed the conditions required for democracy to function, need to be similarly interrogated and considered. It is not by chance that global capitalism is alive and well, and it is highly unlikely that its progressive transformation will be down to luck or chance either.

Andrejevic (2007) argues that, in an information society, information produces potentials that undermine competition yet at the same time also produce new forms of domination and competition. As the internet creates and embeds forms of capitalism, it also brings to the fore the potentials of resistance and *when the conditions are right* they can help bring about a counter-politics and counter-political movements – creating the perfect soufflé. But too frequently people overestimate the capacity of resistive potential to rise up, and forget about the quality of the ingredients or the state of the oven. The potentials for resistance that are evident via the internet may allow for the realisation of cooperation – a solidarity forged through multiplicity; the information society may hold the promise of a cooperative society, it may tantalise us with the prospect of participatory democracy and excite through the spectre of direct democracy. This may be enticing, it may allow radical, oppositional and progressive social and political imaginaries to emerge; but it must not be forgotten that the spaces in which such a politics of hope can take shape must be struggled for and created in a coordinated and systematic fashion in order to transcend the highly coordinated, deftly administered and systemic limitations of the structures of capitalism. Despite all the failures of a centralised politics of the traditional left, clicking the delete button so soon may be tantamount to erasing the lessons of history before they have been learnt.

In this book we have sought to situate the internet in the deceptively simple context of the societies in which we live while also seeking to address the concerns of the specific type of communicational and technological system of the internet. We have also put forward an argument that the contemporary internet is not a democratic space per se. In the complex interrelations of contemporary internet and society there are potentialities for both democratic and anti-democratic formation. The precise manifestation of these interrelations may be suggestive of which particular strategies are appropriate for political progressive transformation in which particular context. Operationally, this creates the need to formulate mechanisms of genuine citizen participation and control of the spaces we inhabit, with new forms of state relations that prioritise the value of the public over profit, patience over productivity, and collaboration over competitiveness. In the final chapter we attempt to outline how this might be realised.

Notes

1 The World Social Forum (WSF) has established itself as the world's largest annual meeting for social movements and activists. It describes itself as 'an international framework for all those opposed to globalization and building alternatives to think and organize together in favour of human development and surmounting market domination of countries and international relations' (WSF official website, March 2011). The European Social Forum (ESF) emerged from the success of the WSF. Its first two gatherings, in Florence (2002) and Paris (2003), attracted over 50,000 participants from across Europe and beyond. More than 20,000 people from nearly 70 countries came to the ESF in London in October 2004.

2 Kettling is a police tactic for the management of large crowds during protests that was used frequently in these demonstrations. It involves the formation of large cordons of police officers who then move to contain a crowd within a limited area. Protesters are left only one choice of exit, determined by the police, or are completely prevented from leaving. Protesters are often denied access to food, water and toilet facilities for extensive periods. The kettling of protestors in these demonstrations is currently subject to legal challenge on the grounds of human rights violations.

3 By contrast, one year later, when WikiLeaks published information from the US Department of Defense, Secretary of State Clinton stated that it amounted to 'an attack on the international community, the alliances and partnerships, the conventions and negotiations that safeguard global security and advance economic prosperity' (Connolly, 2010).

References

Andrejevic, M. (2004) 'The Web Cam Subculture and the Digital Enclosure', in N. Couldry and A. McCarthy (eds) *MediaSpace: Place, Scale and Culture in a Media Age*, London: Routledge, 193–209.

——(2007) *iSpy: Surveillance and Power in the Interactive Era*, Kansas: University of Kansas Press.

Atton, C. (2007) 'A Brief History: The Web and Interactive Media', in K. Coyer, T. Dowmunt and A. Fountain (eds) *The Alternative Media Handbook*, London: Routledge, 59–65.

Benkler, Y. (2006) *The Wealth of Networks: How Social Production Transforms Markets and Freedom*, New Haven: Yale University Press.

Bennett, W. L. (2005) 'Social Movements Beyond Borders: Understanding Two Eras of Transnational Activism', in D. della Porta and S. Tarrow (eds) *Transnational Protest and Global Activism*, Lanham, MD: Rowman and Littlefield, 203–27.

Bhabha, H. (1994) *The Location of Culture*, London: Routledge.

Bimber, B. (1998) 'The Internet and Political Transformation: Populism, Community and Accelerated Pluralism', *Polity* 3: 133–60.

Bohman, J. (2004) 'Expanding Dialogue: the Internet, the Public Sphere and the Prospects for Transnational Democracy', in N. Crossley and J. M. Roberts (eds) *After Habermas: New Perspectives on the Public Sphere*, London: Blackwell, 131–56.

Cartalucci, T. (2011) 'Google's Revolution Factory – Alliance of Youth Movements: Color Revolution 2.0', Global Research.ca, Centre for Research on Globalisation. Online. Available HTTP: <http://www.globalresearch.ca/index.php?context=va&aid=23283> (accessed June 2011).

Carty, V. and Onyett, J. (2006) 'Protest, Cyberactivism and New Social Movements: The Reemergence of the Peace Movement Post 9/11', *Social Movement Studies* 5 (3): 229–49.

Casserly, J. (2011) 'The Art of Occupation', in C. Solomon and T. Palmieri (eds) *Springtime: The New Student Rebellions*, London: Verso, 71–76.

Castells, M. (1996) *The Rise of the Network Society*. Vol. 1 *The Information Age: Economy, Society and Culture*, Oxford: Blackwell.

——(1997) *The Power of Identity*, Cambridge, MA: Blackwell.

——(2009) *Communication Power*, Oxford: Oxford University Press.

Castells, M., Fernandez-Ardevol, J., Linchuan Qiu, J. and Sey, A. (2006) *Mobile Communication and Society*, Cambridge, MA: MIT Press.

Choudhari, H. (2009) 'Beating the Reporting Ban in Iran', in *World Agenda: Behind the International Headlines at the BBC*, September, London: BBC.

Cleaver, H. (1999) 'Computer Linked Social Movements and the Global Threat to Capitalism'. Online. Available HTTP: <http://www.eco.utexas.edu/faculty/Cleaver/polnet.html>.

Connolly, K. (2010) 'Has Release of Wikileaks Documents Cost Lives?', BBC News, 1 December. Online. Available HTTP: <http://www.bbc.co.uk/news/world-us-canada-11882092> (accessed December 2010).

Dahlberg, L. and Siapera, E. (2007) *Radical Democracy and the Internet: Interrogating Theory and Practice*, London: Palgrave Macmillan.

Dahlgren, P. (2009) *Media and Political Engagement: Citizens, Communication and Democracy*, Cambridge: Cambridge University Press.

Day, R. J. F. (2005) *Gramsci Is Dead: Anarchist Currents in the Newest Social Movements*, London: Pluto.

Deacon, D., Downey, J., Stanyer, J. and Wring, D. (2011) 'The Media Campaign: Mainstream Media Reporting of the 2010 UK General Election'. Paper presented to the MeCCSA conference, Salford.

Dean, J., Anderson, J. W. and Lovink, G. (2006) *Reformatting Politics: Information Technology and Global Civil Society*, London: Routledge.

Deleuze, G. and Guattari, F. (1988) *A Thousand Plateaus: Capitalism and Schizophrenia*, London: Athlone Press.

della Porta, D. (2005) 'Multiple Belongings, Tolerant Identities and the Construction of "Another Politics": Between the European Social Forum and the Local Social Fora', in

D. della Porta and S. Tarrow (eds) *Transnational Protest and Global Activism*, Lanham, MD: Rowman and Littlefield, 175–203.

della Porta, D. and Diani, M. (1999) *Social Movements: An Introduction*, Oxford, Malden, MA: Blackwell.

Diani, M. (2001) 'Social Movement Networks. Virtual and Real', in F. Webster (ed.) *Culture and Politics in the information Age*, London: Routledge, 117–27.

DigiActive (2009) Website available at: http://www.digiactive.org/about/.

Downey, J. and Fenton, N. (2003) 'Constructing a Counter-public Sphere', *New Media and Society* 5 (2): 185–202.

Elkin, M. (2011) 'Tunisia Internet Chief Gives Inside Look at Cyber Uprising'. *Wired.co. uk*, 31 January. Online. Available HTTP: <http://www.wired.co.uk/news/archive/2011–01/31/tunisia-egypt-internet-restrictions> (accessed February 2011).

Ester, P. and Vinken, H. (2003) 'Debating Civil Society: On the Fear for Civic Decline and Hope for the Internet Alternative', *International Sociology* 18(4): 659–80.

Fenton, N. (2006) 'Another World is Possible', *Global Media and Communication* 2 (3): 355–67.

——(2008) 'Mediating Hope: New Media, Politics and Resistance', *International Journal of Cultural Studies* 11 (2): 230–48.

Fenton, N. and Downey, J. (2003) 'Counter Public Spheres and Global Modernity', *Javnost – The Public* 10 (1): 15–33.

Ghannam, J. (2011) *Social Media in the Arab World: Leading up to the Uprisings in 2011*. A Report to the Center for International Media Assistance, Washington, DC. Online. Available HTTP: <http://cima.ned.org/sites/default/files/CIMA-Arab_Social_Media-Report_2.pdf> (accessed July 2011).

Ghoddosi, P. (2009) 'Your Turn – Giving Iranians a Voice', in *World Agenda: Behind the International Headlines at the BBC*, September, London: BBC.

Gopnik, A. (2011) 'How the Internet Gets Inside Us', *New York Review of Books*, Digital Edition, 14 and 22 February: 124–30. Online. Available HTTP: <http://www.newyorker.com/arts/critics/atlarge/2011/02/14/110214crat_atlarge_gopnik> (accessed February 2011).

Graeber, D. (2002) 'The New Anarchists', *The New Left Review* 13 (January/February) Online. Available HTTP: <http://www.newleftreview.org/A2368> (accessed 20 November 2010).

Grant, L. (2011) 'UK Student Protests: Democratic Participation, Digital Age', DML Central: University of California, Humanities Research Institute, 10 January. Online. Available HTTP: <http://dmlcentral.net/blog/lyndsay-grant/uk-student-protests-democratic-participation-digital-age> (accessed January 2011).

Guardian Euro Poll (2011) Prepared on behalf of the Guardian by ICM Online. Available HTTP: <http://image.guardian.co.uk/sys-files/Guardian/documents/2011/03/13/Guardian_Euro_Poll_day1.pdf> (accessed October 2011).

Habermas, J. (1989) *The Structural Transformation of the Public Sphere: An Inquiry into a Category of Bourgeois Society*, Cambridge: Polity.

——(1992) 'Further Reflections on the Public Sphere', in C. Calhoun (ed.) *Habermas and the Public Sphere*, Cambridge, MA: MIT Press, 421–61.

——(1998) *Inclusion of the Other: Studies in Political Theory*, Cambridge: Polity.

Hampton, K. and Wellman, B. (2003) 'Neighboring in Netville: How the Internet Supports Community and Social Capital in a Wired Suburb', *City and Community* 2 (4): 277–311.

Hardt, M. and Negri, A. (2000) *Empire*, Cambridge MA: Harvard University Press.

——(2004) *Multitude*, London: Hamish Hamilton.

Held, D. (1999) *Global Transformations: Politics, Economics and Culture*, Cambridge: Polity Press.

Hill, K. and Hughes, J. (1998) *Cyberpolitics: Citizen Activism in the Age of the Internet*, Lanham, MD: Rowman and Littlefield.

Hindman, M. (2008) *The Myth of Digital Democracy*, Princeton: Princeton University Press.

Haywood, J (2011) 'The Significance of Millbank', in C. Solomon and T. Palmieri (eds) *Springtime: The New Student Rebellions*, London: Verso, 69–71.

Holloway, J. (2002) *Change the World without Taking Power: The Meaning of Revolution Today*, London: Pluto Press.

Horwitz, R. (1989) *The Irony of Regulatory Reform: The Deregulation of American Telecommunications*, Oxford: Oxford University Press.

Ilves, A. (2009) 'An Election like no Other', in *World Agenda: Behind the International Headlines at the BBC*, September, London: BBC.

Kahn, R. and Kellner, D. (2004) 'New Media and Internet Activism: From the "Battle of Seattle" to Blogging', *New Media & Society* 6 (1): 87–95.

——(2007) 'Globalisation, Technopolitics and Radical Democracy', in L. Dahlberg and E. Siapera (eds) *Radical Democracy and the Internet: Interrogating Theory and Practice*, London: Palgrave Macmillan.

Keck, M. E. and Sikkink, K. (1998) *Activists beyond Borders: Advocacy Networks in International Politics*, New York: Cornell University Press.

Killick, A. (2011) 'Student Occupation against the Cuts', *Three D*, April, 16: 7–9. Online. Available HTTP: <http://www.meccsa.org.uk/pdfs/ThreeD-Issue016.pdf> (accessed April 2011).

Klein, N. (2000) *No Logo*, New York: Flamingo.

——(2002) *Fences and Windows: Dispatches from the Front Lines of the Globalization Debate*, London: Flamingo.

Kowal, D. (2002) 'Digitizing and Globalizing Indigenous Voices: The Zapatista Movement', in G. Elmer (ed.), *Critical Perspectives on the Internet*, Lanham, MD: Rowman and Littlefield, 105–29.

Laclau, E. (2004) *The Making of Political Identities*, London: Verso.

Livingstone, S. and Bovill, M. (2002) *Young People, New Media*. Research Report Online. Available HTTP: <http://www.lse.ac.uk/collections/media@lse/pdf/young_people_report.pdf> (accessed 28 January 2008).

Livingstone, S., Bober, M. and Helsper, E. (2005) 'Internet Literacy among Children and Young People: Findings from the UK Children Go Online Project', Ofcom/ESRC, London. Online. Available HTTP: <http://eprints.lse.ac.uk/397/> (accessed October 2010).

Loader, B. (ed.) (2007) *Young Citizens in the Digital Age. Political Engagement, Young People and New Media*, London: Routledge.

McKay, G. (ed.) (1998) *DiY Culture: Party and Protest in Nineties Britain*, London, New York: Verso.

Marchart, O. (2007) *Post-foundational Political Thought: Political Difference in Nancy, Lefort, Badiou, and Laclau*, Edinburgh: Edinburgh University Press.

Miladi, N. (2011) 'Tunisia: A Media Led Revolution?' Ajazeera.net, 17 January. Online. Available HTTP: <http://english.aljazeera.net/indepth/opinion/2011/01/2011116142317498666.html> (accessed January 2011).

Morozov, E. (2011) *The Net Delusion: How not to Liberate the World*, London: Allen Lane.

Mouffe, C. (2005) *The Return of the Political*, London: Verso.

Musgrove, M. (2009) 'Twitter is a Player in Iran's Drama', *Washington Post*, 17 June. Online. Available HTTP: <http://www.washingtonpost.com/wp-dyn/content/article/2009/06/16/AR2009061603391.html> (accessed June 2009).

Norris, P. (2001) *Digital Divide: Civic Engagement, Information Poverty and the Internet Worldwide*, Cambridge: Cambridge University Press.

——(2002) *Democratic Phoenix: Reinventing Political Activism*, Cambridge: Cambridge University Press.

Ofcom (2010) *The Communications Market 2010*, London: Ofcom.

Oswell, D. (2006) *Culture and Society*, London: Sage.

Park, A. (2004) *British Social Attitudes: The 21st Report*, London: Sage.

Ribeiro, G. L. (1998) 'Cybercultural Politics: Political Activism at a Distance in a Transnational World', in S. E. Alvarez, E. Dagnino and A. Escobar (eds) *Cultures of Politics/Politics of Culture: Revisioning Latin American Social Movements*, Boulder, CO: Westview Press, 325–52.

Ross, A. (2011) '21st Century Statecraft', LSE public lecture, 10 March. Online. Available HTTP: <http://www2.lse.ac.uk/publicEvents/events/2011/20110310t1830vHKT.aspx)> (accessed March 2011).

Salter, L. (2003) 'Democracy, New Social Movements and the Internet: A Habermasian Analysis', in M. McCaughey and M. D. Ayers (eds) *Cyberactivism: Online Activism in Theory and Practice*, London: Routledge, 117–45.

——(2011) 'Young People, Protest and Education', *Three D*, April, 16: 4–6.

Sassen, S. (2004) 'Electronic Markets and Activist Networks: The Weight of Social Logics in Digital Formations', in R. Latham and S. Sassen (eds) *IT and New Architectures in the Global Realm*, Princeton: Princeton University Press, 54–89.

Solomon, C. (2011) 'We Felt Liberated', in C. Solomon and T. Palmieri (eds) *Springtime: The New Student Rebellions*, London: Verso, 11–17.

Spivak, G. (1992) 'French Feminism Revisited: Ethics and Politics', in J. Butler and J. Scott (eds) *Feminists Theorise the Political*, London: Routledge, 54–85.

Sreberny, A. (2009) 'Thirty Years on: The Iranian Summer of Discontent', *Social Text*, 12 November. Online. Available HTTP: <http://www.socialtextjournal.org/periscope/2009/11/thirty-years-on-the-iranian-summer-of-discontent.php#comment-212> (accessed November 2009).

Sreberny, A. and Khiabany, G. (2010) *Blogistan*, London: I. B. Tauris.

Sunstein, C. (2001) *republic.com*. Princeton: Princeton University Press.

Tapper, J. (2009) 'Clinton: "I Wouldn't Know a Twitter from a Tweeter" and Iran Protests US Meddling', ABC News Blog site, 17 June. Online. Available HTTP: <http://blogs.abcnews.com/politicalpunch/2009/06/clinton-i-wouldnt-know-a-twitter-from-a-tweeter-iran-protests-us-meddling.html> (accessed June 2009).

Tarrow, S. (1994) *Power in Movement*, Cambridge: Cambridge University Press.

Tarrow, S. and della Porta, D. (2005) 'Globalization, Complex Internationalism and Transnational Contention', in D. della Porta and S. Tarrow (eds) *Transnational Protest and Global Activism*, Lanham, MD: Rowman and Littlefield, 227–47.

Terranova, T. (2004) *Network Culture: Politics for the Information Age*, London: Pluto Press.

Tormey, S. (2005) 'From Utopian Worlds to Utopian Spaces: Reflections on the Contemporary Radical Imaginary and the Social Forum Process', *Ephemera* 5 (2): 394–408.

——(2006) *Anti-capitalism: A Beginner's Guide*, Oxford: Oneworld.

Traugott, M. (1995) 'Recurrent Patterns of Collective Action', in M. Traugott (ed.) *Repertoires and Cycles of Collective Action*, Durham: Duke University Press, 1–15.

Ward, S. and Lusoli, W. (2003) 'Dinosaurs in Cyberspace? British Trade Unions and the Internet', *European Journal of Communication*, 18: 147–79.

Warschauer, M. (2003) *Technology and Social Inclusion: Rethinking the Digital Divide*, Cambridge, MA: MIT Press.

Wellman, B., Haase, A. Q., Witte, J. and Hampton, K. (2001) 'Does the Internet Increase, Decrease or Supplement Social Capital? Social Networks, Participation and Community Commitment', *American Behavioural Scientist* 45 (3): 436–55.

Wilkinson, H. and Mulgan, G. (1995) *Freedom's Children*, London: Demos.

Yla-Anttila, T. (2006) 'The World Social Forum and the Globalisation of Social Movements and Public Spheres', *Ephemera* 5 (2): 423–42.

Part IV

Looking forward

Chapter 7

Conclusion

James Curran, Des Freedman and Natalie Fenton

This book has two central themes. The first is that a narrow, decontextualised focus on the technology of the internet leads to misperceiving its impact. This argument is illustrated, in the first chapter, by looking at four sets of technology-centred predictions about how the internet would change society, and then examining what actually happened. The internet did not promote global understanding in the way that had been anticipated because the internet came to reflect the inequalities, linguistic division, conflicting values and interests of the real world. The internet did not spread and rejuvenate democracy in the way that had been promised, partly because authoritarian regimes usually found ways of controlling the internet, but also because alienation from the political process limited the internet's emancipatory potential. The internet did not transform the economy, partly because the underlying dynamics of unequal competition that make for corporate concentration remained unchanged. Lastly, the internet did not inaugurate a renaissance of journalism; on the contrary, it enabled leading news brands to extend their ascendancy across technologies, while inducing a decline of quality not offset, so far, by new forms of journalism. All four predictions were wrong because they inferred the impact of the internet from its technology and failed to grasp that the internet's influence is filtered through the structures and processes of society. This explains, it is argued, why the influence of the internet has varied in different contexts.

The second central theme of this book is that the internet itself is not constituted solely by its technology but also by the way it is funded and organised, by the way it is designed, imagined and used, and by the way it is regulated and controlled. In the second chapter, devoted to the history of the internet, it is argued that the internet was originally shaped, after its military conception, by the values of science, counterculture and European public service. This largely pre-market formation was then overtaken by commercialisation and increasing state censorship. We are now in the midst of a battle for the 'soul' of the internet, which has a global dimension as well as a Western one.

This second theme, concerned with influences on the internet, is developed more fully in the second part of this book. Chapter 3 describes the lyrical, 'second wave' interpretations of theorists like Chris Anderson and Jeff Jarvis who see the internet as a technology that promotes a new form of economy and a new state of being: one that abolishes scarcity in favour of abundance, replaces standardisation with diversity, and substitutes hierarchy with participation and democratisation. However, apart from a communitarian strand linked to non-commercial developments of the internet, these accounts are all based on a market model of the internet. What they overlook is the multiple distortions that a market-based internet has developed: corporate dominance, market concentration, controlling gatekeepers, employee exploitation, manipulative rights management, economic exclusion through 'tethered appliances' and encroachment upon the information commons. The internet market, on closer scrutiny, turns out to have many of the problems associated with unregulated capitalism.

Should we, then, think the unthinkable and contemplate a different way of managing the internet? This seems to disrespect the much-lauded system we have now. This system is said to be ideal because it entails soft governance rather than oppressive state control, self-regulation through experts and users rather than a regime of oppressive bureaucracy. But recent analysis has shed light on what this complacent self-presentation conceals. In fact Western governments are not as absent as they appear to be, and retain a strategic oversight over computer networks that have increasing military and economic significance. This can take the form of arbitrary interventions, as when the US government exerted pressure on credit card companies to refuse payments to WikiLeaks in a bid to muzzle its embarrassing disclosures. Furthermore, control of the internet is increasingly vested in powerful internet corporations, supported by software and hardware restrictions. Self-regulation frequently means corporate regulation in a form that can threaten the freedom and public-good features of the net. So it is now legitimate to consider whether a better system of regulation – independent of government and market control – should be preferred. To this we shall return.

Chapters 5 and 6 focus on the spectacular rise of social media, which has led to speculation that they will profoundly change social relations. Technology that gives a means of communication to individuals and social networks, it is reasoned, must be collectively empowering. Positive concepts like autonomy, access, participation, multiplicity and pluralism are regularly invoked to reinforce this image of a transformative force. While it is true that social media provide a pleasurable means of self-expression and social connection, enable people to answer back to citadels of media power and in certain situations (as in Iran) may support the creation of a radical counter-public, Chapter 5 introduces a sceptical note. Social media are more often about individual than collective emancipation, about presenting self (frequently in consumerist or individualising terms) rather than changing society, about entertainment and leisure rather than political communication (still dominated by old media) and about social agendas shaped by elites and corporate power rather than a radical alternative. For example, Twitter is centred more on eavesdropping on the thoughts of celebrities than on political change. Social media, in other words, are shaped by the wider envir-onment in which they are situated rather than functioning as an autonomous force transforming society.

What, then, is the connection between the internet and radical politics? Young people who have rejected traditional party politics, who have moved away from class-based concerns to a radical politics of identity and who express political interests and hopes that are borderless have adopted the internet as an organising and campaigning tool. There is natural affinity between the global, interactive technology of the internet and the development of a more inter-nationalist, decentred and participatory form of politics. But this politics is enabled by the internet rather than being the product of it. Indeed, a look at specific examples underlines the point that internet-assisted protests have underlying causes: among other things, broken promises, which were the prelude to the 2010 student protests in Britain; and the allegation of a stolen election, which precipitated the 2009 Iran protests. And while the internet has introduced a new degree of creative autonomy and effectiveness in the mobilisation of protests, the radical politics with which it is associated may have limitations. Multiple voices of protest may fragment rather than build solidarity: fluid, issue-based and institution-less politics may not add up to a coordinated project for transforming society.

Of course, in acknowledging the dangers of binary traps – the internet is *or* is not transformative, that it strengthens *or* weakens existing political forces – and the importance of evaluating the internet in quite specific circumstances, we ourselves have found it difficult to contextualise everything, despite our warn-ings. In particular, we are aware that our chosen examples and case studies are taken from a fairly narrow range of countries and perspectives and that there may be other, countervailing arguments.

However, we stand by our approach and our conclusion: that although it was said, and continues to be said, that the internet was going to virtually single-handedly change the world, this has not been the case. Like all previous tech-nologies, its use, control, ownership, past development and future potential are context dependent. If we are to realise the dreams of the internet pioneers, then we need to challenge that context and demand a fresh set of proposals to empower public oversight of and participation in online networks.

The internet, we have argued, is a creature of public policy, developed initially not for profit but for collaboration and communication. It has long been regulated – by governments, markets, code and communities. Sub-sequent developments have changed this fundamentally, so that its collaborative and communicative potential for all citizens is in danger of being enclosed and privatised. According to Tim Berners-Lee, the web that he helped to found

is being threatened in different ways. Some of its most successful inhabitants have begun to chip away at its principles. Large social-networking sites are walling off information posted by their users from the rest of the Web.

Wireless Internet providers are being tempted to slow traffic to sites with which they have not made deals. Governments – totalitarian and democratic alike – are monitoring people's online habits, endangering important human rights.

(Berners-Lee 2010)

This, then, is a critical moment in the internet's history.

In this situation, it may be useful to draw on debates from another industry facing a similar critical juncture: banking. After the collapse of Lehman Brothers in 2008 and the financial crisis that followed, more far-sighted commentators and regulators realised that serious reforms were needed if public trust and stability were to return to the sector. One such figure was Lord Adair Turner, chairman of the Financial Services Authority that regulates the City of London. In a speech in 2009, he argued that the sector had to learn from its mistakes and transform the way it does business if a similar catastrophe was to be avoided in the future. 'We need radical change. Regulators must design radically changed regulations and supervisory approaches, but we also need to challenge our entire past philosophy of regulation' (Turner 2009). Two years later, frustrated by the very slow pace of reform (despite the emergence of the International Financial Stability Board and proposals for tighter control of banks themselves), he once again called for the sector to embrace 'radical policy options', including the possibility of new taxes or state intervention in the running of banks (Turner 2011).

Applied to the internet, the first objection would be that such measures would act as a brake on creativity and a distortion of market principles. Indeed Turner acknowledges precisely these objections, noting that these proposals have been routinely rejected by critics on the basis that 'they would have a "chilling effect" on liquidity, product innovation, price discovery and market efficiency' (Turner 2011). He then dismisses these objections on the basis, somewhat surprisingly for a figure utterly embedded inside the City of London, that 'not all financial activity is socially useful' and that free and competitive financial systems 'sometimes deliver neither stability nor allocative efficiency' (Turner 2011). This is a polite way of saying that a lightly regulated banking sector has failed consumers and undermined the entire financial system.

We draw on the arguments not because the banking sector has indeed been transformed (it has not) or because, as an industry, it should somehow serve as a model for the internet (it should not), but simply to suggest that regulation of vital public resources is both possible and desirable in order to promote 'socially useful' outcomes and to check the power of unaccountable forces, whether they be market or government based. We are therefore calling for a particular form of intervention: of 'market-negating regulation', as the economist Costas Lapavitsas calls it (2010) in his analysis of the global financial crisis. There is no reason why principles that radical economists are proposing, not without good reason, for the banking sector – state regulation of prices, ceilings on interest rates, control of capital markets, all in the name of the public good – could not be applied to the internet. Lapavitsas argues that we have had too much of the 'wrong' sort of regulation (he calls it 'market-conforming regulation'), and this is precisely what has happened in relation to the internet as governments, supranational bodies, large telecoms and internet companies have sought agreement on terms of trade and custom and practice that best serve them and not the public at large.

Of course this will also have to be a 'state-negating regulation' in the sense that it should not lead to the ability of governments (elected or not) to monopolise digital spaces or to use their power to direct what happens in those spaces – a recent example of which was the UK government's proposal to have the ability to switch off social media during periods of national crisis (such as the riots of July 2011), a move that was quickly squashed by both citizens' groups and social media companies themselves. However, the idea that one can use the power of the state to enhance public provision, as opposed to government control, is hardly new: consider Medicare in the US, the French national health insurance system or the BBC in the UK, which, while established by the state, are certainly not the properties of any single administration. Our belief is that it is possible to establish publicly funded bodies (with membership drawn from different parts of society) and systems of oversight (which are accountable to those publics) that have an arms'-length relationship to the state.

We are aware that we cannot make any blanket recommendations, given the situated nature of the internet in specific countries. Instead, we aim to offer our own version of a manifesto for cyberspace, some 15 years after Barlow's libertarian call to arms, that seeks to resurrect public interest regulation and reverse the current relationship between markets and states that has functioned to accrue power for corporations and governments but rarely for the public whom they are supposed to serve. This approach is not counterposed to the many bills of rights already proposed by various organisations and individuals (see Jarvis 2011) that seek to enshrine principles of openness, collaboration and ethical behaviour. Indeed, it is an attempt to find the mechanisms by which these objectives can be protected and nurtured in an environment that increasingly rewards opacity, inequality and unethical behavior.

We want to see *redistributional* public interventions that will foster:

- online journalism that uses the internet's ability to highlight more sources of information and better to link readers and news reports, *not* the speeded-up churnalism that we have all too often seen;
- broadband infrastructures that are constructed as public utilities designed to serve the needs of citizens, *not* the privately constructed toll roads that governments, at a time of economic uncertainty, are keen to see built;
- the protection of public spaces that use the internet's great strengths of interconnectivity, speed and participation, *not* the enclosure of creativity and imagination and the construction of commodified relationships;

- the ability of citizens to talk within and across national boundaries through public funding of sites dealing with major issues of public concern, *not* an artificial international community of branded consumers;
- the circulation of content (whether related to entertainment, news, information or education) on networks regulated in the name of the public and not controlled by major internet players like Google and Facebook with very poor systems of monitoring and accountability.

We are not calling for an international *deus ex machina* to fall from the sky to rescue the internet from today's digital robber barons. We are instead calling for constructive and achievable interventions – acts of deliberate public policy where the public will exists – to create the conditions for a more democratic internet.

This will mean arguing for redistributional policies: for taxes and levies on private communications businesses to help fund open networks and public service content; for changes to intellectual property regimes that will prevent the blockages, copyright extensions and digital rights management that disenfranchise users from networks that are best served by open access; for the creation of a set of conditions, specific to each country, that will allow the funding and regulation of the internet to benefit users, irrespective of wealth, geography, background and age. We understand that these interventions will depend on what is possible in each country at a specific moment in time *but we refuse to believe that change is not possible*. After all, we are calling for measures – for public control of a key utility – that have been applied to other key sections of the economy and society (parts of the automobile industry in the US; banks in the UK; airlines in Argentina; mortgage providers in the US).

Let us give one example of what is possible. Support is growing around the world for a tax on global financial transactions to support international development objectives, the Tobin Tax. If we are agreed that the development of an open internet environment is a policy priority for the twenty-first century, then why should we not press for a mechanism by which those who are benefiting from the demand for information and communication make a full contribution to building and supporting such an environment? A 1 per cent tax on the operating profits of US companies dealing with computer software and hardware, internet services and retailing, entertainment and telecommunications in the Fortune 500 list alone would raise over *one billion dollars* annually. Let us call this a Cerf Tax in honour of Vint Cerf, the architect of the protocols that made the internet possible in the first place, but there could be many international variations.

The internet is at a turning-point. This book has argued that, while many people have exaggerated and confused its real impact and significance, there is little doubt that it is a development that has to be understood, protected and valued. The time has come to demand an internet that is run for the benefit of the public without discrimination by market or state; the pursuit of this demand is urgent and needs to take place nationally and supra-nationally, offline and online, in social movements and social media and in all the networks to which we belong.

References

Berners-Lee, T. (2010) 'Long Live the Web: A Call for Continued Open Standards and Neutrality', *Scientific American*, 22 November. Online. Available HTTP: <http://www. scientific.american.com/article.cfm?id=long-live-the-web> (accessed 5 January 2011).

Jarvis, J. (2011) 'A Hippocratic Oath for the Internet', 23 May. Online. Available HTTP: <http://www.buzzmachine.com/2011/05/23/a-hippocratic-oath-for-the-internet/> (accessed 25 August 2011).

Lapavitsas, C. (2010) 'Regulate Financial Institutions, or Financial Institutions?', in P. Arestis, R. Sobreira and J. L. Oreiro (eds) *The Financial Crisis: Origins and Implications*, Houndsmill: Palgrave Macmillan, 137–59.

Turner, A. (2009) 'Mansion House speech', 22 September. Online. Available HTTP: <http://www.fsa.gov.uk/pages/Library/Communication/Speeches/2009/0922_at.shtml> (accessed 25 August 2011).

——(2011) 'Reforming Finance: Are We Being Radical Enough?', 2011 Clare Distinguished Lecture in Economics and Public Policy, Cambridge, 18 February. Online. Available HTTP: <http://www.fsa.gov.uk/pages/Library/Communication/Speeches/2011/ 0218_at.shtml> (accessed 25 August 2011).

Index